Puberty to Manhood
in
Italy and America

DEVELOPMENTAL PSYCHOLOGY SERIES

SERIES EDITOR
Harry Beilin

Developmental Psychology Program
City University of New York Graduate School
New York, New York

LYNN S. LIBEN. *Deaf Children: Developmental Perspectives*

JONAS LANGER. *The Origins of Logic: Six to Twelve Months*

GILBERTE PIERAUT-LE BONNIEC. *The Development of Modal Reasoning: Genesis of Necessity and Possibility Notions*

TIFFANY MARTINI FIELD, SUSAN GOLDBERG, DANIEL STERN, and ANITA MILLER SOSTEK. (Editors). *High-Risk Infants and Children: Adult and Peer Interactions*

BARRY GHOLSON. *The Cognitive-Developmental Basis of Human Learning: Studies in Hypothesis Testing*

ROBERT L. SELMAN. *The Growth of Interpersonal Understanding: Developmental and Clinical Analyses*

RAINER H. KLUWE and HANS SPADA. (Editors). *Developmental Models of Thinking*

HARBEN BOUTOURLINE YOUNG and LUCY RAU FERGUSON. *Puberty to Manhood in Italy and America*

SARAH L. FRIEDMAN and MARIAN SIGMAN. (Editors). *Preterm Birth and Psychological Development*

LYNN S. LIBEN, ARTHUR H. PATTERSON, and NORA NEWCOMBE. (Editors). *Spatial Representation and Behavior Across the Life Span: Theory and Application*

In Preparation

W. PATRICK DICKSON. (Editor). *Children's Oral Communication Skills*

EUGENE S. GOLLIN. (Editor). *Developmental Plasticity: Behavioral and Biological Aspects of Variations in Development*

Puberty to Manhood
in
Italy and America

Harben Boutourline Young

Pediatrics and Public Health
Yale University
Florence, Italy

Lucy Rau Ferguson

Department of Psychology
Michigan State University
East Lansing, Michigan

ACADEMIC PRESS
A Subsidiary of Harcourt Brace Jovanovich, Publishers
New York London Toronto Sydney San Francisco 1981

ACADEMIC PRESS, INC.
111 Fifth Avenue, New York, New York 10003

United Kingdom Edition published by
ACADEMIC PRESS, INC. (LONDON) LTD.
24/28 Oval Road, London NW1   7DX

Library of Congress Cataloging in Publication Data

Young, Harben Boutourline.
    Puberty to manhood in Italy and America.

    (Developmental psychology series)
    Bibliography: p.
    Includes index.
    1. Adolescent boys--Italy--Longitudinal
studies. 2. Adolescent boys--United States--
Longitudinal studies. 3. Developmental psychology
--Cross-cultural studies. I. Ferguson, Lucy Rau,
1930-   joint author. II. Title.
III. Series. [DNLM: 1. Child development.
2. Adolescent psychology. 3. Cross-cultural
comparison. 4. Puberty. WS 105 Y725p]
HQ797.Y63   305.2'3   80-1687
ISBN 0-12-773150-4

PRINTED IN THE UNITED STATES OF AMERICA

81 82 83 84   9 8 7 6 5 4 3 2 1

*To the 343 young men in Italy and America,
who were the subjects of the study.*

Contents

vii

Preface

In 1955 the Grant Foundation of New York made it possible for Harben Bouterline Young to take advantage of a unique opportunity to study ethnically similar boys in different cultures, following them through the process of puberty and adolescence until they became young men. It was hoped to attain an understanding of physical, mental, and social growth by a careful assessment, not only of the boys, but also of the environment in which they lived, in order to have the chance of relating environmental differences to their development. These differences were large enough to offer the prospect of perceiving differences in the growth patterns of the young men.

There are two major periods in life where changes in growth are sufficiently great to justify a venture of this kind; they are infancy and adolescence. We chose the latter because there is a growth spurt as well as a later deceleration, and because we also would have the opportunity to follow the subjects until they became mature young adults. The study was not intended as one further investigation of growth processes in puberty and adolescence, but rather as a way of finding out how differing environments might affect this phase of development.

Longitudinal studies are difficult in design and arduous in organization. Relatively few have been published. All the same, in human development they provide answers to questions that may not be resolved in other ways, and they will inevitably continue.

Cross-cultural (as opposed to cross-national) studies that encompass a wide range of developmental aspects also are rare and equally difficult to construct and implement. One might imagine that the difficulties of combining a longitudinal and cross-cultural study might be additive, already a task from which the boldest investigator might shrink. In retrospect, one sees that the problems multiply, constituting a series of barriers that continually must be breached as the work proceeds. We report here on a scientific enterprise (design, collection of data through the adolescence and early maturity of our subjects, and analysis and interpretation) that has spanned 25 years.

The contributors represent a small core team that stayed together during the greater part of the study and other professionals who stayed for a period of years or even as little as one year while on sabbatical or special leave from their universities. The director and coordinator, Harben Bouterline Young, remained the same throughout, while Lucy Rau Ferguson joined the project in 1966. The authors were associated with Michigan State and Harvard Universities during the greater part of the study, although Young was on the Yale faculty during the course of collection of some final material. In addition to the authors, other contributors were Elizabeth Janeway and Renata Gaddini (Chapter 2); Elizabeth Bouterline, L. Capotorti, Gino Tesi, and James L. Whittenberger (Chapter 3); Paul Mussen, Robert Knapp, and Pasquale Urbano (Chapters 4 and 5); Richard Jessor (Chapter 6); Irving Torgoff and Frank Barron (Chapter 7); and Leroy Ferguson (Chapter 8).

Acknowledgments

For their participation for periods of time in Florence, we also wish to thank David McClelland, Ludwig Immergluck, Renato Tagiuri, Harry Levin, Gerald Caplan, Joseph Lopreato, Theodore Lidz, Bram Oppenheim, Norman Livson, Norman Bradburn, Eugene Schirchs, Donald Pitkin, and William Kessen.

For consultations and help in the United States, we are grateful to J. P. Guilford, Raymond Cattell, Rose Franzblau, and Juan Cortes.

In Rome we wish to thank Winfred Vagliani as well as Victoria Bongiancino who applied many tests under the supervision of Renata Gaddini.

In Palermo we thank Venerando Correnti, Lidia Morante, and Letitia Casuccio.

We also thank Madeleine McKinney for her assistance in the book's jacket design, and Katherine McCracken for her expert editorial assistance. Our thanks also to Judith Anderson and Marion Aldred for help in the final preparation of the manuscript.

This work was made possible by generous contributions from the Grant Foundation of New York. A grant for a specific purpose also was made by the Wenner Gren Foundation. Small contributions were also made by the Olivetti Foundation, the Fiat Automobile Company (Professor Valetta), the former Montecatini Company, and the Pirelli Company. We thank these organizations, especially for the moral value of this support. We are particularly indebted to the Grant Foundation and its founder, Mr. William Grant, as well as Miss Adele Morrison, associate director of the Grant Foundation, who gave personal interest and support for many years.

PART I

Background

CHAPTER 1

Introduction

We tell the story of three groups of young men. All of them had four grandparents born in the South of Italy, but each group grew up in greatly different environments: the cities of Boston, Rome, and Palermo. Deliberately there were three large cities: one the capital of one of the United States, another a national capital, and the third a former capital city of Bourbon kings.

Though the young men now mostly exceed 30 years in age, they were observed from pre- and early puberty in a series of longitudinal observations of physical, cognitive, and social development. At the same time we tried to assess the effect of the environment upon them.

The study, which after a while took on a life of its own, sprang originally from three related interests: in adolescence, in the relation between measures of physical and psychological development, and above all in the effect on adolescent and young adult developments of markedly contrasting real-life environments.

Our interest in adolescence sprang from the realization that it is a period of growth change, potentially the most susceptible to the impact of different environments, and after which it would be economically feasible to study outcomes in early maturity.

What we inherit and how much this has been affected by the environment has

3

been the inspiration of many studies. The stability of inheritance has been tested in some twin studies (Burks & Roe, 1949; Juel-Nielsen & Morgensen, 1957; Newman, Freeman, & Holzinger, 1937; Scheinfeld, 1968; Shields, 1962; Vandenberg, Stafford, & Brown, 1968); in studies of children reared in adoption and then compared on some aspects of development with their biological parents (Grotevant, Scarr, & Weinberg, 1977; Honzik, 1957; Scarr & Weinberg, 1976; Skodak & Skeels, 1949); and in emigration studies of various kinds. It seems that inheritance may vary in its influence from one developmental area to another and no final acceptable conclusions have been reached in many areas. A considerable problem is the assessment of environmental forces.

Bronfenbrenner (1974) has pleaded for a close examination of the enduring environment in which the child does or might live. He describes two layers, the first consisting of an immediate setting—that is, the home, school, street, and playground. Within this he mentions space and materials; people in differing roles and the activities in which they are engaged. Bronfenbrenner's second layer consists of that in which the other is embedded, such as the geographical, the physical, the social systems, including not only the socioeconomic class but what society provides in the way of services and tangential systems such as shops, public transportation, working hours of parents and many others that influence where children may go, what they may do, and with whom they may stay. Bronfenbrenner looks critically at reports of child development derived from "straightjacket" settings that may bear little relationship to real life.

While the present research does not meet all of Bronfenbrenner's criteria, it does go some way in this direction, and this is in the two main cultures and the two subcultures in one of them.

The Cross-Cultural Approach and Environmental Effects

There is an excellent summary of cross-cultural studies in *behavioral* development by LeVine (1970). He views cross-cultural work as a research strategy and therefore concentrates upon methodological problems. He divided the many studies into three categories: (*a*) the behavior of children in human populations; (*b*) the environment in which they are raised; and (*c*) studies involving relationships between environment and behavior as cause and effect.

The present work is an example of the third category, and LeVine maintains that up to 1970 this kind of study had uncovered few relationships that have had strong evidential support. It is also clear that researchers have tended to concentrate on just a few aspects of behavioral development. In seven pages of references there is not a single cross-cultural study in which a variety of behavioral attributes and physical growth and health were combined.

Effects of environment upon *physical growth* have received increasing attention during the course of this century. Confirmation and explanation of such effects in human beings require some degree of homogeneity of the groups under study but also diverse environmental stimuli prolonged and different enough to produce a variety of perhaps significant effects.

A secular trend in human beings of increasing height and weight has been repeatedly demonstrated in children (Abramson, E. & Ernest, 1954; Gray, 1927; Meredith, 1941a,b; Meredith & Meredith, 1944; Weir, 1952); and in adults (Boyne & Leitch, 1954; Costanzo, 1948; Holmgren, 1952; Morant, 1950). It has also been shown that young adult males are taller than their fathers (Bowles, 1932; Durnin & Weir, 1952). Lundman (1940) has observed a steady increase of stature in army recruits in Scandinavian countries.

It has also been shown that, although the secular trend in the United States is tending to narrow the growth stature differences between groups of individuals of diverse ethnic origin, substantial differences in physical measurements still exist (Meredith, 1939, 1941a,b; Matheney & Meredith, 1947).

The effects of sudden unfavorable environmental conditions upon growth in the Russian famine have been described by Ivanovsky (1923), the effects of poverty in Scotland by Paton & Findlay (1926), and some results of the German occupation of Belgium by Ellis (1945). The effects of climate upon growth have been examined by Mills (1942, 1949, 1950). A review of such findings with an extensive bibliography and discussion has been made by Tanner (1962). Acheson (1960) has also reviewed effects of nutrition and disease.

Authors describing increases in physical measurements with changing environmental conditions have ascribed such results to generally better hygienic conditions, diet, and even climate, but work confirming these interpretations and their relative importance is still awaited.

Studies of Migrants

Studies upon migrants and their offspring constitute one type of research most fruitful in the past and most likely in the future to elucidate the reasons for such changes in growth patterns. The first we have found to take advantage of this natural experiment was Fishberg (1905), who demonstrated that Jews in the United States were taller than those born in Europe, and a fundamental study is that of Boas (U.S. Congress, 1911), who described physical differences apparently caused by modification of growth in a changed environment. These findings were contested by Morant & Samson (1936), but Guthe (1918), Hirsch (1927), and Franzblau (1935) all confirmed the results of the original authors.

Similar studies of Japanese subjects by Iyenaga and Sato (1911) demonstrated that 7- to 16-year-old Japanese in a number of California schools were larger than children of comparable ages in Japan. Spier (1929) compared Japanese children in Seattle with those in Japan and found those resident in America to be taller and larger on some measurements. Suski (1933) showed that American-born

Japanese boys exceeded the means published by the Japanese Ministry of Education in height, weight, chest circumference, and leg length. Ito (1942) compared American-born women of Japanese descent with similar subjects who returned to Japan when young. Those remaining in America exceeded in size those who returned to Japan and to even greater extent those who were born in Japan.

Another fundamental study is that of Shapiro (1939), who examined Japanese immigrants to Hawaii, their children, and relatives born and residing in Japan—in all, 2500 subjects. The Hawaiian-born exceeded the immigrants in height and length of trunk. These differences were more marked when comparison was with the group residing in Japan. Lasker (1946) examined American-born Chinese and compared them with Chinese immigrants; he found in the former greater stature and an increase in all measurements highly correlated with stature. Kaplan (1954) gave a full account of the body of knowledge up to that time concerning physical changes in migrants and their offspring. Greulich (1957, 1958) in a recent study of 898 American-born children of Japanese descent in California has found, in comparing those born and resident in Japan (official Japanese data), substantial differences in height, and sitting height, from 5 to 18 years. At every age concerned, the American-born Japanese boys were taller than the boys of today in Japan by an amount greater than the increases in that country in the past 50 years. The skeletal status of American-born Japanese children was similar to that of the Cleveland white children of superior socioeconomic status of the Brush Foundation Study, on which the Greulich–Pyle (1959) standards of skeletal development are based, in contrast to the relative retardation in skeletal development of Japanese children cited in Sutow (1953). Hulse (1958) demonstrated a number of physical differences between Italo-Swiss, born in the United States, Italo-Swiss migrants, and sedentes in the Swiss Canton of Ticino.

Some of the earlier research workers had suggested that the repeatedly confirmed physical differences demonstrated in these studies might be due to a physical selection of migrants. Goldstein (1943), who also reported that American-born children of immigrants from Mexico exceed the immigrants in total body height and other measurements, presented some evidence of difference in size between immigrants and sedentes. However, he declared that the evidence was not conclusive. Lasker (1952) said that a group of immigrants from a Mexican town differed physically from those left behind but only in the case of those not fully grown (under the age of 27) when they left home. He ruled out physical selection as a major factor, which might explain the differences. Martin (1949), however, had observed that migrants in Great Britain from one part of the country to another were taller than sedentes, and Hulse (1960) noted that Swiss migrating after their army service were a mean of 1.7 cm taller than those still living in Switzerland 25 years later. On present evidence we must agree with Lasker that physical selection appears to be but a minor factor in the explanation of the physical differences described.

Another factor that has been considered is heterosis or hybrid vigor. Trevor

(1953) did not find such evidence in a large sample but Penrose (1955) considers that this may have been due to the parents being insufficiently homozygous. Hulse (1958) has demonstrated clearly that there is an increase on a number of physical measurements in children of exogenous marriages both of sedentes in Switzerland and of migrants in California when they are compared with the offspring of endogenous marriages. It seems, therefore, that any experiment involving measurements of migrants and their descendents, which includes subjects from small isolated villages of less than 1000 as in Ticino, should take this factor into account.

It would seem that the human phenotypes most subject to adaptive change are those influenced by the actions of several genes. Hulse (1960) considers that characters of which the mode of inheritance is relatively simple, such as eye color, blood type, abnormal hemoglobins, show no plasticity under changing environmental conditions; other characters agreed to be complex in their mode of inheritance may show considerable response. For example, skin pigmentation, now known to be the result of several genes, also responds to alteration in the environment: Lee & Lasker (1959).

Given the ignorance of the relative importance of the environment factors that produce such physical plasticity, it is evident that we are at the beginning of studies to elucidate their mechanism. Aspects of psychic development have as yet hardly been touched. Klineberg (1931) has studied performance in intelligence tests in various racial and national groups and demonstrated that most of the conclusions based upon such work confined to the United States could not be substantiated. One early study to examine intelligence in descendants of migrants was by Franzblau (1935), who demonstrated a significant increase in performance in the descendants of Danish immigrants and proposed as cause a probable selection of immigrants or perhaps an effect of environment.

The Longitudinal Method: Advantages and Problems

Neither cross-cultural nor migrant studies, while they suggest environmental effects, illustrate differing growth responses. For this we require the longitudinal method; the rationale has been cogently stated by Kodlin and Thompson (1958):

> The longitudinal approach is the only approach which gives a complete description of the growth phenomenon (p. 8).

In this study an important object was to relate early and actual life experience to predict the consequences in later life. Thus it was essential to observe aspects of development in the same subjects over time. Only the expensive longitudinal approach may achieve this. The approach had to be longitudinal to answer certain questions about cause and effect. In previous longitudinal analyses, Block (1971) has used the adolescent to adult strategy, and Kagan & Moss (1962) reported observations of the Fels subjects from birth to maturity. But each of these admirable studies was limited to one cultural and geographic setting.

Longitudinal studies of *both* physical and psychological development are rare and sometimes are reported in a cross-sectional type of analysis. While physical growth processes and health measures may be measured by the same instruments, many aspects of psychological development must be assessed by methods that must be modified or even changed in form in order to be appropriate to the age of the child. For example, while at one point in adolescence the application of the High School Personality Questionnaire (Cattell, 1958) seemed appropriate, it was no longer so in the late teens and twenties, when the California Psychological Inventory (Gough, 1956) was more suitable. Longitudinal studies suffer also from changes in personnel, which mean also changes in research emphasis. The only safeguard is in the director of the research; and, fortunately, in this study, the director remained the same throughout.

Longitudinal studies are full of obstacles, and it is doubtful whether we would again attempt such an effort unless it were stringently limited in time. The effort of holding subjects over time involves a dedication and renunciation of personal convenience which it is difficult to describe. The present effort required that the principal investigator get to know each subject and each family on a personal basis. He visited their homes; and even now, 20 years after initiation, there are exchanges of visits and of correspondence. No subject was ever paid for his participation, although the principal investigator's own red wine was exported from Italy to the United States with a bottle or two distributed to each family. Friendly critics have referred to this as the "lifeblood" of the study.

CONSIDERATIONS OF DESIGN

After contemplating all of the previous studies it seemed that certain criteria should be observed before a further study could be attempted, so as to assure both genetic simplicity and sufficient environmental flexibility.

First, the environments should be markedly different in as many aspects as possible, including child rearing practices, the school environment and other influences outside the family, opportunities to interact with peers, access to social services, ease of transportation, and many other factors.

Second, the subjects should not be less than a certain number, to be determined after inspired guesses as to how great certain differences might be and ensuring that the subjects be as ethnically similar as possible. An ideal might be to have monozygotic twins reared in different cultures, but the chance seemed remote of obtaining more than a very few of these. An acceptable compromise would be to insist that all four grandparents come from a certain well-defined ethnic area somewhere in the world and that this could be clearly verified.

Third, some obvious confounding factors would receive careful attention: outstanding was socioeconomic class. This involved assessment of socioeconomic class across cultures, a task that might deter even a determined sociologist. Nevertheless, the work of two men encouraged us to believe it might be possible. One was Gilbert (1958) of the Organization for Economic Cooperation and Development, who put together comparative lists of common national products price levels so that their separate economic meaning in different countries might be better understood, and thus provide an adjustment for incomes. The second was Graffar (1956), who devised a more complex approach to cross-cultural socioeconomic conditions. After much thought it was decided to include some acceptable "culture fair" test which might reflect mental ability, and Raven's Progressive Matrices (Raven, 1956) seemed to provide a solution, even if a partial one. Clearly performance in such tests is determined by genetics only up to a certain point. Newman *et al.* (1937) had shown an uncorrected corelation coefficient on the Binet of .91 for monozygotic twins reared together and .67 for those reared apart, very close to dizygotic twins (.64). With McNemar's attenuation correction the correlations were .88 and .76, with dizygotic twins reared together at .63.

In contemplating the twin studies we became interested in methods used to distinguish types of twins. These included blood groups, ability to test phenyl-thiocarbamide (PTC), and color blindness. We considered that these might also be applicable to groups for reassurance as to ethnic origin, and for good measure we added eye, skin, and hair color and lateral dominance. Observations of these should be carried out at least on two occasions on all subjects.

Fourth, it was essential that behavioral development should receive attention, and for this it would be necessary to use methods already shown to be valid cross-culturally, or else to work out new approaches, or perhaps both.

It seemed to us that a study that might make further progress in this field should have some or all of the following characteristics:

1.   The subjects in both cultures should all derive from a limited area characterized by a defined homogeneity, in the mother country; migrants should derive if possible from village units of not less than 3000 population in order to reduce possible effects of subsequent exogenous marriages.

2.   The subjects should be the children and grandchildren of migrants and sedentes.

3.   In addition to the group of sedentes and their offspring, there should be a second group of those who migrated from the original area to elsewhere within the mother country, to compare with those who had gone to a widely different culture; the basic comparison should be between the two ethnically similar groups of migrants in the widely different cultures. Different patterns of migration of individuals from population groups residing in limited geographical areas that have been relatively homogenous over some period of time provide an unparalleled natural experiment. Such migrations to cultural and geographical settings differing sharply among themselves and from the original environment

allow us to examine the possible effects of environment on both physical and sociophysical characteristics. One group, which exemplifies such patterns of migration rather well, derives from southern Italy. During the late nineteenth and early twentieth centuries, large numbers of southern Italians emigrated to America. Somewhat later, many other southern Italian families also emigrated to Rome and to northern Italy to take advantage of the better economic opportunities in that part of the country. It is thus possible to compare three groups of southern Italian origin, now residing in three very different geographic, economic, and cultural environments.

4. The children should be examined over several years during a period of active growth in order that increments of growth might be examined to obtain a better understanding of the mechanisms involved. The choice of age groups of such children would thus be limited to the period from 10 to 14 onward, comprising the pubertal growth spurt in boys, or from one to two years earlier in girls. If an adolescent group were studied it should be carried to termination of physical growth in height.

5. Physical examination should be thorough enough to assess present state of physical health and a record should be made of past and present influences upon health for each individual.

6. Features of psychic growth should not be neglected as in the past. It appears possible that aspects of such growth (for example, intelligence) are determined by several genes and that therefore a certain plasticity might be anticipated here also; there would be an advantage in examining the children for several successive years not with constant instruments as in measurements of physical growth, given the difficulty of assessing increments in psychic growth and to avoid learning effects on a particular test, but with a variety of instruments and with repetition sufficient to give evidence of reliability.

7. Given the well-attested relationship between socioeconomic class and physical growth (Jenss, 1940) and between socioeconomic class and certain aspects of psychic development (Bene, 1958) and also intelligence levels (Havighurst & Breese, 1947; Havighurst & Janke, 1944; Maxwell, 1953), a method of socioeconomic classification should be developed that would be good for both cultures under consideration. Analysis should be made between similar socioeconomic spectrums. Comparison of such social classes within cultures might also be useful as an eventual comparative tool.

8. At the same time greater efforts should be made to understand and describe aspects of family life, local and general culture, so that those aspects held in common might be canceled out and the gross differences reserved for testing as to their possible influence in producing change in the subjects.

In 1956 we obtained the opportunity of assessing physical and mental growth and health for three or more successive years in several hundred adolescent and

˙ preadolescent boys, all with four grandparents from the same limited geographical zone of southern Italy. Of these, one-third lived in Boston and the rest resided in two cities in Italy: Rome and Palermo.

Hypotheses

We had a number of expectations.

1. Because of better nutrition, that the American boys would be taller and heavier and reach puberty earlier and the increased weight would be made up by increased amounts of fat, muscle, and bone

2. That there would be a difference in results on physical fitness tests (Italian superior to American) as observed by Kraus & Hirschland (1953, 1954), and Kraus (1954, pp. 68–69), but that this would be made insignificant when social class was controlled for and allowance made for body fat

3. Because of the less intense scholastic program, that American children of comparable intelligence and social class would have fewer intellectual resources

4. That American children would be more independent and more aggressive because of differing family practices and differences in cultural norms for behavior in children

5. That American children would be more "civic minded" because of cultural norms and the character of their formal education

6. Because of better nutrition, that American children would have a generally higher level of physical health except in certain respects, such as dental caries

7. Because of differing political orientation and practices, that American children would feel more in a position to control their own destinies and developments in their own societies

It was expected that incidental findings during the study would generate a number of additional hypotheses.

Selection of Subjects

To arrive at genetic simplicity it was vital that all of the subjects have all four grandparents originating from an area of Italy that could be demonstrated as sufficiently homogenous. There were the six southern Italian regions of Sicily, Calabria, Lucania, Pughlia, Campania, and the Abruzzi (the "Mezzogiorno"). These regions have been demonstrated to be similar in various respects and as a group to differ from the rest of Italy. Sardinia differs enough from the other regions to warrant exclusion, although together they comprise the economically depressed South (Costanzo, 1948); similar observations have been made upon the growth of children (Bacchetta, 1951). From what is known of the distribution of blood groups, gene frequency of A, B, and Rh D are also fairly homogenous and differ from the rest of Italy (Wolstenholme & O'Connor, 1959); there was also some evidence that the prevalence of color blindness differed from the rest of Italy.

A further advantage was the relative largeness of the village units. Communes of less than 3000 inhabitants are infrequent, and there is a marked tendency for those cultivating the land to live in the village.

The opportunity provided by the historical circumstances of migration from this region seemed unique; and in 1957 we began selecting the boys. We drew a line from Anzio on the west coast, north of Naples, to Pescara on the east coast and accepted all grandparents coming from below it.

To confirm the homogeneity of the subjects it was necessary to test them on a variety of characteristics considered to be hereditary and in which the South was thought to be different from the central and northern parts of Italy. Also it was necessary to compare the ages of the grandparents, their socioeconomic status, and a number of other family factors.

Girls were excluded in order to remove one major variable and because of potential logistic difficulties. At the time in Italy girls were highly protected and it was anticipated that there would be a large initial refusal rate and an equally high proportion of dropouts. This would cause a bias that would be well-nigh impossible to control for. There is also evidence that the male is more susceptible to adverse environmental influences (Douglas & Blomfield, 1958; Miller, Court, Walton, & Knox, 1960; Spence, Walton, Miller, & Court, 1954; Tanner, 1962).

Thus it was decided to find out how many boys of age 10–14, a sensitive period in developmental terms, all with four grandparents from the specified area of Italy, could be identified in the Boston area. Ideally, to reduce selection bias, the names or whereabouts of the subjects should be obtained from various sources. Similarly, enquiry was made in Italy where immigrants from the same area might be found. Clearly two emigrant groups should be compared in order to avoid the "contamination effect" of previous studies, which made a direct comparison of emigrants and those who stayed home.

At the time Rome seemed the most natural choice. Many had immigrated there from the South of Italy, not only before the Second World War but also during it and immediately afterwards. The great flood of southern families to the industrial North had not yet begun. Thus enquiry was made in Rome about the availability of subjects of comparable ethnic origin and it was established that many could be found.

These people had moved at different times and for different reasons. The majority of the subjects in Boston were the second generation born in the United States, that is, their grandparents had gone there mostly between 1890 and 1912. Many of those in Rome, on the other hand, were first generation born there, and some had arrived as young children. Most of the families who went to Boston had been, to some extent, "driven out" of Italy, in that the appalling home conditions had made the adventure across the sea seem attractive. But only about half of those in Rome had chosen to come there out of their own hopes for advancement or adventure. The rest, while subject to the same dire general economic situation, were minor government officials or employees of companies who made the transfer to the capital as part of a civil promotion system.

In order to complete the design, it was necessary to choose an area in the Italian South which would provide certain environmental conditions comparable to the other two sites. That is, the subjects would have to be urban dwellers, in a city of not less than 500,000 people, and to be established as having resided there or in the immediate countryside for a considerable number of years.

There were only two choices: Naples and Palermo. Naples was rejected as it had itself a sizable number of immigrants. Therefore Palermo was the choice. Thus, we had a potential study of the development of young males in Palermo (families never or rarely moved), Rome (all moved from the "South of Italy"), and Boston (all moved from the "South of Italy").

The Boston Sample[1]

Selection began in 1957. Enquiry was made from individuals with a good knowledge of Boston, from agencies such as the health and food departments of the city administration, the boys' clubs, and schools. It appeared that subjects would be more easily found in certain areas: East Boston, Boston North End, Charlestown, Somerville, and Newton. We were advised that the parochial schools might contain more such boys than the public schools.

The director of parochial schools suggested three schools (two grade schools and one high school) situated in predominantly Italian areas where such subjects might be found more readily.

In the two grade schools all boys in the fourth to eighth grades were asked to supply data on the birthplaces of their grandparents. Total population of these grades was 185 boys and 206 girls; 43 boys were identified as eligible and the parents were invited to consent to their participation in the study; 41 families accepted.

Boys with Italian surnames in the ninth grade of the high school were also requested to provide information on the birthplaces of their grandparents. Of the 20 boys identified as acceptable, 15 joined the study with their families. Eighteen subjects were also recruited from the Boys' Clubs of Boston.

[1]We thank the Right Reverend Timothy F. O'Leary, then superintendent of parochial schools in Boston, for his much appreciated help in obtaining the samples and his ready cooperation throughout the duration of the study. We also thank the principals of the schools that opened their doors to us, the Boston School Board as well as principals, the principals of public schools in Chelsea and Somerville, the director and principals of the Newton School System, and the director of the Framingham Heart Study.

We were permitted to examine the grandparental origin in the information files of the Framingham Heart Study (total number of subjects: 5234). Of this number, 1018 reported one or more parent or grandparent born in Italy. Six suitable families with boys aged 10–14 were identified and agreed to join the study.

At the end of the first year 73 subjects out of 86 identified (from a total population of 7599) had accepted.

Between 1957 and 1959, 12 subjects were lost through moves or refusals, or because it was subsequently discovered that one or more grandparent did not come from southern Italy, and a further 23 subjects were recruited. Thus, 91 boys and their families were examined in 1959 and all were available for analysis. In all, Boston subjects were examined one to six times between 1957 and 1964, and totaled 96.

By 1959 the boys were scattered in 30 educational institutions situated in seven separate municipal administrations; 55% were in public schools and 45% in parochial schools.

The public schools are obliged to accept all children up to the minimum school leaving age: 16 for Massachusetts, although the mentally retarded and some of those with behavior problems were excluded. The parochial elementary schools accepted all children who wished to enter but it is our opinion that the rigid standards for behavior produced some selection at this level and there was further selection produced by the high entry requirements at the high school level.

The Rome Sample[2]

Upon request, also in 1957, the Inspectorate of Education of the province of Rome identified some 150 boys, with four grandparents from the selected zones, in the classical junior high schools of that city. Six of thirty such schools were chosen by the Inspectorate as being most likely to contain such potential subjects and at the same time represent a reasonable geographical cross section of the city. They contained a total population of about 9000.

In accordance with our practice, the boys and their parents were invited to participate for a minimum of 3 years in the study which involved medical and psychological examinations and home visits. Experience from previous studies in Florence indicated that between two-thirds and three-quarters of the families would accept. Surprisingly almost all the boys appeared for the examination; only later was it found that attendance had been made obligatory. Some of the boys examined were found to have been wrongly selected in that some had only three grandparents from the selected areas. In view of the lack of children from professional families in the Boston group, three boys, whose parents were physicians, were excluded from further consideration, even though examined once. In

[2]In Rome and in Palermo we are indebted to the chief inspector of education and to the school principals; we extend them our thanks.

each successive year a few boys were discovered who did not fulfill the ethnic characteristics. This was either because important information had been suppressed or not recalled at the appropriate moment or, in a few cases, perhaps because of the temptation to accept the good medical care that was provided by the research, without careful thought of its aims.

Ineligible children were removed from the list of subjects when their true status became apparent and they have not been considered in the data presented here. In a few cases, children examined once had moved before the social worker's visit and were not traceable. As their ethnic origin had not been confirmed, it was not thought desirable to include them in the analysis.

Because of the compulsion of the first year and also the unfamiliarity of the Roman families with such studies, a higher percentage than anticipated (33 boys) did not appear for examination in 1958. An additional 59 boys were accepted from the same schools to make the total number 149 for 1958.

Toward the end of 1958, an experienced full-time social worker took over in Rome and this ensured a smaller wastage between 1958 and 1959 and also the recovery of 10 boys from 1957 who agreed to return to the study.

The original plan was to limit examinations to 3 years in Rome and Boston and to 2 years in Palermo. This was adhered to in Boston and Palermo, but it was found possible to reexamine a number of the boys in Rome on a fourth successive occasion; no great effort was made to persuade those who felt that because of heavy scholastic programs or other commitments they would prefer not to undertake an examination that occupied 5 hours (not including the social visit). Thus the losses between the third and fourth years have no great relevance. To confirm this we examined some characteristics of this group of refusals and they were found not to differ significantly from the Rome group as a whole in respect to age, height and weight for age, intelligence, and social class. Examination of the earlier refusals in Rome shows that there was a tendency for those higher in the socioeconomic scale to refuse the examination.

It has been repeatedly demonstrated that there is a relationship between social class and height and weight; analysis of these refusals presents no exception to the rule. Mean percentiles (Meredith, 1954) for height and weight for those in the different classes refusing to participate are presented in Table 1-1. Thus there was a tendency for those losses to reduce slightly the mean height and weight of those remaining. However, for our purposes the effect is to make the socioeconomic distribution of the Rome sample a little more like that of Boston, and this is an advantage.

Because of differences in regional distribution between the Boston and Roman samples and to reduce still further the influence of the factor of selection for higher education, an additional 13 boys with four grandparents from Campania were selected from 3 of the 43 vocational high schools of Rome. Thus a total of 123 boys were examined in Rome in 1960. These 123 boys were in 43 different

TABLE 1-1

MEAN PERCENTILES

Class	Height	Weight
2	51	52
3	34	39
4	23	26

institutions made up as follows: 57 subjects were in junior high schools; 22 were in senior high schools; 13 were in junior vocational and technical schools, and 30 were in senior vocational schools.

The Palermo Sample

Selection began in 1959. One junior high school, of the nine in the city, was nominated by the Palermo Inspectorate of Education. It was situated in a new middle class section and contained all male classes (there were no mixed classes in this or other such schools in Palermo). Out of the total of 392 boys aged 11–13 in their first and second year classes, 333 accepted the examination for 2 years. Of these, 120 were selected at random, half from each year level: 108 were reexamined in 1960. The balance of 12 refused or had moved away; none was rejected as having been wrongly selected. Of those examined, 96 remained in the original school; the rest (12) had moved to other schools.

Examination of the 12 refusals in Palermo shows that in height and weight for age and in socioeconomic condition they were not different from those who remained. However, their performance on intelligence tests (Raven mean percentile: 23) was significantly lower than those who remained and their scholastic record was disastrous. Their withdrawal should have the effect of raising the average Palermo intelligence test performance for 1959–1960. All these 12 losses were subsequently recovered to restore the total to 120.

Comparability of the Samples

A number of sources of bias may have been introduced by our selection procedures. We have estimated their influence as follows:

Initial Refusals

Over the period of the study, there were 8 initial refusals in Rome, 14 in Boston, and 3 in Palermo. A certain number of initial refusals may have been masked by those deliberately withholding information on family origins. The number cannot be calculated, but it is not believed to be large.

Subsequent Refusals

Excluding those who rejoined or who were ineligible, but including those who moved away in the course of the study, there were 74 in Rome, 6 in Boston, and 12 in Palermo. All of the Boston and Palermo dropouts were later recovered.

The total refusals in Rome are artificially swollen by the 27 of 1960; if the usual efforts had been made to recall all the subjects, this figure would have been cut in half. The demonstration that these refusals do not differ significantly on some key variables from those that remained reduces greatly the possibility that significant bias was caused. As noted, the earlier losses of 1958 and 1959 (47 boys in all) had the effect of making the remaining group more similar socioeconomically to the Boston subjects.

The number of refusals in Boston is not judged sufficient to warrant further investigation.

It has already been suggested that the Palermo refusals have had the possible effect of raising the performance on intelligence tests of those later examined in 1960.

It is interesting that Palermo, which shows a 10% loss as compared with 17% in Rome for 1958–1959, had a much higher proportion of families who disapproved of one or more aspects of the research (30% as against 6%; the Boston figure is also 6%).

Schools Sampled

We have already suggested that the selection of the Boston sample primarily through the parochial schools may have introduced a bias toward higher ability.

We felt that more information on the Italian samples could be obtained from a further study of the factors that determined the child's decision to take the examination for entry into junior high school. This study was undertaken in 1959 on a cluster sample of 1166 fifth-grade children and is reported in Young (1962a). To summarize the results, the weights of the four factors established by a regression analysis were socioeconomic class, .41; intelligence test performance, .30; urban or rural dwelling, .12; sex, male or female, .10. This shows the relative influence of all the factors considered. The factor of intelligence is less than what we anticipated and is possibly almost equalled by the selection factor already described in Boston. It is seen that socioeconomic class remains the outstanding point to control; the remaining two factors have no importance as our subjects were all males drawn from urban centers.

Performance on a relatively culture-free intelligence test (Raven) was chosen as control variable for intellectual function. The results are discussed in Chapter 4.

Unequal Representation from Regions within the Southern Zone

Owing perhaps to a misunderstanding of instructions in 1956, practically no children from the regions of Campania and Abruzzi were chosen for the Rome sample for 1957. This error was partially redressed later. When we examine the distribution of the grandparents between the regions, the principal differences are that the Rome sample has about 47% of Sicilian origin as compared with 30% for Boston, while when we look at those who come from Campania there are 45% in the Boston group and only 16% in the Rome group. As expected, the Palermo group was of predominantly Sicilian origin. Nutritional studies (Bacchetta, 1951) have demonstrated that the heights and weights of children from these regions is closely similar; as a group these regions have shorter and lighter children for equivalent ages than those from nothern and central Italy.

Selective Migration

In addition to biases introduced by our sampling procedures, other sources of noncomparability in the three samples may have derived from the different patterns of emigration from the South to Rome and to the northeastern United States, including Boston.

Time and Reason for Emigration

Of the 91 Boston families examined in 1959–1960, there were 14 instances where either a father or a mother was born in Italy; these parents came to the United States mostly as small children. In three cases both parents were born in Italy. In the majority of families, the grandparents made the change and the mean year of emigration for paternal grandfathers was 1905 and the range was 1877–1914 (excepting one whose wife and child emigrated, and he did not follow them until 1941); for paternal grandmothers the mean year was 1906, the range was 1885–1919 (excepting two who arrived in 1939, long after their husbands); for maternal grandfathers the mean year was 1904, the range was 1883–1926; and for maternal grandmothers the mean year was 1907, the range was 1881–1920.

The majority of the Roman families emigrated from the South before, during, or shortly after the Second World War, it being the parents of the boys studied who made the change. Thus, the majority of the Boston boys are the second generation born in America, while the Rome sample are the first generation born there. On the other hand, it is likely that the process of assimilation in Rome is considerably faster than in Boston and thus the "assimilation equation" is perhaps not too far different.

We have made an attempt to determine whether migration was active or passive. Included in the active group were those "seeking their fortune," "wanting to better themselves," "looking for work," "land of opportunity," etc. The passive group included children accompanying parents or other relatives, wives accompanying or joining husbands, and, in the Rome group, government employees on transfer.

Using such rough criteria, we found that the distribution of active emigrants for the Boston and the Rome groups was 79 % and 42 %, respectively. However, within the Rome group "active" migration varies with social class as shown in Table 1-2.

We selected subjects from the predominantly actively and passively emigrating families in the Boston group and compared them on a number of variables. Chosen were height and weight of father and mother, both now and at 20 years of age, a clinical judgment on aggression in the boy, and his scores on Factor "H" of the High School Personality Questionnaire. This factor—timidity versus adventurousness—is considered by Cattell (1958) to be the most highly correlated of all the Questionnaire factors with hereditary traits. Differences between the "active" and "passive" groups were small and insignificant. These comparisons indicate that motivation for emigration may not be an important factor in explaining the differences later to be described; however, this possibility cannot be entirely excluded, as the real reasons for emigration may be obscure after such a passage of time. This subject will be discussed further.

Urbanization and Socioeconomic Stratification of Grandparents

Table 1-3 shows the derivation of the grandparents from four density groupings: communes with fewer than 3000 inhabitants, those with 3000–10,000 inhabitants, towns with 10,000–50,000 people, and cities greater than 50,000. There are moderate differences in the distribution between Boston and Rome; as anticipated both differ markedly from Palermo. Further, to examine the possible influence of these differences, we took 58 subjects in social class three from Rome, divided them into three density groups, and compared these groups on some variables. Chosen were two indices of intelligence, one the Raven, and Factors "B," "A," and "H" of the High School Personality Questionnaire (HSPQ), representing "intelligence," "schizothymic/cyclothymic," and "timidity/adventurousness." The size of the commune of origin had no significant influence upon these variables. Table 1-3 also shows in the last column that effects of exogenous marriages in a formerly endogenous population are not likely to be appreciable in this experiment because of the small number of subjects with all four grandparents from the same village.

We determined the socioeconomic stratification of the grandparents from information about profession or occupation, educational level reached, and whether they were landowners or not. This was fairly satisfactorily obtained for our Rome subjects, but was recalled with difficulty by the Boston group as a

TABLE 1-2

Social class	1	2	3	4	5
Percentage "active" immigrants	50	21	23	72	75

TABLE 1-3

VILLAGES, TOWNS AND CITIES OF ORIGIN OF GRANDPARENTS
(Percent of Subjects)

Place	Communes with less than 3000 population	Communes with 3000-10,000 population	Communes with 10,000-50,000 population	Communes with more than 50,000 population	Boys with all four grandparents deriving from the same commune of less than 3000
Rome	13	28	25	34	6
Boston	20	31	31	18	1
Palermo	2	10	21	67	1

whole. Accordingly, the commune of origin of a number of the Boston families was visited by the principal investigator with the object of verifying and amplifying information already obtained. It was found that the information given was substantially accurate and that the extra material obtained did not have the effect of varying appreciably the place already allotted on the socioeconomic continuum. In view of the retrospective nature of this data, the socioeconomic classification of the grandparents must, however, be accepted with caution.

Table 1-4 shows the socioeconomic stratification of the grandparents and the present socioeconomic level of the Boston, Rome, and Palermo groups. This table also illustrates the social mobility, in which Boston, Rome, and Palermo may be listed in descending order. The overall socioeconomic superiority of the Palermo and Rome grandparental groups (within which Palermo is ahead) is in contrast to the present comparability of all three groups.

TABLE 1-4

SOCIOECONOMIC STRATIFICATION OF PATERNAL GRANDFATHERS
AND SUBJECTS UNDER STUDY
(Percentage Distribution)

Social Class	Rome		Boston		Palermo	
	Paternal Grandfather	Families under Study	Paternal Grandfather	Families under Study	Paternal Grandfather	Families under Study
1	4	7	-	2	5	6
2	3	14	-	15	12	18
3	37	44	6	60	38	47
4	33	29	27	21	35	22
5	23	6	67	2	11	7

Table 1-5 presents the influence of socioeconomic stratification of the grandparents upon certain key variables (present socioeconomic class held constant). It is seen that there is a tendency for those formerly in class five to be more intelligent and those formerly in classes one and two to be less so. These differences are more significant for the Raven. There is also a tendency for those formerly in class five to be more adventurous (Factor "H," HSPQ, see Chapter 4). This, however, is also shown by those formerly in classes one and two. The heights of the fathers follow the typical socioeconomic gradient downward from classes one and two to class five and it is seen that the families who have descended from classes one and two to class three weighed less (father at 20 years) than those who moved up from class five. There were no significant differences among the subjects grouped according to grandparental social class (on Meredith percentiles to eliminate the variation due to age) in either height or weight.

Type of Person Who Emigrated

Although this is to some extent controlled, we wished to be reassured that those who went were not predominantly the adventurous muscular types, different both physically and mentally from those who stayed at home or emigrated within their own country. (There are no records of observations upon Italian migrants at the time of the great emigration prior to the First World War.) We discarded an examination of the grandparents in view of the number already deceased. We examined the heights and weights of the parents in socioeconomic class four, now and at 20 years of age. This showed that there was already

TABLE 1-5

INFLUENCE OF SOCIOECONOMIC CONDITION OF GRANDPARENTS UPON CERTAIN VARIABLES
(All Subjects from Socioeconomic Class Three - Rome)

MEANS

Social Classes Grand-parents	Number of Subjects	Subjects Under Study							Fathers of Subjects		
		Raven Percent	High School Personality Questionnaire - Factors				Weight Percent (Meredith)	Height Percent (Meredith)	Weight (kg)	Weight at 20 years (kg)	Height (cm)
			B	A	H	I					
1 & 2	5	48	6.8	6.0	7.0	3.5	50	31	68	57	169
3	29	62	7.3	5.0	5.4	3.7	47	32	77	61	169
-4	15	65	6.4	5.2	5.3	3.5	53	40	71	60	168
5	12	73	7.6	5.1	6.5	3.3	60	27	76	61	164

significant difference in height (2.2 cm) of fathers but not of mothers and that the American parents were some 10 lb (4.5 kg) heavier both now and at 20 years of age. It might be desirable to determine what proportion of this significant difference is due to fat, muscle, or bone, but, as the majority of parents were exposed all their lives to the new environment, the results would not be of much help to us as far as control of physical selection is concerned.

The following additional variables were chosen in order to examine the comparability of the groups further:

1. Mean date of birth of parents and grandparents
2. Blood groups (ABO and RH)
3. Color blindness
4. Lateral dominance
5. Taste sensibility (to phenylthiourea)
6. Color of eyes of subject and his parents
7. Color of hair

The choice of 2–7 was determined by intra-European differences in respect to these variables and intra-Italian differences already known for 2 (Mourant, Kopec, & Domaniewska-Sobczak, 1958) and 3 (Dunn, 1957). It was suspected that the other variables might also show intra-Italian differences and, in spite of the relatively small number of subjects, since the extra expenditure of resources was also small, the data were collected. The results are presented in Appendix A.

The remaining variable that we wished to examine for comparability was intelligence, despite the fact that it was regarded as a questionable factor in view of the likelihood that intelligence is subject to plasticity. The results of the Raven Progressive Matricies (a relatively culture-free test) are presented in Chapter 4.

In summary, the main point of difference between the samples is that the Boston group started, two generations ago, from a markedly lower social level but their social velocity has been such that the distributions for social class are now very comparable among the three groups. This broad comparability should not mask the fact that in the Italian socioeconomic classification relatively more value is placed upon education while in the United States group there is more emphasis upon material wealth (Young & Tesi, 1962a).

The other major point of difference concerns the Rome control group which has been exposed to the new environment for one generation only. This is less important than it seems, for the function of this group is to control to some extent for the various factors associated with emigration and not to examine the effect of the Rome environment upon the families. However, it must be remembered that emigration may have isolating effects which have even been described as provoking psychosis in susceptible subjects; this isolation may be reduced in proportion to the number of other migrants who remain close and to the assimilation into the new society. As far as we are able to judge, both samples retain some contacts with families from points of origin; this is greater in the Rome group who are also able, when they wish, to return physically to their old homes. As regards assimilation, this appears more difficult in the United States; on the other hand, these families have now been there for more than 50 years and thus taking account of time we hope that the results of the "assimilation equation" are not too different in the two centers.

The other social variables considered do not appear to have had an effect in impairing the comparability of the groups and the genetic factors have on the whole demonstrated an overall homogeneity of our three southern groups when they are compared with a sample of some 400 boys in central Italy.

SUMMARY

We set out to examine the effects of differing environments on physical, psychological, and social development during adolescence—a period of peak growth and change. The study combined the longitudinal and cross-sectional methods—an arduous undertaking, but essential to grasp the phenomena of interest. Only the longitudinal approach makes it possible to chart the course of growth in contrasting groups of individual subjects and to study the impact of the environment on separate aspects of development at different stages in the change process. Studies of migrants have made an important contribution to our understanding of the effects of contrasting environments on population groups sharing a common genetic and ethnic background. The wave of emigration from southern Italy to the United States around the beginning of this century provides an excellent opportunity to identify subjects for such an investigation, particularly since substantial emigration from the South to central and northern Italy at a later period offered the possibility of contrasting the effects of such internal migration with those of a more drastic move to a very different geographical, political, linguistic, cultural, and economic setting.

We anticipated that the better nutrition available to the American immigrants would result in the third generation in earlier and greater physical growth, in improved health, but not necessarily in better physical fitness if socioeconomic differences were taken into account. We also expected that differences between Sicily and the United States in economic opportunities, social mobility, educational and political systems, and cultural values would be reflected in variations in family life, in modes of child rearing, and in the cognitive, social, and emotional development of the subjects during adolescence and in their status as young adults.

Our subjects were 339 male adolescents, all with four grandparents from the same limited geographical zone of southern Italy, residing in three urban settings: 96 in Boston, 123 in Rome, and 120 whose families had remained in Palermo.

Boys aged 10–14 with the appropriate family background were identified in Boston and Rome, mostly with the help of school authorities; all subjects in Palermo came from a single junior high school. We made elaborate efforts to ensure the comparability of the three groups, both through the use of a number of genetic markers such as blood group and eye color and through checks on our selection procedures. An initial bias in the Rome sample towards upper socioeconomic status was detected and partially corrected. The families in the three locations present a very similar distribution of current social and economic class (see Table 1-4). An inevitable difference between the groups was introduced by the varying times and causes of migration of the Rome and Boston samples, resulting in much greater mobility in Boston from the originally poorer economic status of the grandparent generation. Other possible sources of noncomparability between the three samples (initial refusals, subsequent drop outs, type of school attended, unequal representation from regions within the southern zone, genetic differences as judged by physical indicators) were examined and judged to be within acceptable limits. Data collection began in 1957 and continued until 1968.

CHAPTER 2

The Environment

SOUTHERN ITALIAN CULTURE

It is beyond the scope and purpose of this volume to attempt a general discussion of southern Italian culture, as contrasted with that of the northeastern United States in which so many Italian immigrants found themselves at the beginning of this century. A vivid and, so far as we can judge, accurate portrayal of this cultural transition is probably familiar to many readers from the film, "The Godfather, Part II." We do wish, however, to make a few personal observations on the contrasts between life in Italy and in the United States and to provide some background information on the three cities that were the setting for this research.

Barzini (1964) in *The Italians* has attempted to describe the Italian temperament, and his book serves to amplify and complement our description in much greater detail. His subsequent book (1971) helps one to understand the southern Italian just as Puzo (1969) gives us insight into the life of southern Italians who may have migrated to North America. Further insight into the reaction of Italians to American life may be gained by reading Torrielli (1941).

The visitor in an Italian city, even coming from one of the metropolitan centers of the eastern United States, will be struck by the noise, the bustle, the liveliness, and the apparent disorder and confusion of the life in the streets around him. Traffic is heavy, fast, and erratic. Its flow may be suddenly impeded by the motorist who is double- or triple-parked to conduct a quick business transaction or exchange greetings with friends. The visitor who needs to make any business or legal arrangements will quickly find himself caught in a seemingly inextricable bureaucratic maze whose purpose often seems to be to demonstrate authority or official importance for its own sake, overlaid with the most elaborate and elegant courtesy.

When we consider attitudes toward laws and external authority, we observe that in Italy the attitude toward the police is that toward a hostile force. This is seen by many cultivated Italians as a relic of the days when military or police authority was synonymous with foreign domination. The *carabinieri* are perceived in a more kindly role. Americans seem to regard the police less cordially than do the English, but more so than do the Italians, and, except in areas where they are notoriously corrupt or where there are sharp tensions, they are not viewed with the same suspicion.

In Italy, we are dealing with the southern Italian culture where there are deep family bonds and loyalties that far transcend respect for public authority. This introduces difficulties in law enforcement. The prestige of a family is affected by its perceived inviolability. If there occurs an open insult, such as malicious comment or a seduction, then family honor must be sustained by a settling of accounts. This is not to say that there are not also difficulties within the families. A man who has the slightest suspicion of infidelity in his wife may take violent action. It seems that arguments are more frequent, but perhaps this is because of more vocalization, which may even act as a safety valve.

The Italian seems to have many fewer friends than those who have gone to America, but this is perhaps the interpretation of the word. With the Italians' few real friends, the ties are strong. They will do much to protect and help them. Our subjects in Boston reported four times as many "friends" as those in Rome and Palermo.

It is similar for hospitality. Invitations to dinner or to stay the weekend are not made as easily in southern Italy as in the United States. A casual acquaintanceship is not sufficient for an introduction into an Italian's home life. Here only close friends are admitted. Another aspect of this reticence lies in the fear that the guest may be disappointed by the welcome he receives, that he may be used to better food, more elaborate furnishings, more scintillating conversation. All this is true if one meets people under ordinary circumstances, through profession or business, or at least in the house of common friends. On the other hand, the traveler is saved in the Homeric sense of the word. No effort is spared to help him, to make him feel at home, to resolve his difficulties.

Elegance of dress and of conduct are much prized in Italy. "La bella figura" is frequently in the thoughts of Italians. This may lead to a masking of reality and to deception, which may include the person or his foreign acquaintance. But many others in the same culture will know the truth.

There is much more verbal communication and gesturing in Italy than in the United States; certainly the flight of words and gestures serves as a demonstration of manners, for appropriate emotional response and perhaps as a way of releasing tension, but also there is the intellectual pleasure for people of every social class to express opinions and views on various problems with friends and acquaintances, a pleasure in the mechanism of reasoning for its own sake. It is also customary to be critical of people and events, and if this may appear frequently destructive, without suggestions for productive alternatives, it is discounted by those who know the culture.

It is our impression that there is more sense of frustration in the southern Italian culture, and this will be supported by some of the data discussed in Chapters 6 and 8. This is possibly generated in part by population pressures, with lack of good employment possibilities, the knowledge that a good job may depend more on influence perhaps than upon one's own abilities. In old age, frustration becomes less, as older people enjoy considerable prestige and power, in contrast to the United States, where it could almost be recommended that all people over the age of 65 emigrate to Italy.

Social mobility both in the sense of moving one's residence and of changing one's social class appeared to be substantially greater in the United States, but is undoubtedly increasing in Italy, where there has been a movement both from the south to the north (including to the other heavily industrialized nations of western Europe) and, in as great a degree, from the countryside into the cities.

Education carries social prestige, and in the late 1950s and early 1960s, even the junior high school was important. Now the emphasis has shifted to senior high schools and the universities. In general, the mothers of our subjects had less education than their husbands, and the age difference was 5–10 years. Thus in Italy, the housewife was not only less prepared for outside work if this should prove necessary or attractive but there was even social disapproval of this, except in the more privileged social classes.

There is a great love of small children, who are made much of by parents, relatives, and friends. They are greatly indulged but, as in any culture, there is a point when indulgence stops. Adolescents must be home by rather early fixed hours, and we have even seen one family where an unmarried son who was over 30 and a doctor of medicine was required to be in by 10 P.M. However, this is perhaps an exception, as the young man in his twenties is not discouraged from "having his fling," in contrast to the girl who is protected against any possibility of premarital experience.

We observed that older children were praised for different things in the Rome, Boston, or Palermo cultures. Success in school work was the most frequent reason in Rome and Boston, but in Palermo the unfortunate adolescent has almost a 50% chance of not being able to remember when he was praised as compared to 17% in Rome and none in Boston. Success in "sports" is more praised in Boston (22%), but not at all in Palermo or Rome. We shall amplify these differences in family life and in the experience of our adolescent subjects in a later section.

Dietary Differences

Some differences in patterns of eating and drinking are important in relation to growth. In Italy there is a more critical and appreciative attitude towards food. Culinary intelligence seems more developed. The more inhibited appreciation of material things in the United States may reflect the Puritan inheritance. Conversely, infants are satiated from an early age in the American culture. Our American subjects began to consume carbohydrates at an average of 3.0 months, and eggs or fish or meat at 5.6 months. This is later than the norm for the average Massachusetts infant, but much earlier than Rome and Palermo, whose respective ages were 8.1 months (carbohydrates) and 12.0 months (protein) for Rome, and 7.7 months (carbohydrates) and 10.7 months (protein) for Palermo.

The animal protein consumption per head per year for the United States in 1959, calculated from data published in the *Economist Diary* in 1961, was approximately 20 kg per head, or more than 50 gm per person per day. Horwitz (1960) estimates 66 gm; this was far in excess of that available per person in Italy.

Preliminary analysis of our nutrition data confirms this picture. Our Boston boys had a somewhat greater daily total protein intake and the animal protein proportion was much higher. The provisional figures are given in Table 2-1.

Widdowson (1947) reported London secondary school boys consume 99 gm of protein a day, of which 64 gm were of animal origin. She observed that school children require 2–3 gm of protein per kilogram of body weight to produce maximal storage. Work by Belousov and Gilman (1934, 1936) and Holt and Fales (1921) indicated that 60–70% of the protein intake should be from animal sources in order to promote optimum growth.

Retrospective inquiry suggests that proportional differences between the

TABLE 2-1

DAILY PROTEIN INTAKE

Place	No. of Subjects	Vegetable Protein (grams)	Animal Protein (grams)	Total Protein (grams)
Boston	61	39	69	108
Rome	111	56	46	106
Palermo	53	51	43	94

groups have been fairly constant since infancy. It has been noted that the Boston group start animal protein supplements at a considerably earlier age. In a pilot study we have noted acceleratory effects upon growth of such supplements in infancy (Young, Young, & Flori, 1957).

Although extra meat products account for a great deal of this difference, a considerable amount is contributed by milk and a smaller amount by cheese. Milk drinking habits in the two cultures are entirely different.

Consumption of sugar was 18 kg per person per year in Italy (1957), the lowest level of the Common Market countries, while consumption in the United States was 41 kg per person per year.

Although wine is liberally consumed in southern Italy, it is most unusual to see anyone the worse for drink. In part, this may because the working man uses wine for calories and it is rapidly metabolized, while the white collar groups did not seem to need alcohol to alleviate whatever social pressures might be upon them. Colleagues in the pharmaceutical industry stated that barbiturates were consumed much less in Italy than in the United States. The same appeared true for tranquilizers, even when allowance was made for the differences in purchasing power.

It is in the Italian tradition to keep children up late, especially if company is present. To counterbalance this is the "siesta," but this appears to be more enjoyed by adults than children. In fact, when we asked our subjects to report on hours of sleep, we found that Boston group slept more (at least 9 hr), the differences being approximately 1 hr at the earlier stages to ½ hr or less over the age of 14. No satisfactory correlations between hours of sleep and physical and mental growth are available in the literature.

We also attempted to measure exercise by attaching pedometers to random subgroups. The Boston group habitually exercised less (see Table 2-2). It seems that organized sports in the United States do not make up for the long walks to school, errands, and the lack of elevators in Italy.

THE THREE CITIES

We turn now to the physical political setting of our subjects' lives, and some facts about the three cities themselves. Concerning local statistics, the *Compendio Statistico Italiano* (1960) estimated that there were 1,963,000 people in Rome and 591,000 in Palermo. At the same time Greater Boston had also about 2,000,000 inhabitants (the city of Boston: 800,000, 1951 Census).

Rome, built over its famous seven hills not far from the coast of central Italy, enjoys a fairly mild climate, though it can be cold and wet in winter and oppressively hot in summer. It is a capital city and administrative center and is of great international and historic importance. It is also the world center of the Roman

TABLE 2-2

EXERCISE HABITS: KILOMETERS WALKED PER DAY

Place	Number of Subjects (Subsamples)	Mean	S.D.
Boston	20	8.9	3.33
Rome	29	12.8	4.85
Palermo	14	11.3	4.25

Catholic church. There is a considerable floating population of pilgrims, business men, government officials, tourists, visitors to international organizations (e.g., FAO), and others.

The proportion of population engaged in government service is much higher than in industrial Boston or Palermo.

The presence of the Vatican affects the Roman way of life, but less than might be expected, because of the traditional rivalry between the city and the Vatican.

The frequent invasions over the centuries have played their part in the formation of the Roman character, which has been described as superficially cordial but deeply self-centered and indifferent to others.

Although there is a large thriving university and some independent research institutes of importance, Rome cannot be considered a national education center as is Boston.

The city administration is centralized in Rome and Palermo, whereas in Boston there is the city proper both enveloping and flanked by a number of independent cities and towns that retain their administrative independence but all form part of Greater Boston.

Certain practices in local politics do not seem much different. Both Boston and Rome have had leading local political figures involved in financial scandals but who continued in office regardless and were reconfirmed by the electors.

Palermo is an international city, set on the north coast of the island and backed by a fertile agricultural plain (the "Concha d'Oro") and a semicircle of mountains. The climate is mild (quite hot in summer) and much of the life is out of doors. It still preserves something of the atmosphere of a capital of the Bourbons, its beautiful old buildings lending an air of elegance shading into picturesque decay. It is, in fact, the capital of the Sicilian region and has a parliament, as has Boston, with its state legislature. There is also a large university. During 1959 the scandals of the regional parliament provoked much national and international interest.

The province of Palermo has one of the highest homicide rates in Italy (205 per million of population per year) as compared with 35 for Rome, 21 for Florence, and 54 for all of Italy. (The U.S. rate was 47 in 1959.) The incidence of less serious crime is not much different between the Italian centers. This suggests that either there are more aggressive impulses or else they are more easily expressed in the south. Suicide and attempted suicide rates are available only for regions. For suicides, Sicily (44 per million) is well under the national average (64 per million), but the reverse is true for attempted suicide (103 versus 86 per million), which suggests a value that may attach to the dramatic gesture. For comparison there were 5298 suicides (3175 males and 2123 females) in England and Wales in 1958, a figure of almost 120 per million. In the United States the male rate is 12% higher than in England and Wales while the female rate is some 50% less. The overall U.S. suicide rate is 107 per million. It would appear that there is less tendency in the South of Italy to turn aggression against the self, but the difference may be explained by the strong moral strictures against suicide in a traditionally Catholic country.

There is some industry in Palermo, less relatively than in Rome, but neither can compare with Boston. The three cities have considerable slum areas, which are being cleared. Palermo is the worst in this respect, and the slums comprise 15% of the dwelling units, much more than Rome and Boston, which are more comparable. Some 3% of the units in Palermo are without running water and lavatory facilities.

The infantile mortality rates and the death rates are presented in Table 2-3. We have included Tuscany for comparison. The infantile mortality rates may be taken to reflect the health of populations; the order is Boston, Florence, Rome, Palermo. The figures for Palermo are certainly greatly augmented by the slum areas in which, however, only a very small proportion of our subjects reside.

The crude death rate is rather better in Sicily and Lazio than in Tuscany. The overall Italian and United States rates are similar. The higher Massachusetts level reflects an older population.

Those who are unable to read and write in these three Italian cities are Florence, 4.3%, Rome 4.1%, and Palermo, 18%. These figures are all reduced but still comparable proportionally if only the population of school age is considered.

THE ITALIAN AND AMERICAN SCHOOLS: DIFFERING EDUCATIONAL EXPERIENCES[1]

Since the initiation of this study in 1956, there have been many changes in the Italian schools, and we refer only to the circumstances encountered by *our* subjects.

[1]We thank Professor Lamberto Borghi, Professor of Education at the University of Florence and formerly at Columbia University, New York, for his scholarly review and for his suggestions, which have been adopted.

TABLE 2-3

INFANT MORTALITY RATE, CRUDE DEATH RATE AND BIRTH RATE
FOR SICILY, LAZIO, TUSCANY, ITALY, MASSACHUSETTS AND THE U.S.A.

Rate	Sicily	Lazio	Tuscany	Italy	Massa-chusetts	U.S.A.
Infant Mortality Rate (Per 1000 live births)	55.4 (1957)	41.1 (1957)	33.1 (1957)	48.2 (1958)	22.8 (1958)	26.9 (1958)
Death Rate (Per 1000 pop., 1959)	8.6	8.0	9.7	9.3	11.6	9.4
Birth Rate (Per 1000 pop., 1959)	21.6	19.0	13.1	17.9	23.5	24.1

Prior to college or university, the United States and Italy provide 12 and 13 years of education, respectively.

Education was compulsory up to varying ages for different states of the union; the highest was 18 (Ohio, Oklahoma, Utah); the lowest was Hawaii (15); Massachusetts had compulsory schooling to age 16.

In Italy education was then compulsory until 14 years of age, but a number of children, especially in country areas and in the south, managed to leave school before this. The situation was changing rapidly, and within a few years education was effectively universal up to 14 years of age.

In both countries school starts at age 6, although in many American states it is not compulsory until age 7. In the United States promotion from one year to the next is usual even if the standard of performance is not satisfactory. In Italy promotion depended upon the standard reached. In recent years there has been some relaxation in the elementary school, but from the classical junior high school upwards the percentage of failed students rose appreciably. For instance, failure rates for Florence in 1960 are presented in Table 2.4. Total failure means

TABLE 2-4

FAILURE RATES FOR FLORENCE, 1960
(Percentages)

Level	Passed June Exam	Passed Sup-lementary Sept. Exam	Total Passed	Total Failed
Media I (6th grade)	41	39	80	20
Media II (7th grade)	43	35	78	22
Media III (8th grade)	57	36	93	7

the year must be repeated. Partial failure in June obliges the student to work during the summer, in order to sit for the September exam. One of the junior high schools in which we worked in Rome stated that 21% of the students who took the exams in June and in September were failed in all three grades.

The American student thus starts college at 18, while the Italian starts at 19 and frequently later, owing to the probability that he has been failed once during school career.

Scuola Media (Junior High School), Italy

Unlike the junior high schools in the United States, the *scuola media inferiore* in Italy was not one common school for all children.

After the five grades of elementary school, for their education from 11 to 14, children were expected to choose between the vocational (commercial, industrial, or agricultural) school and the classical junior high school which prepared students to go on to the senior high schools (*liceo ginnasio, liceo scientifico,* or *magistrale*). The *magistrale* is a special high school adapted to the training of future elementary school teachers. Graduation from these senior high schools allowed admission to the university. Graduates from the *magistrale* were limited to entrance to the teaching and language faculties only.

Figure 2-1 illustrates the overall situation for the 13 years of preuniversity education with various alternatives available. The width of the channels indicates the volume of children. The distribution indicated in this figure is for the whole country and not solely the urban culture from which our subjects were derived. Clearly marked are those schools from which our subjects were drawn or to which they passed while under observation.

It is important to note that the system was rigid for individual students. One who took the less appropriate of the two main lanes at 11 years might find it very hard to remedy the situation. One may imagine a membrane between the two main streams; students might pass through in the downward direction but the difficulties of passing up were almost insuperable. The lack of transverse paths with two-way traffic caused preoccupation among those who were aware that the nation may thus lose precious talent. Separation at the junior high school level has been demonstrated to be socioeconomically determined (Young, 1962a). A new law has now been passed that has abolished the separation and made the junior high school equal for all students 11–14 years of age.

Article 34 of the Italian Constitution states, "School is open to all. Instruction for the first eight years is obligatory and free."

In theory this is true, but in practice school has not been entirely free. There were books to be bought, fares to be paid, still a few small taxes for examinations, etc., and the poorer families had to do without the important small sums of money that the child might earn by full-time work between 11 and 14; parents

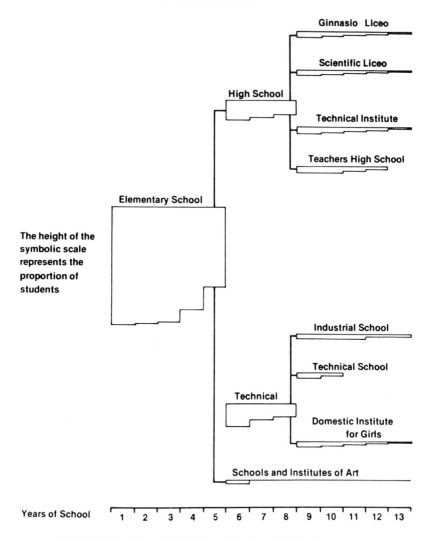

FIGURE 2-1.   National distribution of students in the Italian school.

might pay as much as $20 for books, which usually had to be purchased new each year. Children whose parents were not able to help them with their homework because of their own lack of learning found themselves at a disadvantage if they needed such help because lessons then cost up to $2 an hour. Usually the parent who could not help directly also could not afford these outlays.

In the province of Rome, 47% of the boys who received an elementary school diploma were admitted to the classical junior high school. By analogy with

Florence, where data were available to us, it would be expected that 54% of *city* boys would pass from the fifth elementary class to the classical junior high school.

To be admitted at that time to the classical junior high school, one had to pass a special state exam. If the main exam in June (pass rate 49%) and the supplementary exam in September (pass rate 29%) are considered together, the pass rate was 78%. For boys, the total number of hours in the first school year was 720, and 780 in the second and third. This did not include music and singing, which none of our subjects seem to have taken.

As seen, about 20% of children were failed at the end of their first and second years. A student might repeat the same class not more than once before he was expelled from that school. He might then try to make up the class privately or study in a nonstate school, perhaps returning to the state school later if he was successful, or else he might transfer to a vocational school.

Teachers in the elementary schools must have a diploma from the *magistrale,* described above. The secondary school teachers must possess a university degree. (The teachers of purely technical subjects, such as typing, in the technical schools were an exception.)

The clearest summary on the American high school at the time of our study has been provided by Conant (1959). The curricula in the various Italian high schools and technical schools attended by our subjects may be summarized as follows for the *ginnasio superiore* and *liceo classico:*

Italian language and literature	4–5 hr
Latin language and literature	4–5 hr
Greek	3–4 hr
History	2–3 hr
Mathematics	2–3 hr
Religion	1 hr
Physical education	2 hr
Foreign language	4 hr in the first 2 years
Geography	2 hr in the first 2 years
Philosophy	3 hr in the last 3 years
Science	3 hr in the last 3 years
Physics	2–3 hr in the last 2 years
History of art	1–2 hr in the last 3 years

for a total of 27–29 hr of classes per week each year.

The program in the *liceo scientifico* was very similar, with a slightly greater emphasis on natural sciences and mathematics and with Greek omitted. The curriculum in the *Istituto Magistrale* also omitted Greek, and included some psychology, educational theory, teaching practice, and additional music.

There were three types of technical institutes, emphasizing training in commercial, industrial, or construction subjects, and providing a 5-year secondary education alternative to the *liceo* or *magistrale*. They offered a reduced program in most of the subjects included in the *liceo* curriculum (with the exception of Latin and Greek) and provided an increasing number of hours per week of technical subjects (up to 16-24 hr in the final year). In addition, the industrial curriculum included up to 17 hr per week of practical work.

As we have seen in Chapter 1, most of the Rome sample were originally selected from the "classical" junior high schools and went on to a *liceo*. However, by 1960 one-third of the sample was enrolled in a vocational or technical junior or senior high school. All of the subjects in Palermo came originally from a single "classical" junior high school, although they represented a range of socioeconomic classes and went on to a number of different high schools. The Boston sample was enrolled in a number of parochial and public schools, most of them located in the North End and other neighborhoods with a large Italian population.

Consideration of the respective curricula and rates of failure leads to the conclusion that there was considerably more scholastic pressure in Italy and that, age for age, the pupils were obliged to learn more. On the information available it cannot be concluded that the Italian children learn to reason better, age for age, although it is possible that they do.

In Italy extracurricular activities were few and contact between students outside the classroom or "gymnasium" was limited to individual friendships. It was unusual to find competitive sports between schools. Physical education was often limited to indoor gymnastics, since sports fields were lacking. During the year one or two opportunities were given to the children to make 1-, 2-, or 3-day bus trips together, to a center of outstanding historical importance or of modern significance (e.g., the Olivetti or the Fiat factory). These trips were optional and might be costly.

The passing of the examination for admission to the *scuola media* was evidence that the pupil was capable of carrying out the 3 years satisfactorily. Theoretically there was no further grouping by ability; in fact, there was a trend for the brighter students and the more able and experienced teachers to be assigned to the A, B, and C sections, but this was only in several schools.

A class once formed, usually about 30 pupils, stayed together for all 3 years, sometimes with the same teacher or sometimes with another, as the Italian promotion and transfer system for teachers is flexible. The room may change from one year to the next but remains the same through any given year. The children stay in the room; the teachers move. The teacher of Italian, Latin, history, and geography is the home-room teacher, and considerable bonds of affection and understanding may develop between this teacher and the pupils during the 3 years. The majority of teachers are women.

Generally, one morning a week is allotted for individual teacher–parent discussions. Problems of scholastic achievement mostly occupy this time; however, the teacher does comment upon the child's behavior if this seems necessary.

There was, at the time of this study, no student council nor were there elections for class officers.

In Boston there was a wide range of extracurricular activities in all the schools, with many clubs and sports teams in which most boys participate. Competitive sports between schools is the rule. Most schools provide a partial mechanism of self-government, which the students may manipulate with guidance.

The normal course in civics, which is part of the history course, does not seem to explain success in developing a sense of responsibility towards the community. Rather it seems to be due to an underlying philosophy of education. The school newspaper might assist in this.

Generally there was no grouping by ability in either type of elementary school: those less able had been prevented from entering.

In many of the public junior and senior high schools there was a complex system of grouping by ability in that boys might enter the precollege, the commercial, the general, or the vocational course (Conant, 1959). Other public high schools were already specialized (e.g., the Boston Latin School, which provided a classical education and had higher standards for entry).

Almost all schools had a parent–teacher association that provided an opportunity for discussion of individual problems but is primarily a forum for the discussion of school programs and philosophies.

The Italian school climate, therefore, differed from that of the United States in encouraging higher standards of scholarship at the expense of extra pressure on the student; the range of communication between students was much more limited, although bonds between individual students and their teachers might be even stronger than in America; and there was less opportunity for effective participation in the working of the school society. As will be seen, the school was put to less use as a general social instrument.

Health Services

There was a health service for the Italian *scuola media*. Outside the great cities, it was uneven. In some areas it had not yet been initiated.

The service was generally limited to a physical examination and the detection and control of infection; the examination was frequently superficial, and there was not yet a national policy about how many examinations or what screening or follow-up services a child should have within the 3 years. There was no dental service. Little provision was made for the detection of emotionally disturbed children, although outside clinics existed where parents might take children who seemed to be disturbed.

The schools did not provide counseling to assist children in making a choice between alternatives, but most of the provincial administrations supported by the Ministry of Public Instruction (Education) have a center where children may go for vocational testing and advice.

In most of the Boston schools, parochial and public, attended by our subjects, opportunity was taken to detect departures from physical and mental health and public medical facilities were sought if the family did not have a doctor. There was also a counseling service, though not an equally good one in all schools. Overall, the quality of the school health service in Massachusetts was higher than in Italy.

School Plants

The end of the war found Italy with outdated and inadequate school buildings and grounds. Many new schools had been built, but the problem was still serious. When the study began, a great many schools had afternoon sessions and a few even had three sessions; in the following year in our group this was reduced to three schools. In 1960, only one of these schools still had double sessions. A room was occupied by one class for its school day from 8:30 until 12:30 or 1:30, and by another class from 2:00 until 6:00 or 7:00.

Many teachers thought that classes confined to the afternoon achieved less. In the interest of justice, some schools alternated afternoon sessions from day to day, week to week, month to month, or term to term.

In Boston many of the schools were modern and well equipped and provided good accommodation and areas for recreation. Generally, the public schools were superior to the parochial schools in this respect, but there were some exceptions.

The pupil–teacher ratio was generally greater than in Italy. This possibly reflects the relatively lower prestige of the teacher in America and the attendant difficulties of obtaining well qualified personnel. There were classes of up to 40 in the elementary public and parochial schools. In the junior high and high schools, 30 was the more usual number but this was frequently exceeded.

We applied a sociometric instrument, the "California Class Play," developed by Bower (1958), to seven classes (200 children) in Palermo, three classes (100 children) in Rome, and seven classes (200 children) in Florence. The number of roles allotted and number of negative roles in each center did not differ greatly from California, where the instrument was developed.

This suggests that intragroup hostilities and tensions are approximately the same in the school populations of both countries.

THE FAMILY IN ITALY AND AMERICA

Sociologists, anthropologists, and many popular writers have stressed the central significance of the family in southern Italian life. The family is the basic social and economic unit in the southern Italian village, and the bonds of loyalty, authority, and support that tie the individual to the family so outweigh the claims of any other social system that the culture has been characterized as "familistic" (Banfield, 1958). Although the broadest definition of *famiglia* (see Tomasi, 1972) subsumes a kinship network of all blood and in-law relatives up to the fourth degree, and also includes godparents, the functional family unit in the society from which our subjects derived was generally the extended nuclear family of a husband and wife, their unmarried children of both sexes, and generally the wives of any married sons; close ties to godparents were also recognized. A sharp boundary separated the social world of the family from all outsiders, especially those not from the same village, and, as we have already mentioned, any fiscal or political claims from that outside world were generally viewed with the profound suspicion deriving from centuries of oppression by absentee landlords. In later chapters we shall deal with the implications of "familism" for the individual's sense of moral values and his relation to the political system. Here we are more concerned with the family as a set of intimate relationships and as a child-rearing unit.

The southern Italian family has been described as patriarchal, but mother centered. The father (or oldest surviving male) is the undisputed head of the family, and retains authority in most vital matters over both wife and children. The mother, on the other hand, has the central responsibility for child rearing and for running the household, and carries out many decisions in her husband's name. Parental authority and control are maintained over offspring even into middle life. Another impression of south Italian life is of strict sexual mores. A woman was required to be a virgin at marriage (evidence to the contrary was considered a deep dishonor), and contact between the sexes at adolescence and beyond was strictly limited. Sexual taboos were somewhat undermined, in reality, by a marked double standard, with much greater latitude extended to men than to women. The individual's relation to the family was both more supportive and more restrictive, altogether more enveloping, than in American culture with its emphasis on independence and individualism. Adolescents in America are likely to have more freedom from family rules and limits and to come under the influence of a much wider range of socializing agents. The influence of the peer group, in particular, is likely to be more powerful and more at odds with parental standards than would be the case in traditional southern Italian communities. American parents are more likely to permit and encourage early involvement with peers of both sexes, as well as participation in sports and other competitive activities. (We have seen that sports were much more prominent in the school programs of our American resident subjects.) The educational system in America functions in many ways to reinforce individualistic and competitive values, and thus might be seen to be at odds with traditional southern Italian family values. Educational opportunities have also been much more limited in Italy, although this has changed markedly in the past 30 years or so. Thus higher prestige attaches to educational attainment in the Italian system of values, but education has not played the part in social mobility that it has in America. For this and other reasons, we would expect to find, among the families who remained in Sicily, a closer adherence to a traditional way of life and a sense of the individual's role in society being more thoroughly predetermined by his family's status and economic position than in the more mobile American system.

As we have seen, the families who moved to Rome did so more recently and for different reasons than those who emigrated to America. Where we find differences between them and the Sicilian group in patterns of family life, these differences may well reflect this selective emigration process which tended to send a disproportionate number of minor civil servants (as contrasted to impoverished peasants) to the national capital. Ties to families in the south have generally remained close, however, and we would expect considerable correspondence to the traditional way of life.

Our sample in Boston consists of second-generation immigrant families. There is a considerable literature that chronicles the process of adaptation of the rural southern Italian family to life in (for the most part) the urban, industrialized northeastern United States. Since the Italians, in contrast to other ethnic groups, tended to migrate in extended family networks, the traditional structure of the family was often maintained or reconstituted. The supports provided by the family were often helpful in the process of individual adaptation to the demands of the new setting; this has been described, for instance, by McLaughlin (1971) in her study of first-generation Italian immigrant families in Buffalo who found work in the canneries. On the other hand, the notorious (though not typical) contribution of the Italian community to organized crime has also been attributed by some to the persistence of family loyalties (Ianni and Ianni, 1972). Some writers suggest that the traditional family structure has operated to retard assimilation (Child, 1943), the integration of the individual into the educational system (Covello, 1967); by comparison with other second-generation immigrant groups, Italian–Americans have been found to be less individualistic, less competitive and achievement oriented (Strodtbeck, 1958).

Other investigators have been less concerned with the influence of the Italian family on individual assimilation into American culture than with the impact of the assimilation process on the family itself. Spiegel (1972), for instance, contrasts the values of the Italian–American and the Anglo–American family systems, and sees the discrepancy as producing conflicts within the Italian family that may lead to a variety of more or less successful resolutions. Some analyses (e.g., Campisi, 1948; Feminella, 1970, pp. 127–141) have focused on the changes across generations since immigration; these authors document a shift toward greater maternal power, a more open and democratic family system, less restrictive sexual mores (including freer heterosexual social contacts before marriage, mate selection by partners rather than by parents, practice of birth control

leading to smaller families, and more willingness to discuss and otherwise ac-
knowledge sexual matters), and greater mobility and emphasis on individual
achievement. However, the most recent comparisons of Italian–Americans with
other ethnic groups (e.g., Greeley & McCready, 1974) attest to the durability of
some basic characteristics and values of the southern Italian family. They have
found evidence of the persistence of fatalism, sexual restrictiveness, especially
for females, and reluctance to participate in the democratic process. On the
positive side, lower rates of alcoholism (as compared for instance with Irish and
Scandinavian ethnic groups) are attributed to the more supportive and nurturant
atmosphere of the Italian family (see Chapter 6 for data on this last issue).

Since this project was not conceived as a study primarily of family life or the
acculturation process, our data can make only a limited contribution in this area.
We did not include a contrast group of families from other ethnic groups resident
in the United States, as have such investigators as Spiegel and Greeley. Thus,
where our Boston families are found to differ from the Italian families in our
sample, we can only assume but not precisely document that these differences
reflect the process of cultural assimilation to the American way of life.

Despite the many impressionistic accounts and more global analyses of differences between Italian and American family life, there is little in the way of
empirical literature on parent–child relations and child-rearing practices. The
only relevant recent study is one by Peterson and Migliorino (1967), comparing
the responses of a group of Sicilian parents interviewed in Palermo with a group
of parents from a Midwestern American university community. They used a
modification of the Sears, Maccoby, and Levin (1957) parent interview schedule
(as have most recent cross-cultural studies), appropriately translated, with Sicilian interviewers and raters for the Palermo sample. The ages of the children
involved, however, ranged from 5 to 14, and both sexes were included in the
sample. Peterson and Migliorino report their most striking finding, and one very
much in line with general impressions of cultural differences, to be one of
marked differences along the general factor of Permissiveness/Control. Sicilian
parents reported maintaining a much stricter control over their children than did
the American sample, particularly with respect to sexual and aggressive behavior. They seemed to countenance practically no sexual behavior in their
children, most of whom had not yet reached adolescence. They were also less
likely than American parents to permit aggressive acts towards themselves or to
encourage aggressive interaction with peers. There is also a slight reported difference in affection in favor of American parents, but on the whole no great
difference in the apparent warmth in family life. Somewhat more surprisingly, in
view of the usual stereotypes, these investigators also failed to find any clear
differences in the distribution of parental authority. The Sicilian husband is, if
anything, even more likely than the Midwestern American husband to leave
everyday financial decisions to his wife.

Peterson and Migliorino found the general structure of parental attitudes and reported child-rearing practices to be quite similar for their Sicilian and American samples, so that they were justified in comparing the two groups of parents along the same dimensions. We would expect our groups to be even more similar, since they were much more carefully matched with respect to age of offspring and socioeconomic factors, and all derive from the same southern Italian ethnic background. To the extent that the Boston sample may have absorbed some of the child-rearing mores of the American culture, however, we would look for differences from the Italian groups especially along the dimensions of control, permissiveness toward sexual and aggressive behavior, and pressure towards independence.

The Parent Interviews

Our data on family relations and child-rearing practices were collected primarily in two rounds of interviews with the families in 1957–1958 and 1959–1960. Essential objectives of these interviews were to collect information on health history and to permit a cross-culturally valid estimate of socioeconomic status (SES). Much information was also collected on family life and parents' attitudes toward many aspects of their sons' behavior. The interviewers were professional social workers, one in each of the three cities; some interviews were also done by the project director. The observer went by appointment to the home and interviewed the mother and if possible the father. The interview was made as "free flowing" as possible, but the observer always had in mind the standard form she must complete afterwards. The interviews lasted on average of 2 hr, and it took about the same amount of time to write up the case. In subsequent yearly visits, less time was required in the home and some items required verification only.

The earlier interviews in 1957 and 1958 were concerned with establishing socioeconomic conditions and observing certain family practices. In 1959 and 1960 there was more emphasis on family dynamics, and the observer was required to make a 4-point judgment on a number of variables that might be influenced by family life (e.g., dependence/independence, sex education, aggression, affection). Obviously ensuring comparability of information and of observers' judgments for the three groups of families, particularly where subjective ratings were involved, presented formidable problems. Earnest efforts were made to overcome these difficulties by having each of the interviewers visit a small number of families either together or on subsequent days, and by intensive group discussions of methods and criteria. In addition, the project director made visits to four Boston families in 1959 and to 25 families in Rome and 15 in Palermo in 1960. He established good agreement with the social workers in Boston and Rome, and fair agreement with the worker in Palermo. The interviewer in Boston spoke only English, whereas the interviewer in Rome was bilingual and acted as interpreter for her colleague on the joint visits. The interviewer in Palermo was a native of that area, with somewhat less professional experience than her two colleagues. This may account for the generally somewhat lower, although satisfactory, reliability.

The SES measure was derived according to an index developed by Graffar (1956). It involves five component variables: occupation and education of the father, family income, condition of the home, and location of the dwelling (type of neighborhood). Occupation was rated on a scale running from one to eight. Years of education was reduced to five categories (see Young & Tesi, 1962b), introducing a correction for the differences in structure of the Italian and U.S. school systems. Family income was similarly categorized in five steps, equating for rate of exchange and discrepancies in purchasing power between the lira and the dollar. Condition and location of dwelling were also rated from one to five. The five components averaged to derive an overall index of SES, running from one (the highest) to five (the lowest social class). The distribution of SES in the three groups has been discussed in the preceding chapter, in connection with subject selection.

We also obtained some information on family structure. Tables 2-5a–c show the distribution of numbers of children among the three groups of families and of the ordinal positions of our subjects. We see that the majority of families in all three groups had two or three children (55% in Boston, 62% in Rome, and 72% in Palermo). However, there was a disproportionate number of first-borns in

TABLE 2-5a

FAMILY CONSTELLATIONS: BOSTON

Number of Children	Place of Subject										Number of Families	Percent
	1	2	3	4	5	6	7	8	9	10		
1	6										6	6.2
2	14	13									27	28.2
3	7	9	10								26	27.1
4	5	3	1	5							14	14.6
5	1	4	1	2	4						12	12.5
6	1	1	1		1	2					6	6.3
7					1	1					2	2.0
8			1								1	1.0
9	1										1	1.0
10										1	1	1.0
Total											96	100.0

TABLE 2-5b

FAMILY CONSTELLATIONS: ROME

Number of Children	Place of Subject										Number of Families	Percent
	1	2	3	4	5	6	7	8	9	10		
1	14										14	10.9
2	16	13									29	23.6
3	12	19	18								49	38.4
4	3	7	8	4							22	17.2
5	2	2	1	2	1						8	6.2
6	1										1	0.7
7						1	1				2	1.6
8											0	0.0
9				1							1	0.7
10										1	1	0.7
Total											127	100.0

TABLE 2-5c

FAMILY CONSTELLATIONS: PALERMO

Number of Children	Place of Subject											Number of Families	Percent
	1	2	3	4	5	6	7	8	9	10	11		
1	7											7	5.8
2	28	14										42	35.9
3	17	7	10									34	28.3
4	6	4	4	4								18	15.0
5	2	4	1	1	3							11	9.3
6		1		3	1	1						6	5.0
7							1					1	0.8
8												0	0.0
9												0	0.0
10												0	0.0
11											1	1	0.9
Total												117	100.0

Palermo (45% as contrasted to 36% in Boston and 38% in Rome) and a dispro-portionate number of very large families (five or more children) in Boston (24% as contrasted to 10% in Rome and 13% in Palermo). The number of only children in Rome is somewhat larger (11% as contrasted to 5% and 6% in the other two groups). We are not sure what these differences in family size may mean, except that perhaps the group of families in Rome have adapted to a larger and more industrialized setting with a trend towards smaller families whereas the group in Boston, with somewhat better conditions of nutrition and medical care, have stretched the tendency of southern Italians toward large families in the opposite direction. The greater number of first-borns in Palermo might suggest a somewhat more vulner-able sample, both medically and psychologically, but also a group somewhat advantaged in early nurturance.

At the same time, the interviewers inquired about the amount of contact each subject had with grandparents. In Palermo, of course, most subjects had frequent or daily contact with grandparents, so long as they were still living. In 118 families where information was available, 88 subjects had one or more grandparents living in Palermo or within easy travel. Of these, 30 were living in the same dwelling as the subject. For the remaining 20 subjects all four grandparents were reported as having died. This was when the boys were 12 to 13 and many of these grandparents must have known the subjects when they were younger. In only one family were all four grandparents from outside Sicily. They were from Puglia. All grandparents came from the South of Italy. On the whole the Palermo grandparents were reported as socioeconomically more privileged than the Boston grandparents, but in Palermo there are some transparent over-statements, as where the grandparent, an evident sharecropper, was described as a landed proprietor. Instead, in a subsample of some 15 Boston families where the places of origin in Sicily were visited by the principal investigator, the socioeconomic report was substantially correct. Perhaps in the United States there is less disadvantage and even some pride in admitting to humble forefathers.

Table 2-6 shows the respective situations in Boston and Rome among the two emigrant groups of families. The proportions of families in which grandparents lived in the home are very similar, particularly if one takes account of the fact that in Rome almost all lived within the family, while in Boston some lived in an apartment above or below that of our subjects but in the same building. The proportions of Boston subjects who knew their grandparents was substantially higher than in Rome, reflecting the circumstances noted in Chapter 1, that extended family groups tended to emigrate from southern Italy to the United States. The grandparents with whom the Rome boys had contact were mainly still living in the village or town of origin; the subject usually visited them at summer vacation time for a period up to 3 months. Some of these grandparents had died before 1960, but all had known the subject until he was at least 5 years old. In

TABLE 2-6

KNOWLEDGE OF GRANDPARENTS

Knowledge of Grandparents	Boston (N=96)		Rome (N=127)	
	Number	Percentage	Number	Percentage
Grandparents living in the same apartment or dwelling	15	15.6	16	12.6
Subject did not know any grandparents	8	8.3	31	24.4
Knew paternal grandfather	50	52.1	41	32.3
Knew paternal grandmother	65	67.7	53	41.7
Knew maternal grandfather	51	53.1	50	39.3
Knew maternal grandmother	75	78.1	80	63.0

both cities, contact with grandmothers was higher because of female longevity. Thus we see that for the majority of our emigrant subjects, but especially for the Boston group, grandparents were an important presence in the family and a strong potential source of influence. This is significant for the persistence of traditional patterns of socialization and family life, which we shall note repeatedly in later sections. On the other hand, a quarter of the Roman subjects had no contact with grandparents, and thus experienced growing up in a more isolated nuclear family unit, a situation more typical of modern urban living than of traditional life in southern Italy or of the "urban villages" of "Little Italy" or the North End of Boston.

Socialization Dimensions

Since the items in the interview records referring to various aspects of family life and child-rearing practices were so diverse in nature, it did not seem reasonable to proceed by means of factor analyses to establish empirical dimensions of socialization that might be unique to this population of families. Rather we selected rational groupings of items which were presumed to reflect aspects of socialization or family relations found in previous cross-cultural studies and which we supposed might differentiate among our groups. These sets of items were then subjected item by item to tests of discrimination among the three groups (generally by means of chi-square comparisons), and also analyzed for internal consistency by means of intercorrelations. (Since many items were dichotomous or poorly distributed, tetrachoric correlations were used.) The subsets of items that survived this internal consistency analysis were then totaled to yield combined scores on eight socialization variables. The means and standard deviations of the scores on these variables for the families in each of the three cities are given in Table 2-7 along with an indication of which of the comparisons between cities yielded significant differences. Each of these areas of socialization and family relations will be discussed in terms of these comparisons of combined

TABLE 2-7

SOCIALIZATION VARIABLES

Variables		Boston	Rome	Palermo	Comparisons of Means		
					Boston-Rome	Rome-Palermo	Boston-Palermo
1. Control	$\bar{X}$	9.18	10.87	10.18	t= 7.04	t= 2.30	t= 3.85
	SD	1.31	2.06	2.17	p= .01	p= .05	p= .01
	N	92	127	112			
2. Sex	$\bar{X}$	4.26	4.02	5.72	t= 1.41	t=12.14	t=10.43
Restrictive-	SD	1.34	1.16	.77	p= N.S.	p= .01	p= .01
ness	N	92	124	112			
3. Freedom of	$\bar{X}$	4.69	6.92	5.61	t=10.14	t= 5.95	t= 5.41
Expression	SD	1.06	1.83	1.36	p= .01	p= .01	p= .01
	N	95	127	112			
4. Early	$\bar{X}$	72.07	86.09	81.44	t= 3.79	t= 1.21	t= 2.48
Socialization	SD	25.54	26.71	27.79	p= 01	p= N.S.	p= .01
(Age)	N	94	125	112			
5. Indulgence	$\bar{X}$	86.63	101.85	97.60	t= 3.86	t= 1.07	t= 2.82
	SD	27.03	28.63	27.99	p= .01	p= N.S.	p= .01
	N	95	127	112			
6. Peer	$\bar{X}$	13.25	15.54	13.37	t= 7.63	t= 7.04	t= 1.23
Relations	SD	2.11	2.21	1.73	p= .01	p= .01	p= N.S.
	N	95	127	112			
7. Cohesion	$\bar{X}$	4.33	5.67	5.24	t= 6.75	t= 2.15	t= 6.57
	SD	.93	1.60	1.20	p= .01	p= .05	p= .01
	N	92	127	112			
8. Academic	$\bar{X}$	12.04	13.78	14.09	t= 4.24	t= .76	t= 5.54
Pressure	SD	2.61	3.13	2.60	p= .01	p= N.S.	p= .01
	N	95	127	112			

scores and in terms of individual differentiating items, which generally give a more precise picture of the content of the differences in family life observed.

Control (Permissiveness/Strictness)

The dimension of the degree of control that the parent exercises (or attempts to exercise) over the child's behavior, usually labeled as running between the two poles of permissiveness and strictness, has emerged in almost all studies of parent–child relations as one of the two major axes defining the psychometric "space" of parental attitudes and behavior (the second major dimension being that of warmth versus hostility or rejection). In their comparison of the child-rearing practices of Sicilian and American parents, Peterson and Migliorino found the greatest differences along this factor of parental control. In particular they found that Sicilian parents expressed much more restrictive attitudes with respect to sexual behavior and aggression toward peers. As we have seen, the comparison groups in their study were much less closely matched than ours on a number of relevant variables, such as SES and age of child; furthermore, all of our families derived from the same southern Italian ethnic background. Consequently, one would expect less contrast in child-rearing practices between our Italian and Italian–American groups of parents. It is thus of considerable interest that our findings very clearly confirm the main conclusions these other investigators drew from their data.

A series of 14 items in the interview schedule (B 75 . . . 79, C 5 . . . 13) may be considered to reflect different aspects of the control the parents exercised over the conduct, choices, and everyday lives of their sons. Of these 14 items, the Boston group responded to 11 clearly and significantly in a more permissive, less controlling fashion than both of the Italian groups. On only one item (C 13: Does the parent see that the boy is neat and clean?) was this trend reversed; the Palermo parents were more permissive than the Boston parents, although the Rome group was the least permissive. The differentiating items were as follows:

B 75   May he go out alone outside of going to school?
B 76   Must he seek permission every time?
B 78   May he choose any friends he wishes?
B 79   May he develop interests and hobbies on his own?
C 6   May he belong to youth clubs or similar organizations on his own?
C 7   May he dress as he likes?
C 8   Has he chosen his own school curriculum?
C 9   Will he have full freedom to choose his own profession?
C 10   Would his parent like him to achieve what they themselves have been unable to achieve?
C 11   Does he have pocket money?
C 12   Do his parents control the way in which the money is spent?

To all of these items the Boston parents responded in the more permissive direction.

The differences in response between the Rome and Palermo parents are less consistent and generally of smaller magnitude. In 8 out of the 14 items, however, the Rome group responded more frequently in the controlling direction (items B 76, 78, 79, C 6, 8, 9, 11, 12). On only four items did the Palermo parents express stricter attitudes (items B 75, C7, 10, 13). This would indicate that the parents in Rome generally exercised somewhat tighter control over their sons' lives, and that the Palermo parents were somewhat more permissive, although clearly less permissive than the parents in Boston.

Out of this group of items, seven (B 75, 78, C 5, 7, 8, 9, 11) were found to have an acceptable degree of internal consistency (a Kuder–Richardson [K–R] coefficient of .68). Responses to these items were accordingly summed in order to derive a total score for each family on the dimension of Strictness versus Permissiveness of Control (high scores indicate strictness). The mean scores for the three groups are listed in Table 2-7. The differences between each of the cities are significant at the .01 level.

These overall differences on the variable of control confirm the conclusions derived from the comparisons of responses to the individual items. In general, parents in Boston describe themselves as considerably more permissive than did either of the two Italian groups, and the parents in Rome exercised somewhat more control over their sons, on the average, than did parents in Palermo. (In the two Italian groups, degree of control tended to be related to the boy's age; correlations of $-.23$ and $-.24$ indicating that parents of older boys were slightly more permissive. This association may reflect the fact that the two Italian samples included somewhat younger subjects than did the sample in Boston.)

Attitudes toward Sex

Peterson and Migliorino found that within the general Control factor, the sharpest differences between the Sicilian and American parents were on items that had to do with sexual behavior, the Sicilian parents being much more restrictive in this area. Our interview with the parents did not cover the same items of sexual behavior as those included in the modified Sears, Maccoby, and Levin schedule used by Peterson and Migliorino, but did include a number of questions reflecting the parents' openness in discussing sexual matters with the boys and informing them about sex, and their willingness to permit heterosexual social contacts. Of the seven items in question, one (C 36) did not yield enough responses to be useful and another (C 34–35: Age at which the boy asked the first questions about sexual matters) could not be analyzed in the same way as the others. All of the other five items yield highly significant differences, and on each item the Boston parents express the most permissive attitudes, the Palermo parents are the most restrictive, and the Rome group falls in between. These items are

B 64 Are they opposed to games and friendships between friends of the opposite sex?

C 31 Sexual education: Do the parents prefer to inform the boy themselves or do they prefer him to be informed by others?

C 32 Do they speak of sexual problems in the boy's presence?

C 33 Do they prefer to inform him in a realistic manner, or have they taken refuge in tales of storks, etc.?

C 37 To what extent has the family faced up to the problem of the sexual education of the boy?

It is of some interest to note that by far the greatest proportion of failures to gain information on these items occurred among the Roman parents. This might reflect a difference in interviewing technique, but it is also possible that these parents as a group met the questions about sexual matters with more evasiveness, while the Palermo parents more openly expressed their restrictive attitudes and the Boston parents were more permissive. In any case, these data support the general conclusion that the atmosphere of the Sicilian family is extremely non-permissive about sex, at least in so far as the education of adolescent boys is concerned. The Italian–American parents, on the other hand, reflect the generally greater freedom and openness in this area of the American culture.

Three of the sex items (C 31, 32, 33) were sufficiently internally consistent (K–R reliability, based on 321 cases, of .76) to justify summing them to yield a total score (see Table 2-7). To judge from the combination of these three items, the Palermo parents expressed significantly ($p < .01$) less open attitudes toward sexual matters than did parents in the other two cities. The difference between Rome and Boston is not significant.

Aggression toward Peers

Unfortunately, the social inquiry does not provide any information about attitudes on aggression within the family. There were no questions dealing with aggressive acts toward parents, and to the one question (B 62) about quarreling among siblings there were too few responses to be useful.

There were five items, however, that concerned the manner in which parents would advise their sons to respond to aggressive acts from peers. Four of these (C 38, 39, 41, and 42) yielded clear differences between the Boston and Italian parents; the two Italian groups did not differ significantly, although there was some indication that the Palermo parents were even less likely than those in Rome to encourage an aggressive response. The parents in Boston were much more likely to advise that the boy respond immediately and aggressively to such an attack. Almost no parents in Boston indicated that they would advise their son to withdraw in the face of an attack by a peer, whereas a majority in Rome and in Palermo (68%) would advise this. Secondarily, the Italian parents would allow the boy to make his own decision as to how to respond. The parents in Boston also indicated that they were more likely than those in either Palermo or Rome to advise other ways of dealing with the situation but, interestingly enough, this response tended to be associated with encouraging counteraggression in Boston and with advising withdrawal in Rome. The parents in Rome were the most likely to use adages and proverbs to influence their sons' behavior in such situations; this response was very rare in Boston, and did not occur at all in Palermo. It seems that the parents in Rome are even more likely than those in the other two groups to use much verbal exhortation in their attempts to influence their sons.

These aggression items were neither sufficiently numerous nor internally consistent enough to justify a summary score. It seems clear, however, that in aggressive situations with peers, the Italian–American parents are much more likely to encourage an active, aggressive response, whereas the Italian parents encourage a more passive response and the inhibition of overt aggression toward peers. As we shall see in the boys' interview responses, there are indications that, especially in Palermo, aggression within the Italian family is even more severely inhibited, whereas the generally greater permissiveness and freedom of expression in the Boston families would suggest that a certain amount of aggression might be tolerated.

Freedom of Expression

Four items were judged to reflect the variable of Freedom of Expression, conceptually related to the general Control dimension. Their content is as follows:

B 71   Does the boy discuss his personal problems with his parents?
B 72   May he question an order?
B 73   Do the parents explain the why and wherefore of orders or prohibitions?
B 74   When there is an important decision which affects the whole family do they take his opinion into consideration?

For three of these four items, the parents in Rome are least likely to allow freedom of expression, while on the fourth item almost equal minorities of the Rome and Palermo parents (30% and 31%) respond in the permissive direction. These four items were found to constitute a reasonably internally consistent group (a K–R coefficient of .63). Accordingly they were summed to derive a total score on the dimension of Freedom of Expression. The means for the three cities, with higher scores in this case meaning *less* freedom, are given in Table 2-7. Each of the differences between means is significant at the .01 level. We may infer that there is more open communication in the Italian–American families than in those in Italy, and that these parents have been influenced by some of the more typically American values in favor of democratic child rearing. Again, the parents in Rome appear to be the most controlling—more so, on the average, than those in Palermo.

Early Socialization

We have been considering the general dimension of the strictness versus permissiveness of child rearing from the standpoint of the degree of control the parents currently exerted over their adolescent sons' lives, as contrasted with the amount of freedom allowed them in action and expression. Another aspect of child rearing generally found as part of the Control factor has to do with the degree of pressure towards socialization, especially at early developmental stages. Relatively late ages of weaning, toilet training, cleanliness training, etc., and relatively little emphasis with the young child on honesty, obedience, and other aspects of self-control may be considered to reflect a relatively indulgent pattern of child rearing. A total of 18 items appeared to reflect some aspect of socialization pressure versus indulgence. The first group of items refers to ages of beginning and completing training of bladder and bowel control, and the amount of time the training required (B 22–23, 24–25, 26–27, 28–29, 30–31, 32–33). Item B 44–45 refers to the age when tooth cleaning started; items C 18–19 and 20–21 refer to the ages at which the child began to wash and dress himself.

Comparisons on specific items did not seem especially meaningful, since parents' retrospective reports, after a lapse of 10 years or so, of the exact ages at which certain milestones of early socialization were passed, are subject to considerable unreliability. However, it did seem useful to average these items for each case to obtain an overall estimate of the degree of indulgence, as compared to pressure for early socialization, which the parents described as characterizing their early child rearing. The means for these ages of early socialization scores are given in Table 2-7, variable 4. The differences between Boston and each of the Italian cities are significant at the .01 level. The difference between Rome and Palermo is not significant. It seems that the Italian–American group of parents exerted clearly greater pressure towards early socialization in the areas of elimination, cleanliness, and self-care than did the Italian parents.

A few other items seemed related conceptually to this same dimension of child rearing. Of these, four (B 46, 48, 50, and C 71) either had too many missing scores or did not discriminate among the groups; to four others the Boston parents clearly responded in the least indulgent direction:

B 43   Tooth cleaning—regular versus irregular?
B 47   Is he obedient?
B 49   Type of maternal upbringing—rigid versus indulgent (the equivalent item for paternal upbringing did not differentiate the groups).
C 17   Responsibility in the home.

On a fifth item, already reported in the previous section (C 13: Do the parents make sure he is neat and clean?), the Palermo parents seemed the strictest, the Rome parents the most indulgent. Of the previous four items, the Rome parents were the most indulgent on two (B 43 and 49) and those in Palermo on two (B 47 and C 17). Thus it seems that the two groups of Italian parents do not differ from each other, but show a consistent trend toward greater indulgence than the Boston parents.

This entire group of items was found to have very high internal consistency (a K–R coefficient of .96, based on the 243 subjects from all three groups who gave sufficient information). The three groups of parents can thus be compared very reliably in their mean total scores on the dimension of socialization pressure versus indulgence. The means for the three cities appear as variable 5 in Table 2-7. Again the Boston parents were significantly different at the .01 level from the two Italian groups, which did not differ from each other, although the Rome parents have the highest mean score on indulgence.

On taking these findings together with those on current control over the boy's behavior already reported, there emerge quite different patterns of child rearing for the Italian–American as compared to the Italian parents. The parents in Boston combine earlier pressure toward cleanliness and self-control with greater current permission for freedom of expression and self-determination. The Italian parents, on the other hand, and this pattern is especially marked in Rome, combine indulgence in early childhood with greater restrictiveness and control in adolescence. These differences would seem to constitute a consistent contrasting pattern if we assume that the parents in Boston, influenced by prevailing American values and ideas about child development, have held higher expectations of maturity in their sons than have the Italian parents. In Palermo and especially in Rome, on the other hand, the boy is expected to remain immature and subject to more parental control for a much longer period of time. Thus he is treated both more indulgently as a small child and more restrictively as an adolescent.

Independence

In line with the preceding set of conclusions, there seem to be some marked differences between the Italian and Italian–American parents in the degree to which they encouraged self-sufficiency and responsibility when the boys were in early adolescence. More of the Boston parents than either of the two Italian groups were judged by the social worker as "favoring the boy's independence, respecting his personality." In Boston, 69% of the parents, as against only 48% in Rome, and 39% in Palermo, considered the boy capable of "facing up to his own difficulties." Perhaps even more impressive are some of the differences on such concrete items as work, pocket money, and amount of responsibility in the home. In Boston, 39% of the boys have done some work (outside of school and home), whereas none have in Rome and only two in Palermo. To be sure, this item may reflect the more demanding nature of the school program in Italy, which might leave less time for work; certainly the economic pressures would be as great in the Italian families, but there may be more of a feeling among the Boston parents that work is useful in teaching responsibility. Possibly related is the fact that a much higher proportion of the boys in Boston are reported as having chosen their future occupation. More of the boys in Boston, and fewest in Palermo, have some pocket money of their own. In Boston, 88% of the boys have some responsibility in the home, whereas 75% in Rome and 88% in Palermo have none. This last item may reflect the sharper differentiation of sex roles in the Italian culture. However, these items taken as a group certainly support the impression of earlier independence training in the American than in the Italian culture.

Peer Relations

We have already seen that the parents in Boston, particularly as contrasted with those in Palermo, are much more likely than the Italian parents to encourage heterosexual social contacts. They are also somewhat more likely to encourage the boys to belong to groups (clubs, etc.) and to say that they may choose any friends they wish, whereas the Rome parents are the most controlling in this area.

It is not surprising then, that the Boston parents report that their sons participate in group activities to a much greater extent than do the Italian boys: 64% in Boston as against 26% in Rome and only 10% in Palermo. Apparently the Italian parents are much more likely to differentiate between those of their sons' friendships that are purely scholastic and those that are nonscholastic; relatively more of the latter type are reported in Rome than in Palermo. In Boston, on the other hand, most parents (76%) describe the boy's friendships as "both"; apparently for the American boys there is much more continuity in their social contacts between school, the neighborhood, and other situations.

A number of other items reflect the generally greater permissiveness and positive attitudes toward friendships among the Italian–American than either Italian group. Most parents in all three cities say that they are pleased that the boy has friends, but this is 99% in Boston, whereas a few parents in Rome and 34% in Palermo indicate that they are not pleased. Italian parents are more likely to say that they prefer that the boy play at home rather than at the house of others or elsewhere, whereas the majority of the Boston parents indicate that they have no preference in this regard. Most of the parents in all three cities indicate that the boys' friendships are free rather than arranged, but this response is most frequent in Boston and least so in Rome; 24% of the Rome parents report arranged friendships, as against almost none in the other two cities. The parents in both Boston and Palermo seem to prefer that the boy take the lead in social situations, whereas most in Rome express no preference. The parents in Rome were the most likely to be described by the interviewers as intervening a great deal in problems the boy might have with others, and the Boston parents were most rarely so described. While the Palermo parents in general were intermediate between the other two groups in amount of intervention, a small proportion (10%) were described as not intervening at all. Thus, although the pattern of differences between the two Italian groups is not entirely clear, it seems that the parents in Palermo are more likely to hold negative or indifferent attitudes toward their sons' friendships, whereas those in Rome are somewhat more likely to attempt to exercise control over them. In any case, it is clear that the Boston parents, as a group, are much more permissive and encouraging of social contacts. They also seem to be more sociable themselves: 92% of them report that they get together with friends very frequently, whereas 71% in Rome indicate that they very rarely or never see friends. The Palermo parents are intermediate in their sociability. It is possible that the Rome families tend to be more socially isolated as a function of their more recent emigration.

There is one final indication of the greater positive value the Boston families seem to put on social relations. When asked the three most important things the boy should learn to do, the majority of parents in all three groups emphasized achievement (hard work, getting a diploma, a profession, intelligence). This is the more prevalent tendency among the Italian parents, whereas about 40% in Boston, but very few in either Rome or Palermo, mention aspects of human relations (getting along with others, moral qualities).

Seven of these items (B 57, 60, 61, C 25, 30, 61) proved to have sufficient internal consistency to justify combining them into a summary score. The means for the three cities on this variable of attitudes toward peer relations (high scores meaning interference) are given in Table 2-7, variable 6. Rome and Palermo do not differ significantly.

Family Relations

The following group of items was considered to reflect the variable of *cohesion* in the life of the family:

C 47   Do they take their meals together?
C 48   Does the mother work outside the home?
C 50   Do they have common interests?
C 51   Do they talk together?
C 52   Do the husband and wife go out together?

On all of these items, significantly more of the Boston than of the Italian parents responded in the affirmative direction; differences were not as great between Rome and Palermo. The item having to do with mothers' work proved interesting. It had originally been thought that the mother working outside the home would reflect a lack of cohesiveness. In Boston, where 53% of the mothers did work, this proved to be the case; the item correlated negatively with the other cohesiveness items. In Rome and Palermo, on the other hand, where very few of the mothers worked (15% and 12%, respectively), working was *positively* related to cohesiveness. This may well be an artifact of differential socioeconomic status; it is probable that in Italy only wives in families of relatively high status worked outside the home (see Table 2-8).

Of this group of items, four (C 47, 49, 50, and 51) were found to have sufficient internal consistency to justify combining them into a summary score (a K–R coefficient of .68, based on 329 cases). The mean scores for the three cities on total cohesion are given in Table 2-7, variable 7; higher scores reflect less cohesiveness. All three differences are significant at the .01 level, although the greatest contrast is between Boston and the two Italian cities.

One or two additional items add to the general impression that the Boston families were more cohesive than the Italian ones. The families in Boston were judged by the social worker to be significantly more united than the ones in Rome, and the ones in Rome significantly more united than those in Palermo. This difference runs counter to the summary score just reported. There were no significant differences, however, on the question about how much each member of the family participated in the life of the others. In answer to the question whether they would advise their sons to marry, most parents in all three cities responded affirmatively, but fewer in Rome said ''yes'' unconditionally.

Although most of the families in each of the three cities said they were satisfied with their work, the level of satisfaction seems to be somewhat greater in Boston, and least in Palermo. Incidentally, the parents in Boston earned more, on the average, and their incomes seem to have been somewhat less fixed; more of them report either an increase or a decrease in the last 10 years.

There are somewhat different patterns of interests in the three cities, both among the boys and among the parents. The parents in Boston are most likely to report participation in sports, and those in Palermo are least likely to report active involvement in sports; if they do participate, it is purely as spectators. The Palermo parents are most likely to report ''professional'' interests. This somewhat passive pattern of interests is reflected in the pastimes ascribed to the boys, which are most likely to be passive in Palermo (watching movies, television, and sporting events). However, active participation in sports is reported most frequently for the Rome boys rather than for those in Boston, as we might have expected, and least frequently in Palermo. The Boston boys were most likely to be described as interested in mechanical things—constructing and cars—whereas the Italian boys are somewhat more likely to be interested in reading and imaginative games. The last was most frequently mentioned in Rome, which is interesting in view of the greater productivity of that group on the Imagination Test and the later measures of creativity. The data obtained directly from the boys on degree of interest in sports places the Boston group as highest and shows better correspondence with the parents' own interests, thus fitting better with a notion of parental modeling. Interestingly enough, the Boston parents report that they read books and newspapers more frequently than do the Italian parents. The

TABLE 2-8

CORRELATES OF SOCIALIZATION VARIABLES

Variables	1 Control			2 Sex Restrictiveness			3 Freedom of Expression			4 Age of Socialization			5 Indulgence			6 Peer Relations			7 Cohesion			8 Academic Pressure		
	B	R	P	B	R	P	B	R	P	B	R	P	B	R	P	B	R	P	B	R	P	B	R	P
1. Control							.32		.28								.21						.30	
2. Sex Restrictiveness							.37											.20						
3. Freedom of Expression	.32		.28	.37							.28	.22	.29	.22		.24			.41	.32	.43			
4. Age of Socialization		.21					.28	.22					.99	.99	.99	.20								
5. Indulgence							.29	.22		.99	.99	.99				.22								
6. Peer Relations						.20	.24			.20			.22							.18			.19	
7. Cohesion							.41	.32	.43								.18							
8. Academic Pressure		.30															.19							
9. Father's Profession						.22			.38										.22				.70	
10. Father's Education	.27			.34	.19				.33											.19	.58			
11. Mother's Education					.24	.31		.29	.29				.28							.18	.52			
12. Ordinal Position							.23																.20	
13. SES				.33					.39											.21	.61			
14. Income				.24	.23				.34											.26	.50			
15. Cuddled																								
16. Truth																								.24
17. Obedient																			.22	.19	.22	.34		
18. Relationship with Father								.25	.37	.22			.23						.20	.33	.34	.49	.38	
19. Relationship with Mother							.33													.19	.21	.20		
20. Responsibility at Home							.29						.27			.37								
21. Aggression							.26	.19		.23		.26	.27		.25	.24							.38	
22. Affection from Family							.23		.34				.29			.45				.30	.39			

All correlations significant at p < .05

57

interviews were carried out before television came into general usage in Italy, so this was not inquired about. There is some indication, however, that the Boston families experienced greater exposure to mass communication media.

As to the quality of the relationships of the boys to their parents and other members of the family, there do seem to be differences between the groups, although here we must depend almost entirely on the judgment of the social workers in each of the three locations, which may not have been strictly comparable. Significantly, more poor relationships are reported in Rome with both parents and with other members of the family, but this is especially true for relationships with the father (56% are described as "indifferent" or "bad," as against only 13% in Boston and 8% in Palermo). We have already seen that the Rome boys as a group are also much less likely than the boys in the other two cities to discuss personal problems with their parents. We may infer that more of the Rome sample have experienced some rejection, or at least lack of closeness, in their family relationships, particularly with their fathers. (This is an inference which seems to be borne out by some of the personality data on the boys, but not by the little information contained in the Social Inquiry on possible symptoms of emotional disturbance. Thumb-sucking, nail-biting, and sleep disturbances are reported only rarely in any of the three samples, but slightly more often in Boston and least often in Palermo.)

Affection and Nurturance

The interviewers also rated the amount of affection the boy received from each parent and from others in the family, and made an overall judgment of the amount of affection he received. These judgments are not systematically related to the items on relations with others in the family reported in the previous section. (Thus an attempt to construct an overall score on warmth was not successful.) There are no significant differences among the three groups on affection from the mother. Again there is a very slight tendency for the Rome boys to have received less from their father; but the only significant difference is between Palermo and the other two groups, the Palermo fathers being rated as significantly more affectionate. Thus the Palermo families are more frequently scored high on the overall rating, but most of the variance seems to be contributed by the fathers' scores. (There is also a tendency for the Boston mothers to be rated as slightly less affectionate than the Italian mothers.) These data certainly do not support Peterson and Migliorino's tentative conclusion that their Sicilian parents were less affectionate than American parents, although they compared only mothers.

Some more concrete items referring to early nurturance may be relevant here, and less subject to interviewer bias. Significantly more mothers in Boston than in either of the Italian cities worked when the child was small but, since he was likely to have been cared for by a grandmother or other relative, this may represent diffusion of nurturance rather than less of it. The Boston mothers reported cuddling the boys most when they were small and those in Palermo reported least of this form of physical affection. It is interesting to note that age up to which the child slept with the mother is positively correlated with the overall rating on affection in both of the Italian groups, but not in Boston. These data do not add up to any very consistent picture of differences in nurturance between the three groups, although these variables have proved useful for internal analyses. The overall rating on affection (C 46) is so highly correlated with the other ratings that it might as well be used in lieu of a summary score.

Mother's Personality

The final set of items in the Social Inquiry is a series of judgments by the interviewer of the mother's personality. We have no guarantee that they are comparable from one group to another, and so comparisons between the three groups based on these judgments are of very doubtful meaning. But we report them here for what they may be worth. The Boston mothers were more likely to be described as anxious than the other two groups. The mothers in Palermo were more likely to be described as tolerant and understanding of the boy's emotional needs, but also likely to be described as authoritative. The Rome mothers were described as the most able to deal with the boy's practical problems and the least able to deal with his emotional problems—perhaps another indication of less closeness in the families of the Rome group.

Interrelations among Family Variables

Table 2-8 lists the correlations among the socialization summary scores and between them and other selected variables describing aspects of family life, socioeconomic status, and child-rearing attitudes. Only those correlations that reach the .05 level of significance are shown. In general the correlations are modest, and give us some assurance that we have measured family variables that are reasonably independent of each other, although we made no attempt to derive orthogonal factors, since the nature of the data did not seem to warrant such an analysis.

A few interesting and generally internally consistent relations do appear. Control and lower freedom of expression are moderately correlated in both Boston and Palermo. In Boston, lower freedom of expression also related to restrictive attitudes toward sex and to intervention in peer relations, but these associations do not appear in the Italian cities. In both Boston and Rome, more indulgent early socialization related to less freedom of expression in adolescence. (This association might be considered an indication of a more traditional Italian pattern of child rearing persisting among some of the emigrant families, but this interpretation in Boston is made less plausible by the association of more indulgent early training with higher maternal education.) In Rome, control is also related to later ages of habit training and to higher academic pressure: in fact, academic pressure relates only in Rome to a set of generally restrictive and somewhat rejecting parental attitudes. Apparently it is among the Rome families that we see the sharpest reversal from early indulgence to later demands for achievement.

Family cohesion is associated with greater freedom of expression in all three cities. Intervention in peer relations is associated in Palermo, to a slight extent, with a more cohesive family life and greater academic pressure. The various indices of SES are modestly related to greater freedom of expression and more open attitudes toward sex in one or both of the Italian cities. There is an interesting difference in the association between family cohesiveness and socioeconomic status in Palermo: the family's SES, as reflected in the overall index, in father's occupation, and in both parents' education, is very strongly predictive (Peterson product-moment correlations, r, of .52 to .70) of family cohesiveness. This is also true in Rome, but to a much lesser extent, and the correlation in Boston is slightly negative ($r = -.13$). This means that in Palermo, to a much more marked degree than in the other two cities, families of lower social class reported much less shared family life. This finding tends to confirm our earlier speculations about the association with mothers' employment. This effect of SES may be a function of greater economic pressures in the South, but more probably reflects the separation between the sexes in interests and activities traditional in Mediterranean societies, and which might be expected to persist to a greater extent in families of lower educational and economic status.

As we might expect, family cohesion is associated with a general pattern of positive family relations and favorable attitudes toward the son in all three of the cities. In addition, in Palermo, it is associated with parental encouragement of aggression in response to attacks from peers. This association is partly a function of the positive relations of both variables to SES, but since the correlation between encouragement of aggression and SES is fairly low ($r = .28$), one is tempted to speculate that Sicilian families tend to preserve closeness and to control hostility within the family partly through the mechanism of displacement of aggression toward peers and others outside the family. This would certainly fit with the folklore about the Italian family system.

In Boston, on the other hand, intervention in peer relations as well as more indulgent early socialization are correlated with higher family affection and lower demands for maturity, suggesting a pattern of rather protective parent–child relations. These two variables do not seem to have the same meaning for the Italian parents, among whom they are considerably more typical. Thus these data on interrelations among the parental variables amplify, but do not essentially change, the interpretations based on the group comparisons.

SUMMARY

For the reader unfamiliar with Italy, we have provided some salient impressions of southern Italian culture and thumbnail descriptions of the three cities. Comparisons of dietary patterns revealed earlier consumption of carbohydrates and proteins by American infants; our adolescent subjects in Boston consumed much higher amounts of animal protein and sugar than the Italian boys, who exercised more. Differences in infant mortality and in literacy rates reflected the greater poverty still prevalent in southern Italy.

School and family are the two main social institutions in the lives of adolescents. We have assumed familiarity with secondary schools in the United States; about half our subjects in Boston were enrolled in parochial schools; the rest attended public junior high and high schools. We have supplied a detailed description of the system of secondary education in effect in Italy at the time of the study. School attendance was compulsory until age 14; entrance to university was generally at 19, but might be later, since many boys failed at least one grade and were obliged to repeat it. More boys in Sicily dropped out of school early. At age 11 Italian students were rather rigidly channeled into either classical or vocational junior high schools, which in turn fed into, respectively, the various types of *liceo* or teacher preparatory schools or into the industrial or technical high schools. The authors believe that scholastic pressures were greater for the Italian boys. They also enjoyed fewer extracurricular activities, opportunities for peer interaction, or organized sports; however, closer bonds might develop with individual teachers. Health services were more limited in the Italian schools and plants older and more crowded; pupil–teacher ratios were generally lower.

While sociologists and ethnographers have described the southern Italian family, both in Italy and in the process of assimilation to American culture, little comparative information existed prior to this study on patterns of child rearing and parent–child relations in adolescence. While parent interviews were intended primarily to secure data on socioeconomic status, family structure, and nutritional history, aspects of child rearing and family relations were also explored. The sample of families in Rome, in contrast to both Boston and Palermo, showed a trend toward fewer children and less contact with grandparents.

The Italian–American parents were found to exercise less strict control over their adolescent sons and to allow them more freedom of expression; the Sicilian parents were particularly restrictive with respect to sex while the Roman parents exercised stricter control in other areas. The Italian parents also placed greater pressure on their sons for academic achievement than did their Italian–American counterparts. Parents in Boston were more likely than those in Italy to encourage counter-aggression toward peers; they were also more supportive of peer friendships. Italian parents were more indulgent toward their sons and placed fewer demands on them for maturity when they were small children; they also allowed them less independence as adolescents. Italian–American parents were more consistent over time in expecting more mature behavior from their sons. Families in Boston seemed more cohesive and more egalitarian, though not necessarily more nurturant, than those in Italy; family cohesiveness was most closely associated with higher SES in the Palermo sample.

PART II

Adolescent Development in Boston, Rome, and Palermo

CHAPTER 3

Physical Growth, Development, and Health

GROWTH, BODY COMPOSITION, AND PHYSICAL FUNCTION

Physical growth and body composition are of interest for any investigator who seeks to discern the long-term effects of the environment. Less than optimal conditions may slow down growth processes, including sexual maturation; adult body lengths, weight, fat and muscle mass may all be affected by hardship.

The problem here was to choose those aspects of physical growth most likely to be affected by the environment. These included measurements used for generations by physical anthropologists, assessments of pubertal maturity, and then an analysis by means of growth increments during the period of puberty. The use of the costly longitudinal method may be justified, if appropriately sensitive measures are chosen.

Measures that present a clear and truthful picture of growth must portray not only body composition but also the three essential components: body mass (e.g., weight), linear characteristics (e.g., height), and fat. Each of these components has many parts.

When Sheldon (1954) chose his first subjects for judgments of physical type, he took them from a line waiting for a movie to open. Despite this doubtful sampling procedure, his ideas have persisted in three types: mesomorphy (substantial in bone and muscle), ectomorphy (tall and usually thin), and endomorphy (plump and moving to fat). Closer comparisons will show differentiating pictures of development within these three broad concepts, and not only in a direct comparison by age. Because of possible different times of arrival at sexual maturity, which is usual for physical and other aspects of development at this time, selected measurements must be seen against the now well-known and accepted maturation scales for puberty and adolescence.

A longitudinal study must present growth functions also in the form of the second mathematical derivative—that is, not only a distance but also a velocity curve, which may focus more sharply on certain details. Selected measures will be shown, at least one from each of the three Sheldon concepts.

As parental heights are available, we shall attempt to compare predicted heights from midparental data. This is a measurement for which prediction equations are at present available, and they may reflect relative changes in the different environments.

What do differences in body composition mean in real life? They may reflect health and efficiency. For health, body mass and especially its fat component may indicate a liability to eventual heart disease, including high blood pressure. Thus it may be important to try to relate these measures to age, blood pressure, abuse of tobacco, and cholesterol. It is regrettable that on this last measure we have no data, but in such a study, short as we were in financial support, we could not examine everything.

The time of arrival at puberty and connected events are important in discerning individual differences (physiological and pathological) as these may have some influence on eventual body shape and form, as well as giving insight into relationships between physical growth and physiology. The observations may also be of help to physicians in adolescent medicine, to see more clearly the differences between chronological age and the differences in time of arrival at maturity in different cultures and diverse socioeconomic situations. The codes used in the recording and analysis of information from the successive physical examinations and the medical history are reproduced in Appendixes B and C.

We shall present data in this way:

1. A comparison by age of the boys on a few selected measurements[1]
2. A comparison of sexual maturity
3. Some related facts that seem to be of importance

Every effort was made to publish the results as they began to emerge. In this way it was possible to make continuing appraisals of the methods and the approaches. For example, 2 years after initiation, it became clear that in Rome there was too high a proportion of subjects from privileged classes. This was remedied by recruiting more Roman boys from underprivileged families.

As already stated, increments of physical growth have been calculated. Thus it may be possible to predict individual growth and, given the relatively large numbers of subjects involved in this study, to understand the limitations on such predictions.

At the beginning of the study, the subjects, all male, were between 10 and 14 years of age. They were followed until over the age of 20. Tables 3-1 to 3-9 show the differences in respect to weight (Table 3-1), height (Table 3-2), leg length (Table 3-3), arm circumference (Table 3-4), dynamometer (Table 3-5), puberal age (Table 3-6), skinfold triceps (Table 3-7), Harvard Step Test (Table 3-8), and fat-free arm circumference (Table 3-9) in these subjects. The following additional measures are not shown here, but are available from H. Boutourline Young[1]: sitting height, arm length, chest circumference, skinfold biceps, skinfold subscapular, and fat-free calf circumference.

The main results follow.

Table 3-1: Body Weight   Boston subjects were superior to Rome and Palermo subjects at all ages from 11 to 19+ (young adult status). The differences were of the order of 6 kg at age 11, to 12 kg at age 17, and so on, being reduced to 7.5 kg at age 19. All these differences were highly significant. Of interest was the finding that the Rome and Palermo subjects were closely comparable with the old Stuart and Stevenson (1954) and Meredith (1939; see also Nelsen, 1954, pp. 58–59) U.S. scales. It was the emigrant adolescents in Boston who were far in excess, although their weight pattern corresponds to the latest figures for the United States Health Survey (Hamill, Drizd, Johnson, Reed, & Roche, 1977).

When they were about 15, the boys in the Palermo sample were shown six photographs of boys all about the same height but ranging from one (lean) to six (fat). The subject chose his "ideal" type. There proved to be a significant association with the subject's own fat level, both at the time and at later ages. This same trend was evident in a subsample of the Boston group. The boys who chose the fatter photographs had higher fat levels themselves, both at age 15 and at ages 18 to 19. It is difficult to know if these choices are an approval of self or an expression of an ideal.

Table 3-2: Height   At all ages the Rome groups (internal emigrants) were comparable to the sedentes in Palermo. On the other hand, the Boston groups were significantly taller at ages 12, 14–17, and 19.

In general, the Rome and Palermo adolescents were broadly comparable, with just a few advantages in Palermo at all ages. Further references will be mainly to the two emigrant groups—that is, those in Boston and those in Rome.

---

[1]In this chapter we have omitted a number of variables important and useful for reference but unnecessary here to show a general picture. The expert in this area may wish to consult the more detailed data. They are available from H. Boutourline Young, Via Venezia 10, 50121 Florence, Italy (complete data on physical growth and health).

TABLE 3-1

WEIGHT BY AGE: BOSTON, ROME, PALERMO

	Boston				Rome				Palermo			t-Ratio		
Age	No. Ss.	Mean Weight (kg)	S.D.	Age	No. Ss.	Mean Weight (kg)	S.D.	Age	No. Ss.	Mean Weight (kg)	S.D.	Boston/ Rome	Boston/ Palermo	Rome/ Palermo
11	30	41.94	10.75	11	27	35.92	6.82	11	22	38.78	8.14	2.49**		
12	25	44.91	10.85	12	84	38.53	6.02	12	76	39.57	8.31	4.22***	2.84***	
13	53	48.39	11.40	13	100	43.70	7.94	13	79	42.13	8.88	2.99***	3.54***	
14	52	55.81	11.29	14	85	48.76	8.39	14	55	48.87	11.75	4.18***	3.11***	
15	58	60.19	10.76	15	55	53.81	8.92	15	67	57.58	10.55	3.42***		2.10**
16	42	66.47	12.04	16	28	56.07	9.02	16	72	57.20	8.47	3.90***	4.81***	
17	42	70.32	12.76	17	25	58.51	7.00	17	47	61.17	11.11	4.25***	3.62***	
18	20	67.88	11.67	18	26	61.62	7.58	18	58	61.71	8.83	2.13**	2.40**	
19+	68	72.24	10.73	19+	99	64.87	9.78	19+	52	64.29	11.31	4.60***	3.90***	

```
  *  .05< p <.10
 **  p <.05
***  p <.10
```
Only probabilities less than .10 are expressed.

In sitting height (not shown), the Boston boys were significantly superior to those in Rome at 14, 15 and 19+ years—that is, as mature young adults.

Table 3-3: Leg Length The Boston boys were superior to those in Rome at ages 11–17 and 19+ (mature adults). In arm length (not shown), the Boston boys were significantly superior to the Rome subjects at ages 11, 12, 14–16, and 19+. In chest circumference (not shown) taken at the sternal xiphoid–sternal junction, Boston subjects were superior to Rome at ages 12, 14, 16, 17, and 19+, while Palermo subjects were superior to Rome subjects only at 15 and 16 years of age.

Table 3-4: Arm Circumference Boston is significantly superior to Rome at ages 11–18 and 19+ at .01 level. Palermo is superior to Rome at 15 years of age.

Table 3-5: Dynanometer (Static Strength) Boston is superior to Rome at all levels ($p < .01$) except ages 17 and 18. Palermo is also superior to Rome at most ages.

Table 3-6: Puberal (Biological) Age Puberal age is measured by clinical observations of secondary characteristics checked by an equation (Young, 1969). Boston is significantly superior to Rome at ages 14 and 16—that is, on the average. Boston subjects are judged as more mature.

Table 3-7: Skinfold Triceps The Boston subjects are significantly greater at ages 12 and 17. They are always greater, but not significantly so, at all ages. In

TABLE 3-2

HEIGHT BY AGE: BOSTON, ROME, PALERMO

	Boston				Rome				Palermo			t-Ratio		
Age	No. Ss.	Mean Height (cm)	S.D.	Age	No. Ss.	Mean Height (cm)	S.D.	Age	No. Ss.	Mean Height (cm)	S.D.	Boston/ Rome	Boston/ Palermo	Rome/ Palermo
11	30	144.01	8.30	11	27	141.07	5.86	11	22	142.46	5.77			
12	25	148.45	9.12	12	84	145.48	6.11	12	76	145.92	6.76	2.07**		
13	53	153.81	8.99	13	100	152.40	6.64	13	79	150.29	8.78		2.24**	
14	52	161.85	7.64	14	85	158.11	7.03	14	55	157.38	8.81	2.92***	2.80***	
15	58	166.89	7.82	15	55	163.45	7.32	15	67	165.54	6.98	2.41**		
16	42	170.70	7.04	16	28	165.80	5.96	16	72	166.46	6.01	3.03***	3.41***	
17	42	172.05	6.43	17	25	167.48	6.22	17	47	169.34	6.36	3.09***	2.26**	
18	20	170.91	6.65	18	26	169.63	5.04	18	58	169.97	5.86			
19+	68	172.71	5.79	19+	101	169.57	5.77	19+	52	171.16	5.81	3.46***		

```
  * .05 < p < .10          Only probabilities less than .10 are expressed.
 ** p < .05
*** p < .01
```

TABLE 3-3

LEG LENGTH BY AGE: BOSTON, ROME, PALERMO

	Boston				Rome				Palermo			t-Ratio		
Age	No. Ss.	Mean Leg Length (cm)	S.D.	Age	No. Ss.	Mean Leg Length (cm)	S.D.	Age	No. Ss.	Mean Leg Length (cm)	S.D.	Boston/ Rome	Boston/ Palermo	Rome/ Palermo
11	30	89.60	5.67	11	27	86.19	4.20	11	22	87.52	4.99	2.56**		
12	35	92.58	6.63	12	84	89.29	4.16	12	76	89.88	5.52	3.27***	2.24**	
13	53	96.04	6.25	13	100	93.72	4.57	13	79	92.77	6.13	2.62***	2.98***	
14	52	100.95	5.18	14	85	97.16	4.69	14	55	97.68	6.38	4.41***	2.90***	
15	58	104.00	5.25	15	55	100.09	5.08	15	67	101.82	5.23	4.02***	2.32**	
16	42	105.78	5.59	16	28	100.90	4.55	16	72	101.91	4.60	3.84***	4.00***	
17	42	105.74	4.86	17	25	101.00	4.32	17	47	103.68	4.68	4.02***	2.04**	2.37**
18	20	104.13	4.82	18	26	102.44	3.65	18	58	103.35	4.98			
19+	68	105.25	4.25	19+	101	102.05	4.47	19+	52	103.83	4.66	4.65***	1.74*	2.30**

```
  * .05 < p < .10          Only probabilities less than .10 are expressed.
 ** p < .05
*** p < .01
```

69

TABLE 3-4

ARM CIRCUMFERENCE BY AGE: BOSTON, ROME, PALERMO

	Boston				Rome				Palermo			t-Ratio		
Age	No. Ss.	Mean Arm Circum. (cm)	S.D.	Age	No. Ss.	Mean Arm Circum. (cm)	S.D.	Age	No. Ss.	Mean Arm Circum. (cm)	S.D.	Boston/ Rome	Boston/ Palermo	Rome/ Palermo
11	30	22.61	2.98	11	27	19.94	2.75	11	22	21.56	3.73	3.50***		
12	35	23.15	2.81	12	83	20.38	2.22	12	76	21.21	3.14	5.71***	3.12***	
13	53	23.76	3.06	13	100	21.19	2.53	13	79	21.41	2.71	5.55***	4.64***	
14	52	25.21	2.83	14	84	21.94	3.35	14	55	22.93	3.48	5.86***	3.71***	
15	58	25.95	2.83	15	55	22.83	2.30	15	66	24.93	3.27	6.47***	1.84*	4.01***
16	42	27.65	2.81	16	28	23.41	1.99	16	72	24.49	2.40	6.91***	6.37***	
17	42	28.46	3.15	17	25	24.74	2.24	17	47	26.00	3.11	5.17***	3.70***	1.79*
18	20	28.59	2.81	18	26	25.79	2.36	18	58	25.83	2.52	3.67***	4.10***	
19+	68	29.94	2.94	19+	101	27.32	2.64	19+	52	26.40	2.73	6.04***	6.74***	

```
  * .05 < p < .10              Only probabilities less than .10 are expressed.
 ** p < .05
*** p < .01
```

TABLE 3-5

DYNANOMETER BY AGE: BOSTON, ROME, PALERMO

	Boston				Rome				Palermo			t-Ratio		
Age	No. Ss.	Mean Dynan- ometer Score	S.D.	Age	No. Ss.	Mean Dynan- ometer Score	S.D.	Age	No. Ss.	Mean Dynan- ometer Score	S.D.	Boston/ Rome	Boston/ Palermo	Rome/ Palermo
11	7	34.14	6.49	11	16	21.50	1.71	11	21	30.95	4.06	7.42***		8.72***
12	28	33.50	7.37	12	56	26.46	6.40	12	76	33.02	4.29	4.52***		7.05***
13	34	36.18	10.04	13	90	29.12	6.93	13	79	35.02	5.75	4.44***		5.97
14	30	42.07	7.77	14	83	34.62	8.49	14	55	39.05	6.72	4.21***	1.87*	3.25***
15	48	45.48	8.75	15	55	38.89	9.24	15	67	47.61	6.78	3.70***		6.00***
16	38	50.05	7.58	16	28	42.71	6.98	16	71	48.52	5.68	4.02***		4.29
17	38	51.00	8.74	17	25	47.92	6.26	17	46	51.93	6.97			
18	20	53.25	7.14	18	24	49.79	6.23	18	58	54.47	5.03	1.72*		3.57***
19+	61	58.11	7.17	19+	97	53.77	6.37	19+	51	53.41	5.51	3.97***	3.83***	

```
  * .05 < p < .10              Only probabilities less than .10 are expressed.
 ** p < .05
*** p < .01
```

TABLE 3-6

PUBERAL AGE BY CHRONOLOGICAL AGE: BOSTON, ROME, PALERMO

	Boston				Rome				Palermo			t-Ratio		
Age	No. Ss.	Mean Pub. Age	S.D.	Age	No. Ss.	Mean Pub. Age	S.D.	Age	No. Ss.	Mean Pub. Age	S.D.	Boston/ Rome	Boston/ Palermo	Rome/ Palermo
11	30	1.62	0.72	11	27	1.69	0.65	11	22	1.58	0.76			
12	35	2.30	0.76	12	84	2.14	0.83	12	76	2.15	0.88			
13	53	3.17	0.80	13	100	3.03	0.85	13	79	2.85	1.01		1.94*	
14	52	4.06	0.71	14	85	3.71	0.85	14	55	3.71	0.96	2.49**	2.14**	
15	58	4.75	0.75	15	55	4.46	0.91	15	67	4.99	0.84	1.86*		3.35***
16	42	5.55	0.51	16	28	5.05	0.63	16	72	5.27	0.68	3.67***		
17	42	5.88	0.29	17	25	5.88	0.25	17	47	5.77	0.39			
18	20	6.00	0.00	18	26	5.95	0.15	18	58	5.97	0.14			
19+	68	6.00	0.00	19+	97	6.00	0.00	19+	51	6.00	0.00			

* .05< p <.10
** p < .05
*** p < .01

Only probabilities less than .10 are expressed.

TABLE 3-7

SKINFOLD TRICEPS BY AGE: BOSTON, ROME, PALERMO

	Boston				Rome				Palermo			t-Ratio		
Age	No. Ss.	Mean (mm)	S.D.	Age	No. Ss.	Mean (mm)	S.D.	Age	No. Ss.	Mean (mm)	S.D.	Boston/ Rome	Boston/ Palermo	Rome/ Palermo
11	30	12.45	5.10	11	27	10.36	6.46	11	22	12.22	5.77			
12	35	11.96	4.68	12	84	9.91	4.32	12	76	10.30	5.39	2.30**		
13	53	11.37	5.38	13	100	9.93	4.48	13	79	9.42	4.71	1.76*	2.20**	
14	52	10.51	4.21	14	85	9.39	3.90	14	55	9.75	5.73			
15	58	9.44	4.32	15	55	8.39	3.35	15	67	9.23	5.02			
16	42	9.53	4.15	16	28	8.34	3.68	16	72	8.07	4.28		1.78*	
17	42	9.95	4.68	17	25	7.91	2.78	17	47	8.90	4.48	1.98*		
18	20	9.11	4.07	18	26	8.53	3.32	18	58	8.39	4.21			
19+	68	9.69	4.51	19+	101	8.85	4.21	19+	52	8.20	3.66		1.94*	

* .05< p <.10
** p < .05
*** p < .01

Only probabilities less than .10 are expressed.

the skinfold biceps measure (not shown) there are also consistent superiorities with significant levels being reached at ages 12–17; and in the skinfold subscapular measure again there are consistently higher values in the Boston subjects, but significant differences are reached only at 12 and 14 years, and at 16 years if Palermo is considered. The characteristic reduction in body fat during puberty is clearly seen as we and others have previously described.

Table 3-8: Harvard Step Test (Cardiovascular Resistance)   Here no significant differences are seen; in fact, when small differences exist they mostly favor the subjects resident in Italy.

Table 3-9: Fat-Free Arm Circumference   This variable is derived from the equation $Cbm = C - 2.244(F1 + F2)$. There are highly significant differences between Boston and both Italian resident groups at all age levels 11–20; on three occasions, Palermo exceeds Rome. The fat-free calf circumference was derived in the same manner and also shows highly significant differences in favor of Boston for all ages 11–17. In contrast to the fat-free arm circumference, there appears to be a "catch-up" phenomenon after the age of 17. Both of these measures are highly correlated. This finding should be pondered upon in relation to the lack of superiority for Boston in cardiovascular resistance, since these measures reflect extra bone muscle, which should help physical performance as shown in the table.

A Comparison by Sexual Maturity

For puberal or biological age the scale used was the familiar one from one to six (Greulich, Dorfman, Catchpole, Solomon, & Culotta, 1943; Tanner, 1962; Young, 1969):

Stage 1   As a child, no hair, testicular volume 1–2 cc.

Stage 2   Prepuberal, downy hair pubic area, testicular volume 3–4 cc

Stage 3   First phase of puberty, small quantity curled pigmented pubic hair, testicular volume 5–6 cc

Stage 4   Mid phase puberty, moderate quantity curled pigmented pubic hair, first appearance axillary hair, testicular volume 9–11 cc

Stage 5   Late phase puberty, considerable quantity curled pigmented pubic hair, moderate quantity axillary hair, testicular volume 14–16 cc

Stage 6   Adult status, further growth pubic hair to include frequently upper thighs and triangled up to umbilicus, considerable quantity axillary hair, testicular volume 18–22 cc or more

There is considerable variation in the age at which puberty starts. Actually the process from Stage 2 to Stage 5 takes three years or more. There is also some variation here of up to a year or more.

TABLE 3-8

HARVARD STEP BY AGE: BOSTON, ROME, PALERMO

	Boston				Rome				Palermo			t–Ratio		
Age	No. Ss.	Mean Score	S.D.	Age	No. Ss.	Mean Score	S.D.	Age	No. Ss.	Mean Score	S.D.	Boston/ Rome	Boston/ Palermo	Rome/ Palermo
12	44	72.48	14.69	12	55	72.00	11.21	12	86	71.05	10.50			
14	66	70.59	10.43	14	88	72.39	10.91	14	65	73.00	10.47			
16	32	70.47	9.46	16	40	70.75		16	54	72.60	4.83			
				18	11	71.82	13.93							

  * .05 < p < .10
 ** p < .05   Only probabilities less than .10 are expressed.
*** p < .01

TABLE 3-9

FAT FREE ARM CIRCUMFERENCE: BOSTON, ROME, PALERMO

	Boston				Rome				Palermo			t–Ratio		
Age	No. Ss.	Mean Arm Circum. (cm)	S.D.	Age	No. Ss.	Mean Arm Circum. (cm)	S.D.	Age	No. Ss.	Mean Arm Circum. (cm)	S.D.	Boston/ Rome	Boston/ Palermo	Rome/ Palermo
11	29	18.19	1.76	11	27	16.11	1.48	11	22	17.08	1.97	4.70***	2.00**	1.90*
12	35	18.87	1.81	12	83	16.88	1.43	12	76	17.45	1.82	5.85***	3.84***	
13	53	19.85	2.28	13	100	17.82	1.69	13	79	18.04	1.94	5.64***	3.29***	
14	52	21.48	2.23	14	85	18.97	1.97	14	55	19.23	2.14	6.61***	5.23***	
15	58	22.62	1.94	15	55	19.92	1.82	15	67	21.54	2.27	7.71***	2.92***	4.38***
16	42	24.21	2.16	16	28	20.53	1.38	16	72	21.70	1.70	8.76***	6.61***	3.55***
17	41	24.71	1.95	17	25	22.18	1.18	17	47	22.86	2.41	5.17***	4.02***	
18	20	25.38	2.06	18	26	22.83	1.70	18	58	22.94	1.75	4.55***	4.68***	
19	21	26.08	1.73	19	15	23.28	1.55	19	34	23.08	1.85	5.09***	6.12***	
20	46	26.65	2.11	20	85	24.28	1.96	20	17	24.12	1.87	6.24***	4.60***	

  * .05 < p < .10
 ** p < .05   Only probabilities less than .10 are expressed.
*** p < .01

73

The object in measuring by puberal age, as mentioned before, is to reduce the variability associated with differential rates of maturation when growth measures are put against chronological age.

First, as regards overall rates of maturing (see Table 3-10), there was little difference between the centers apart for a tendency for Boston to start a little earlier and for Palermo to finish somewhat later. Nowhere did the differences exceed 6 months.

We considered the following six variables: weight, height, leg length, chest circumference (at xiphoid), arm circumference, and triceps skinfold at puberal stages 2-5. The findings for Stages 4 and 5 are shown in Tables 3-11 and 3-12. Similar findings for Stages 2 and 3 are available upon request.

When these results are compared with those in the preceding section results in body weight are fully confirmed.

For height there is much the same picture as in chronological age. Naturally the standard deviation is somewhat reduced because of the reduction of variability. Boston exceeds Palermo at Stage 3 and both Rome and Palermo at Stages 4 and 5.

For leg length we have a broadly similar picture. At Stages 2 and 3 Boston is slightly above Rome and Palermo, but this difference becomes highly significant at Stages 4 and 5.

For chest circumference Boston was higher than Rome at Stages 3 and 5, but only weakly so, which corresponds fairly well with the analysis by chronological age.

Instead, in arm circumference in all comparisons for Stages 2-5 Boston was significantly above Rome and Palermo. A similar picture is seen in skinfold triceps.

In short, the analysis by biological age fully confirms that by chronological age. There is some sharpening, but it is not great as might be expected, since there are only relatively small age differences in arrival at maturity in the three centers.

TABLE 3-10

CHRONOLOGICAL AGE

Pubertal Age	Boston	Rome	Palermo
Stage 1	10.47	11.97	12.27
Stage 2	12.19	12.45	12.46
Stage 3	12.96	13.18	13.13
Stage 4	14.02	13.88	14.05
Stage 5	15.06	15.09	15.47
Stage 6	18.36	19.54	17.46

TABLE 3-11

PUBERAL STAGE 4

	Boston			Rome			Palermo			t-Ratio		
	No.	Mean	S.D.	No.	Mean	S.D.	No.	Mean	S.D.			
Weight	65	54.66	9.80	89	49.58	6.61	66	50.14	8.58	B/R	t=3.63	p < .01
										B/P	t=2.79	p < .01
Height	65	161.27	6.20	89	159.34	5.94	66	159.29	5.65	B/R	t=1.95	p < .10
										B/P	t=1.90	p < .10
Leg Length	65	100.52	4.55	89	97.98	4.52	66	98.65	5.02	B/R	t=3.43	p < .01
										B/P	t=2.92	p < .01
Chest Circumference	64	75.43	5.86	76	74.42	4.19	58	76.16	5.33			
Arm Circumference	65	25.92	2.67	89	22.23	1.98	66	22.92	2.79	B/R	t=6.56	p< .01
										B/P	t=4.17	p< .01
Triceps	65	10.36	4.36	89	8.91	3.63	66	9.01	5.12	B/R	t=2.05	p< .05

What is clear in both cases is the better performance of Boston over Rome and Palermo in both types of analysis.

Growth Increments: Longitudinal Analysis

We have chosen five variables for examination. These were body height and weight, bone muscle arm, bone muscle calf, and subscapular skinfold. These

TABLE 3-12

PUBERAL STAGE 5

	Boston			Rome			Palermo			t-Ratio		
	No.	Mean	S.D.	No.	Mean	S.D.	No.	Mean	S.D.			
Weight	64	61.98	9.66	57	56.24	6.94	79	56.28	8.33	B/R	t=3.78	p <.01
										B/P	t=3.75	p <.01
Height	64	168.93	6.01	57	165.64	5.33	79	165.86	5.58	B/R	t=3.19	p <.01
										B/P	t=3.13	p <.01
Leg Length	64	105.18	4.53	57	100.55	4.00	79	102.21	4.48	B/R	t=5.94	p <.01
										B/P	t=3.91	p <.01
										P/R	t=2.27	p <.05
Chest Circumference	64	80.61	5.38	55	78.92	4.68	69	81.08	5.40	B/R	t=1.84	p <.10
Arm Circumference	64	26.34	2.33	57	23.53	1.79	79	24.44	2.73	B/R	t=7.59	p <.01
										B/P	t=4.52	p <.01
Triceps	64	9.08	3.70	57	8.46	3.42	79	8.13	4.16			

represent linear growth, total body mass, bone muscle (by subtracting the skin and subcutaneous tissues), and fat (by skinfolds). We have confined ourselves to Boston and Rome, as the Rome and Palermo patterns are similar.

Height increments are by chronological age. Although the Boston boys started at 11 years with an advantage of some 2 cm in height, the course of velocity during puberty is broadly similar (Figure 3-1). The Rome curve is somewhat more uneven; this unevenness may be eliminated by charting against puberal age (see Young, 1969; Figure 3-2).

We have already seen that with regard to weight increments the Boston boys remain fairly steadily and considerably higher in weight both before, during, and after puberty (Figure 3-3). The analysis by puberal age shows a relative weight gain at puberal age 4–5. It is in the area of bone muscle and fat increments that big differences appear. Figure 3-4 presents the bone muscle arm increments by chronological age. Boston is clearly superior. Figure 3-5 presents both bone muscle calf and supracrestal fat measurements by puberal age. The simultaneous rise in bone muscle and fall in fat velocity probably reflects the influx of hormones at the critical puberal period. These not only influence sexual development, but also have profound metabolic effects.

These various figures show that, except for total body height, Boston has greater velocities during puberty than Rome. It also shows the smoothing effect of measuring by puberal rather than chronological age, a procedure perfectly justified as there is little difference in the timing involved.

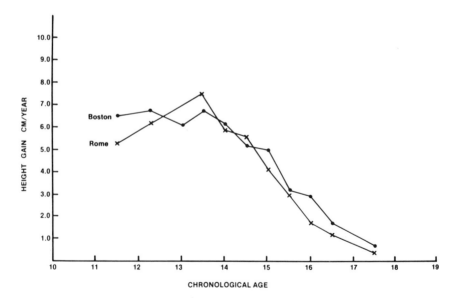

FIGURE 3-1   Height velocity.

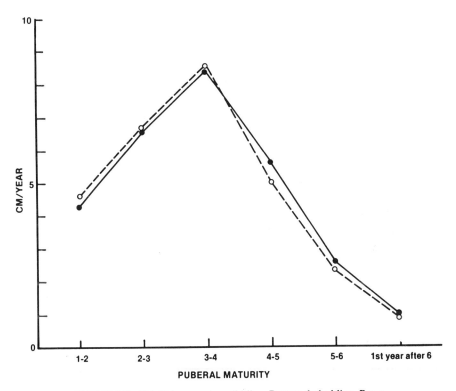

FIGURE 3-2   Height increments: solid line, Boston; dashed line, Rome.

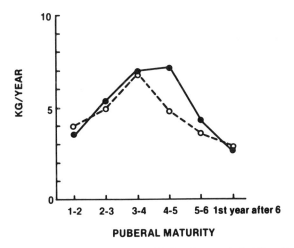

FIGURE 3-3   Weight increments: solid line, Boston; dashed line, Rome.

Physical Growth Intercorrelations

The following somatic variables were intercorrelated at 12, 14, 16, and 18 years: weight, height, sitting height, leg length, arm length, chest circumference (at xiphoid), arm circumference, dynanometer, puberal age, skinfold (triceps, biceps, and subscapular), Harvard Step Test, and bone muscle arm circumference.

At 12 years of age in Boston, weight intercorrelated highly with all variables except dynanometer; and, as expected, there was a negative correlation with the test of cardiovascular endurance (Harvard Step). Similarly in Rome weight correlated positively with all variables except dynanometer. In Palermo the same picture was seen except that chest circumference this time was largely insignificantly correlated with the Step Test—negatively, as in Boston.

Height presented few differences between the three groups, except for no correlation with two fat measurements in Boston and Rome, and none with chest circumference in Rome.

The three linear measurements—sitting height, leg length, and arm length—correlated well with each other in all three centers, but not with the dynanometer in Boston nor with the fat measurement nor the Harvard Step. In general there were negative or insignificant correlations with the Harvard Step throughout. Puberal age correlated well with the somatic measurements but not with the Harvard Step nor with the fat measurements. The dynanometer correlated well with mass and linear measurements in all centers except Boston, where it failed to correlate with height, weight, arm or leg length, chest or arm circumference.

Naturally the three fat measurements correlated well with each other in all three centers, while bone muscle went along well with the other somatic measurements and with puberal age.

At 16 years, the body mass and linear variables were still holding well together although chest circumference was still showing some weakness. The dynanometer was not correlating with body mass and linear measurements and also with puberal age. In general the fat measurements did not correlate too well with the mass and linear measurements but better so in Rome and Palermo. Notable exceptions were with chest and arm circumferences.

At 18 years the arm circumference failed to correlate with many measurements in all three centers except for height, chest, and bone muscle arm circumference. The chest circumference shows weakness in Boston and Palermo. At this age puberal stage mainly was not significant.

Of interest was the general failure of the Harvard Step, with its persistent negative correlations with the mass and linear body measurements, to be associated with growth. This may be because it was applied only in the early years of the project.

Except in the 18-year-olds the bone muscle arm circumference proved a useful

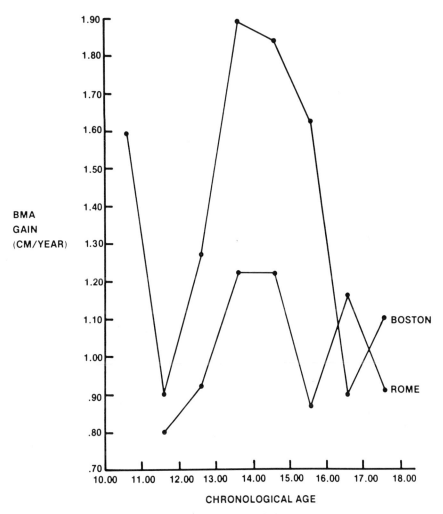

FIGURE 3-4   BMA velocity.

measure. Plausibly, it was frequently negative or insignificantly correlated with the arm fat measure.

The dynamometer proved useful up to the age of 18, except in Boston at 12 years of age, where the instrument used was not easy to manipulate and was later changed.

Antecedents   Predicted adult heights of subjects and midparental heights.

Midparental height correlates .63 with child height in comparison with a theoretical correlation of .71 (Susanne, 1975); stature presents one of the highest

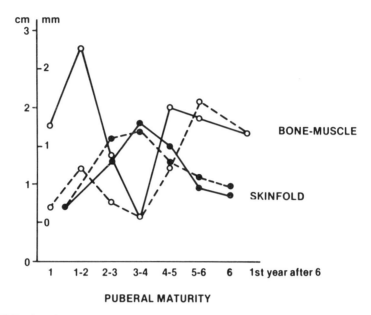

FIGURE 3-5   Bone-muscle calf increments: solid line, Boston; dashed line, Rome. Skinfold supracrestal increments: solid line, Boston; dashed line, Rome.

correlations that exists. In Boston, Rome, and Palermo the total parental heights were as shown in Table 3-13. Thus overall in the preceding generation the Boston-born fathers had the advantage over Rome and Palermo, but the mothers did not.

Using the Fels specific standards of height we calculated expected subjects' heights for 18-year-olds (Garn and Rohman, 1966). In the Fels tables the lowest midparental heights are 163.0 cm, whereas below this figure were 22% in Boston, 30% in Rome, and 29% in Palermo. We took the liberty of extrapolating downwards which is a questionable action, but we thought it worthwhile to try, as environmental influences differentially affect intrafamilial correlations. The new work by Roche, Wainer, & Thissen (1975) was not then published.

The deviations of "predicted" adult height from midparental height by social class in Boston, Rome, and Palermo are expressed in Table 3-14.

Overall there were more child increases and less decreases in Boston versus Rome and Palermo, when actual is compared with prediction, and the decreases were less. There were no consistent social class differences within any city. The differences in favor of Boston fit in with the observed nutritional advantages there.

In the Rome sample of 127 males there wer 29 born in 1943–1944 when food was scarce in Rome as a result of the economic disruptions toward the end of

TABLE 3-13

TOTAL PARENTAL HEIGHTS

Father

Boston			Rome			Palermo		
No.	Mean	S.D.	No.	Mean	S.D.	No.	Mean	S.D.
96	170.8	6.51	127	168.0	5.79	120	169.0	6.51

Mother

Boston			Rome			Palermo		
No.	Mean	S.D.	No.	Mean	S.D.	No.	Mean	S.D.
96	159.3	5.85	127	159.4	4.3	120	159.7	5.04

World War II. Of these 29 subjects, 9 showed heights greater than predicted from parental heights (mean increase of 4.34 cm, S.D. 3.00), 2 were correctly predicted, and the remaining 18 were shorter than predicted (mean 8.14 cm, S.D. 3.76). There were no consistent social class differences. The height deficit was greater than for boys born after 1944. This difference could have been caused by shortness at time of arrival at puberty, early puberty, or a puberal growth spurt in height less than to be expected. Excluding three subjects too old at initial examination to estimate puberal stage 3, we calculated age of arrival at overall puberal index 3 (first stage endocrinological development) along with mean heights for the group of subjects born in 1943–1944 as compared to those born later. The results are given in Table 3-15.

Those born in the famine of 1943–1944 reached puberty a mean of .41 years later, at which time they were shorter, on the average, by .53 cm. This is interesting as the expected height, given more time to grow, would have been 2–3 cm greater. It seems possible that the overall adult height deficit of Rome subjects born in 1943–1944 is related to both diminished height at the time they reached puberal index 3 and less growth in puberty. The height deficit at puberal index 3 is understandable as an effect of the hard conditions upon early childhood growth. More interesting is the deficit in height growth during puberty. Was this already programmed in 1943–1944?

It is also of interest that ordinal position correlated negatively with height and bone muscle in Rome and also number of children with puberal maturity negatively in Rome. That is, the lower the ordinal position the lower the height and less bone muscle in Rome. The later the child and larger the family, the lower the height, bone muscle, and puberal maturity.

TABLE 3-14

DEVIATIONS FROM ADULT HEIGHT "PREDICTED" FROM MID-PARENTAL HEIGHT BY SOCIAL CLASS:
BOSTON, ROME AND PALERMO

	Boston		Rome		Palermo	
Increases	33	34.4%	28	22.0%	26	21.7%
Decreases	55	57.3%	85	66.9%	55	45.7%
Prediction Correct	7	7.3%	13	10.2%	38	31.7%
Not Available	1	1.0%	1	0.9%	1	0.9%
Total	96	100.0%	127	100.0%	120	100.0%

		No.	Mean	S.D.	No.	Mean	S.D.	No.	Mean	S.D.
Average Increase		33	5.12	3.47	28	3.84	2.26	26	5.34	3.69
Average Decrease		55	5.04	2.89	85	6.28	3.68	55	5.79	3.45
Increase by Social Class[1]	1	4	4.65	4.20	8	3.54	2.41	6	3.25	1.07
	2	23	5.45	3.39	10	3.73	1.94	11	6.05	4.59
	3	6	4.15	3.75	10	4.18	2.60	9	5.86	4.00
Decrease by Social Class	1	13	5.42	3.04	16	6.10	3.67	20	5.39	4.44
	2	29	5.14	3.03	43	7.15	3.87	19	6.14	3.39
	3	13	2.41	26	26	4.96	3.03	16	5.60	2.23
No Change by Social Class	1	1	--	--	9	--	--	9	--	--
	2	4	--	--	4	--	--	17	--	--
	3	2	--	--	0	--	--	12	--	--

[1]Social Classes 1 & 2 = 1; 3 = 2; 4 & 5 = 3.

Interpretation

We have previously described the differing exercise pattern and diets of the three groups of subjects. In general, the Italian resident boys exercised much more despite the virtual nonexistence of organized sports at the time of this study, and they habitually ate a diet with less animal protein. The Boston boys, as babies, began animal protein supplements and carbohydrate much earlier, as reported in Chapter 2.

It is suggested that the larger physical dimensions, together with some evi-

TABLE 3-15

MEAN HEIGHTS

	Born 1943-1944 (N=26)			Born after 1944 (N=88)		
	SES	Age	Height	SES	Age	Height
Mean	3.19	13.25	150.10	2.93	12.84	150.63
S.D.	0.80	1.06	7.05	0.92	1.67	5.29

dence of an earlier arrival at puberty, of the Boston subjects may be explained by the nutrition–hygiene hypothesis. The considerably greater amount of bone muscle in the arm would also explain the better performance in static strength (dynamometer). The superiority of Palermo over Rome in static strength may be an illustration of one motivational factor that enters into this test. However, their bone muscle is superior to the Rome group, although not significantly so. On the other hand, the Boston boys, despite more muscle, perform no better on a well-established test of cardiovascular resistance (Harvard Step Test). It is suggested that this is due to the greater fat they must support during this exercise. Although overall the Boston boys may not be described as obese, there were some three instances of obesity in this sample.

Bigger may be better in certain physical performance situations, such as static strength, but the results are more disappointing in the potentially more interesting test of cardiovascular resistance. We suggest that attention might be directed to the fat levels of children of some ethnic groups in the United States, where dietary and exercise patterns have undergone changes since immigration, and appropriate advice given.

PATTERNS OF HEALTH AND DISEASE

As the three study groups proceeded through puberty and adolescence, they underwent regular medical examination. This section points up some similarities and differences of health and disease.

The principle differences were seen in six areas—that is, visual acuity, upper respiratory infections, dental health, days in bed and lost at school or work, work or school performance and behavior, and orthopedic conditions, together with some data on blood pressure. We have also included information upon the physician's clinical impression of sense of security, interest in this research work, and general sociability. There were virtually no differences in hemoglobin levels and skin infections nor in analysis of the urine. Tuberculin testing was not undertaken, and the number of subjects in the study did not warrant an investigation of the thalassemia trait.

Intergroup comparisons of some aspects of genetic makeup have been presented separately in Chapter 1 and Appendix A.

There were differences in visual acuity, where Boston at all ages through 19 years presented better performance. This appears due in great part to higher prevalence of myopia in Italy.

We have reported significant differences only; astigmatism was never significant at any one age point, and seems to make little contribution (see Table 3-16). Examination of ocular imbalance did not show significant differences between Boston and Rome.

The importance of myopia stimulates further thought about its environmental components. Twenty years ago Gardiner (1955, 1956, 1958) presented evidence for myopia's having environmental components, which has been refuted by Sorsby (1972), Sorsby and Leavy (1970); Sorsby, Sheridan, and Leavy (1962); and Sorsby, Sheridan, Leavy, and Benjamin (1960), who have argued for an almost entirely pure genetic influence. Here it seems clear that there is an en-

TABLE 3-16
VISUAL ACUITY

Age	Visual Acuity Right Superiority	Visual Acuity Left Superiority	Myopia Right	Myopia Left	Glasses	Visual Acuity Right W/Glasses	Visual Acuity Left W/Glasses	Astigmatism	Ocular Imbalance
11	B>R B>P	B>R B>P		B<P					
12	B>R B>P	B>R B>P	B<P	B<P					P>B
13	B>R B>P P>R	B>R B>P	P>R	B>R					P>B
14	B>R B>P	B>R B>P	B<R B<P	B<P R>P					
15	B>R B>P	B>R B>P	B<P	B>P		B>R	P>R		P>R
16	B>R P>R	B>R	B<R B<P	B>R		B>R P>R			P>B P>R
17	B>R B>P	B>R B>P	B<P	B<R B<P	B>P				
18	B>P R>P			B<P R P	B>P P>R	B>P P>R			
19	B>P								

\> means better condition.

vironmental component, and we conjecture that poor lighting and long hours of night homework in Italy may have played some part. Of the boys aged 15 and 16, for example, 63% in Boston, 55% in Rome, and 63% in Palermo had 20/20 vision. But it is in the case of severe myopia that the differences emerge: 10% in Boston, 29% in Rome, and 30% in Palermo. We found many boys in need of glasses when the study began, but this was quickly corrected and subsequently those with glasses that did not correct adequately were few.

Recent work on the possible relation between myopia and intelligence (*British Medical Journal*, 1976) raises the problem of a possible sampling bias—the less intelligent having emigrated to America, the more intelligent to Rome. However, these are as yet imponderables; we need more knowledge. Recently Peckham, Gardiner, & Goldstein (1977) have provided more evidence, from a British National sample at 11 years of age, that myopia was more common in children from nonmanual and small families and in children of higher birth order. The myopic performed much better in school and read more often in their leisure time. (The associations held within social class.) It is suggested that a greater quantity of homework might predispose to myopia and this would be consistent with homework differences between Boston and the two Italian cities.

Table 3–17 presents the findings for upper respiratory infections. Here the size of the tonsils is consistently greater in the Italian resident boys. However, it should not be forgotten that tonsillectomy was more widely practiced in the United States and that 65% of our Boston subjects had undergone the operation as compared with 33% in Rome and 24% in Palermo (15–18-year-olds). Moreover, the condition of the existing tonsils was judged better in Boston (the possible confounding effect of the healthier tonsils being left is countered to some extent by the criteria used for recommendation for tonsillectomy) and on the whole in Boston the cervical glands, anterior, lateral, and posterior were smaller—a sign of fewer infections for the throat and adjacent areas. Where there were differences in other glands, such as those in the axillary and inguinal areas, these were generally in favor of Boston. There was a relative absence of significant differences in the auditory apparatus and canals.

It was in the area of dental health (Table 3-18) that we found the most striking differences, especially as we consider the whole picture throughout all ages from 11 to 19. The DMF index (decayed, missing, filled) was much lower in the Italian resident subjects. The methodology was Stage One of the American Dental Association (Young, 1962b). Most observations were made by the principal investigator, who reviewed with the other observer physicians a minimum of 10 subjects a year in Rome and Palermo. Also he examined eight Boston subjects independently seen by a competent dentist using light mirror and probe. In four subjects the DMF index was the same and the overall agreement was 85%. In contrast to the DMF at a number of ages, Boston was superior in gingival health and there was less malocclusion in the years up to 14.

TABLE 3-17

UPPER RESPIRATORY INFECTIONS

Age	1 Nose Condition	2 Nose Infection	3 Tonsils Size	4 Tonsils Condition	5 Cervical Glands Anterior	6 Cervical Glands Posterior	7 Cervical Glands Lateral	8 Inguinal Glands	9 Axillary Glands	10 Hearing	11 Drums	12 Sundry
11			B > R B > P P > R	B > R B > P R > P	B > P	B > R P > R	B > R B > P P > R		B > R B > P			
12	P > B P > R		B > R B > P P > R	B > R B > P R > P	B > P P > R	B > R	B > R B > P P > R					
13			B > R B > P P > R	B > R B > P P > R	B > R B > P P > R	B > R P > R	B > R B > P P > R	R > B	B > R B > P			
14	P > B P > R	P > B	B > R B > P P > R	B > R B > P	B > R P > R	B > R P > R	B > R B > P P > R	R > B R > P	B > P			
15	B > R P > R	P > B	B > R B > P P > R	B > R B > P	B > R P > R	B > R P > R	B > R B > P P > R		B > R B > P	P > R	P > R	P > R
16	P > B P > R		B > R B > P	B > R B > P P > R	B > R P > R	B > R P > R	B > R P > R		B > P			
17			B > R B > P	B > R		B > R	B > R P > R					
18			B > P	B > P			B > P	R > B P > B				B > R
19			B > R	B > R	B > R B > P		B > R B > P					
20					B > R					R > B		

> means better condition.

It should be noted that the level of fluoride in the drinking water in the three communities was about the same during the life of the study and that, although the Italian resident boys were superior in dental health, Palermo presented a better record than Rome. (The eating of fruit after meals is a common practice in Italy, and oranges are cheaper in Sicily.) And perhaps the more frequent tooth brushing reported by our American subjects may have been beneficial to their gums.

In the area of sickness and health records (see Table 3-19) there were few differences in days in bed. On the other hand, there were many differences in diagnoses. Boston generally had fewer diagnoses; those instances where Boston health was worse were almost entirely accounted for by moderate upper respiratory infections, perhaps a reflection of the climate.

The Boston school reports were in general better (but this may be a cultural phenomenon). In clinical impression of general condition, Boston had the advantage.

Table 3-20 presents the orthopedic defects, and here Boston showed surprisingly few advantages: less kyphosis, for example, at 11 and 13, less scoliosis at 13, fewer flat feet at 11 and 13, fewer winged scapular at ages 11–15. (It should be remembered that we are presenting significant group differences only and that in general Boston had a better record—although not necessarily significantly better—in all fields.)

We may consider orthopedic variables as possible indications of later life conditions, since a recent paper clearly associates kyphosis with reduced expectancy of life (Anderson & Cowan, 1976).

In clinical impression of muscle mass and tone, Boston demonstrated impressive and significant advantages. For those who doubt the value of "clinical impressions," it is enough to look at the objective records of arm or calf bone muscle mass presented earlier in this chapter. These amply confirm the clinical impression of muscle mass.

TABLE 3-18

DENTAL HEALTH

Age	1 DMF	2 Number Of Teeth	3 Emergence Of Teeth	4 Dental Health	5 Filled Missing	6 Caries Not Filled	7 Gingival Health	8 Malocclusion
11	R > B P > B		No Signifi-cant	R ≥ B P > B	R ≥ B P > B		P > R	B > P
12	R ≥ B P > B		Differ-erences	R > B P > B	R > B P > B		B ≥ R P > R	B ≥ R P > R
13	R ≥ B P > B			R > B P > B	R > B P > B		B > R B > P	B > R P > R
14	R ≥ B P ≥ B P > R	R ≥ B P > B		R ≥ B P ≥ B P > R	R ≥ B P ≥ B		B ≥ R P > R	B > R P > R
15	R ≥ B P > B			R ≥ B P > R	R ≥ B P > B		B ≥ R P > R	
16	R ≥ B P > B			P ≥ B	R > B P > B		B > R	
17	P > B	P > b			P ≥ B P ≥ R		B > R	
18	R > B P ≥ B	R > B		B ≥ R	P > R			
19	R ≥ B P > B				R > B P > B		B > R B > P	
20						P ≥ B		

> means better condition.

TABLE 3-19

HEALTH RECORDS

Age	1 No. Days In Bed	2 Diagnoses	3 No. Days Lost At School	4 School Report	5 Comportment	6 General Condition
11		B> R P> R		B> P		B > R
12	B > P	B> R P> R	B > R	B> P R> P	B > P	B > R R> P
1?		B> R P> R		B> P R> P	R >P	B > R
14	R > B	R> B P> B P> R		B> R		B > P
15	P >R	R> B P> B P> R	P > B	B> P		B > P
16		R> B P> B P> R		R> P		
17		B> R B> P P> R				
18		R> B R> P			P >B	B >R
19		B> P P> R		B >R		
20		R> B				

> means better condition.

The blood pressure measurements at the last examination showed that the Boston and Palermo samples were practically identical for mean systolic and diastolic pressures (systolic Boston 120.5, S.D. 12.92; Palermo 120.9, S.D. 11.5; diastolic Boston 77.2, S.D. 7.50; Palermo 78.1, S.D. 7.54), although Palermo had a greater proportion of subjects with diastolic pressures above 90—10 in 118 measurements, which is 8%, as compared with Boston's 4 in 96, which is 4%. On the other hand, Rome had systolic and diastolic mean pressures significantly higher than both Boston and Palermo (systolic 126.18, S.D. 14.12; diastolic 81.3, S.D. 8.8), and 16 subjects, or 13%, with diastolic pressures above 90. The comparison yielded results as follows: systolic pressure, $t = 3.62$, $p < .01$; diastolic pressure, $t = 3.76$, $p < .01$. The comparison between Rome and Palermo gave these results: systolic pressure, $t = 3.17$, $p < .01$; diastolic pressure, $t = 3.08$, $p < .01$. These results suggest that the greater quantity of fat carried by Boston subjects was not accompanied by an increase in blood pressures. It is tempting to reflect that greater environmental pressures in Rome might have been related to these differences.

Since an association between fat and elevated blood pressure has been reported in other samples, we examined the association within each of our groups (Table 3-21). In all three cities, there are consistent trends toward increases in both systolic and diastolic blood pressure as fat level increases. The differences in systolic pressure are significant in both Boston and Rome; diastolic pressure proves significant in both Rome and Palermo. Overall, fatter subjects tend to show increased blood pressure, but this relationship, as we have noted, does not account for the greater incidence of high blood pressure in Rome.

We also examined the possible relationship between blood pressure and smoking habits among our subjects. Amount of smoking was recorded either by personal interview or in the questionnaire distributed by Richard Jessor when the subjects were in their early twenties (see Chapter 6). While there was a somewhat greater incidence of heavy smoking in Boston (12 subjects there reported smok-

TABLE 3-20

ORTHOPEDIC DEFECTS

Age	1 Kyphosis	2 Scoliosis	3 Flat Feet	4 Lordosis	5 Winged Scapula	6 Muscle Mass	7 Muscle Tone
11	B > P		B > P R > P		B > P R > P	B > P P > R	B > R B > P
12					B > P	B > R B > P P > R	B > R B > P
13	B > P	B > P	B > P	R > P	B > R B > P	B > P P > R	B > R B > P
14					B > R B > P	B > R B > P P > R	B > R B > P P > R
15					B > R P > R	B > R B > P P > R	B > R B > P P > R
16						B > R P > R	B > R B > P P > R
17		P > R				B > R P > R	B > R P > R
18		P > R			P > R		B > R P > R
19							B > R B > P
20							B > R

> means better condition.

Table 3-21
BLOOD PRESSURE BY FAT LEVEL

Fat Level	Boston			Rome			Palermo		
	N	Syst.	Diast.	N	Syst.	Diast.	N	Syst.	Diast.
4-7.9 mm	24	118.1	76.8	41	124.5	78.6	49	118.7	76.9
8-11.9 mm	40	118.7	76.1	45	128.8	81.8	46	121.9	79.2
12+ mm	32	124.7	79.0	41	132.8	83.9	25	122.6	82.1

ing more than 24 cigarettes a day, as against one in Rome and none in Palermo), there was no correlation between reported cigarette usage and blood pressure either there or in the two Italian samples.

At the suggestion of David McClelland, we also undertook an analysis of the relation between blood pressure levels and need-power expressed in the Imagination Test (see Chapter 4). The results are presented inTable 3-22. Overall, there is a tendency for blood pressure to increase as n-power increases. The differences in both diastolic and systolic pressure are significant in Rome, and for systolic pressure in Palermo. These findings provide some support for the notion that blood pressure is related to motivational variables.

Table 3-23 deals again with clinical impressions, this time the physician's opinion of the boys' sense of security, interest in the research, and his sociability. For security, Boston was most positive at ages 13–15 and also in interest in the research and sociability for ages 11–15. And in these three variables, Palermo scored higher than the traditionally blasé Rome.

TABLE 3- 22

NEED-POWER AND BLOOD PRESSURE

	Boston			Rome			Palermo		
	0-3	4-7	7	0-3	4-7	7	0-3	4-7	7
Number	38	33	17	33	47	16	26	48	10
Percentage	43.2	37.5	19.3	34.4	49.0	16.6	31.0	57.1	11.9
Systolic									
Mean	120.2	121.3	116.4	132.5	126.2	124.7	125.2	119.5	123.3
S.D.	11.70	13.20	11.93	16.55	12.76	9.01	10.96	10.08	6.04
Diastolic									
Mean	78.6	76.1	75.5	83.6	79.5	78.31	80.4	78.5	76.9
S.D.	7.56	5.49	10.67	8.69	7.10	8.00	7.97	7.80	5.80

TABLE 3-23

CLINICAL IMPRESSIONS

Age	1 Security	2 Interest	3 Sociability
11		B > P R > P	B > P
12		B > R	B > R
13	B > R P > R	B > R P > R	B > R
14	B > R P > R	B > R P > R	
15	B > R P > R	B > R P > R	B > R P > R
16	P > R	P > R	P > R
17			P > R
18			B > R
19			
20			

> means better condition.

It is concluded that there was need for further investigation of possible environmental correlates of myopia, that there was need for more preventive pediatrics in Italy in the upper respiratory tract (which has since been largely met), that there was a great need for programs of dental conservation in the United States (although it should be remembered that much work has been done on fluoridation since these subjects were young), and that more organized sports or gymnastics would be of undoubted benefit in Italy both for orthopedic defects and for muscle mass and tone. It is likely that the steadily improving nutritional facilities in Italy will also play an important part.

SUMMARY

The Boston subjects were clearly superior to the two Italian groups on a number of measures of physical growth taken throughout the course of adolescence: body weight, height, leg length, and arm circumference. They also reached puberty earlier than the Italian boys and excelled on a measure of strength (dynamometer) but not on a measure of physical efficiency (Harvard Step). They were also fatter than the Italian subjects.

When growth measures were plotted against puberal rather than chronological age, the same picture of superiority for Boston as against both Rome and Palermo was evident. Growth measurements were similarly intercorrelated for the three groups, except that fat measures were less closely associated with mass and height in Boston than in Italy. More of the Boston subjects attained a greater height than would have been predicted from parents' stature; this is interpreted as resulting from Boston's nutritional advantage, especially in protein intake. There was evidence that some subjects born in Rome during the famine of 1943–1944 reached puberty later and were shorter than expected.

Myopia was more prevalent among the Italian subjects; this difference may reflect environmental factors. Dental caries was much lower among the Italian subjects, although gums were healthier in Boston. There were few other differences in health. Mild upper respiratory infections were reported a bit more frequently in Boston, perhaps related to climate, but enlarged tonsils were observed more frequently among the Italian subjects. Although blood pressure and fat levels tend to be correlated, blood pressure differences among the three groups did not parallel the difference in fat. While Boston subjects were fatter, there was more tendency among the Rome subjects toward elevated blood pressure, perhaps a reflection of greater stress.

CHAPTER 4

Psychological Development
in Adolescence

INTELLIGENCE AND COGNITIVE DEVELOPMENT

In this chapter we shall first discuss data from a variety of measures of intellectual functioning that have been administered to the subjects at various points in the study. These include the Raven Progressive Matrices (1956 Revision), a digit-reordering task designed as a measure of capacity for concentration, the Gottschaldt Embedded Figures test, and a battery of tests of creativity. Taken as a group, these tests may give us a picture (not, to be sure, as systematic as we would like) of the impact of the different educational and social environments of our three cities on the course of intellectual development and the patterning of various cognitive abilities in adolescence.

The Raven Progressive Matrices

Originally the Raven was thought of as one check on the genetic equivalence of the three samples. It may perhaps better be interpreted as an indicator of intellectual functioning and scholastic aptitude in the three samples which is a resultant both of genetic endowment and of the differential impact of social and educational experiences. The Raven was chosen as the most apparently "culture-free" of available measures of general intelligence. The 1956 revised order of the test was administered by the project staff to a sample of children in and around Florence constituting about 4% of the school population between the ages of 10¾ and 16¼, as reported in Young and Tesi (1962b). Although on the average the performance of the Florentine children was very slightly superior to that of the English standardization group, ranges and distributions of scores, as well as age increments, were very similar. It was concluded that percentile scores based on Raven's norms would be an appropriate way of representing the performance of the groups in the longitudinal study. The test was accordingly administered twice to most of the subjects, in succeeding years (1958–1959 and 1959–1960), when the subjects were on the average 13–15 years of age. No second testing on the Raven is available for the group of subjects in Rome who were recruited in 1960 in an effort to make the socioeconomic level more comparable to that in the other two centers.

The results of the first and second administrations of the Raven, by cities and by social class groupings within each city, are given in Table 4-1. A two-way analysis of variance on these figures reveals the main effects both of cities and of social class to be significant at the .01 level. The interaction is not significant, and thus the influence of SES would seem to be equivalent within each of the three locations. The mean score for Rome is consistently higher than that for the other two cities, but only the difference in means between Rome and Palermo is significant (at the .001 level); the mean performance in Boston is intermediate between that in the two Italian cities, and not significantly different from either. To the extent that the Raven is a valid measure of general intelligence for this population, we may conclude that the subjects in Boston are of generally similar ability level to the combined Italian group and to Raven's standardization group.

TABLE 4-1

RAVEN: MEAN SCORES

First Testing		Boston	Rome	Palermo	Total
Social Classes	N:	16	25	32	73
1 & 2	Mean:	63.56	70.0	55.22	62.35
Social Class	N:	55	51	43	149
3	Mean:	46.56	51.3	36.97	45.41
Social Classes	N:	31	51	31	113
4 & 5	Mean:	37.68	52.5	35.58	43.79
Total	N:	93	127	106	
	Mean:	47.39	55.6	42.05	
Second Testing	N:	81	110	105	
Total	Mean:	52.54	68.54	51.73	

There are a number of reasons to suppose, as discussed in Chapter 1, that the group of families in Rome who were included in the study represent a somewhat different population from the group sampled in Palermo of families who had stayed in the South, as reflected among other indices in superior scholastic aptitude.

Each group of subjects improved on the average in performance, relative to the normative group for the test, from the first to the second administration. Each of the comparisons between means for first and second testing is significant at the .005 level. However, the magnitude of the difference is somewhat less for Boston, and this may reflect the greater familiarity of American adolescents with tests of this general kind. The consistency of individual subjects' performance from first to second testing was measured by means of product moment correlations (see Table 4-2). The highest reliability figure is for Boston, but the correlations for the two Italian groups are very similar, and in all three groups the temporal consistency of the test over about a year's interval would seem to be very satisfactory. More recently we examined the long-term consistency of the Raven scores for very small samples of subjects in each city. These results are also shown in Table 4-2. These tests were given in 1968, approximately 10 years after the original administration. The correlation for Boston is quite high (.71) and, although the very small number of subjects makes it fairly unreliable, it suggests that in this group the Ravens administered in early adolescence had good long-term predictive validity. The correlations for the two Italian samples are quite low, however, and although positive are not significant with these small samples. It is hard to know how to interpret this difference, and we are reluctant to conclude that the earlier Raven scores were any less valid for the Italian subjects, although they did not have the same long-term significance. Perhaps the more varied educational experiences of the Italian boys between the time of first testing and the re-test when they were in their early twenties may account for this difference.

Digit Ordering

This test was developed by Rey (1957) as an instrument reflecting capacity for concentration. It involves reassembling groups of scrambled numbers in ascending order. Since such a task would seem to be relatively culture-free, at least among western societies, it seemed a good candidate for inclusion in the battery of measures of intellectual functioning for this cross-cultural study.

The test presents the subject with four columns of numbers; in each column there are 24 groups of 7 numbers in random order, 96 groups in all. The task is to rearrange each group in ascending order. The task may be group administered. Rey originally recommended a time limit of 20 min, which was shortened to 10 in this study. At the end of each minute the examiner called the time and the

TABLE 4-2

RAVEN: LONG-TERM AND SHORT-TERM CONSISTENCY

Correlations		Boston	Rome	Palermo
Test I	N:	81	110	105
with Test II	r:	.83	.70	.78
Test I	N:	8	10	12
with Test III	r:	.71	.37	.29
	rho:	.65	.13	.37

subject marked the point he had reached. The test may be scored qualitatively, in terms of the speed and accuracy of performance during the 10 min, or strictly quantitatively, in terms of numbers reordered correctly. As there was a marked tendency for subjects to sprint during the first minute, slow up in the second minute, and then proceed toward a more steady rate, the first and second minutes were scored separately and the third to tenth minutes were averaged.

Before application to the subjects in the longitudinal study, the test was administered to samples of high school students in both Florence and Boston. The results suggested that this test is an appropriate measure of cognitive functioning for subjects in both cultures. It shows regular increments with age, and there were no marked differences in performance between the two standardization samples. In the longitudinal sample there is a low positive correlation with the Raven. Motivational as well as ability factors seem important in determining scores on this test.

The results of the administration of the digit reordering task to the subjects of the longitudinal study are shown in Table 4-3. Overall, the performance of the subjects both in Rome and Boston is superior to that of the standardization groups, while that in Palermo is inferior. This parallels the mean differences in percentiles on the Raven, but in view of the modest overall correlations with the Raven (r between digits, minutes 3–10, and Raven: in Boston, .19; in Rome, .17; in Palermo, .23; correlations for first and second minutes range from .12 to .25) it is likely that other factors are involved, especially in the difference for Palermo. Turning to comparisons among the three groups in the longitudinal study, we note that the Boston group is clearly superior to the two Italian groups in the first minute (t's of 5.43 and 4.92, both p's $< .01$), possibly reflecting initially greater confidence in attacking the task. In the second minute, where all groups exhibit the typical slump in performance, the Rome and Boston subjects do about equally well, and the boys in Palermo are distinctly inferior; this same pattern of differences is repeated in the averaged performance for the remaining minutes. (Significance of differences: second minute, Boston vs Palermo, $t = 7.04$, $p < .01$; Rome vs Palermo, $t = 6.85$, $p < .01$; third to tenth minutes, Boston vs Palermo, $t = 6.86$, $p < .01$; Rome vs. Palermo, $t = 7.52$, $p < .01$.) Part of the difference between Palermo and the other two cities might be attributed to the generally younger ages of the boys there at the time of testing (mean age for Palermo: 13.5, as against 14.4 in Boston and 14.7 in Rome). However, when we group 12–13-year-old subjects in Palermo and the 14–15-year-olds, and compare them with the equivalent age groupings in Boston (see Table 4-3), we see that the differences are of approximately equal magnitude and equivalent significance among the older as compared to the younger subjects (the t's run from 4.11 to 2.73 and all are significant at the .01 level). Thus we must look to other differences between the groups, above and beyond age and general intelligence, to account for these differences in performance. The project staff observed that boys in Palermo are notoriously diffident when faced with

TABLE 4-3

PERFORMANCE ON DIGIT ORDERING TASK — LONGITUDINAL STUDY

	1st minute		2nd minute		3rd-10th minutes	
	Boston	Rome	Boston	Rome	Boston	Rome
N	84	111	84	111	84	111
Mean	50.43	42.19	38.37	36.36	39.00	38.69
SD	12.82	8.32	12.95	10.19	10.10	8.72
t		5.43		1.24		0.23
p		.01		NS		NS
	Rome	Palermo	Rome	Palermo	Rome	Palermo
N	111	104	111	104	111	104
Mean	42.19	40.97	36.36	27.66	38.69	30.25
SD	8.32	13.34	10.19	8.66	8.72	7.99
t		.81		6.85		7.52
p		NS		.01		.01
	Boston	Palermo	Boston	Palermo	Boston	Palermo
N	84	104	84	104	84	104
Mean	50.43	40.97	38.37	27.66	39.00	30.25
SD	12.82	13.34	12.95	8.66	10.00	7.99
t		4.92		7.04		6.86
p		.01		.01		.01

12-13 year olds

	1st minute		2nd minute		3rd-10th minutes	
	Boston	Palermo	Boston	Palermo	Boston	Palermo
N	29	80	29	80	29	80
Mean	50.21	40.12	35.34	27.52	37.31	30.01
SD	11.39	11.14	11.20	8.40	10.08	8.07
t		4.15		3.92		3.90
p		.01		.01		.01

14-15 year olds

	1st minute		2nd minute		3rd-10th minutes	
	Boston	Palermo	Boston	Palermo	Boston	Palermo
N	38	18	38	18	38	18
Mean	49.79	43.50	40.84	29.11	39.00	31.67
SD	14.02	21.42	14.85	9.01	10.10	8.36
t		1.32		3.09		2.68
p		NS		.01		.01

something new, and thought anxiety generated by this test might have been sufficient to impair performance to a large extent; there was greater variability in performance among these subjects. There is also the generally less permissive atmosphere of the family in Palermo, and less support for achievement, as we noted in the analysis of the parent interviews (see Chapter 2). We shall see to what extent these possible explanatory variables gain support from an analysis of the interrelations of the cognitive and the personality and child-rearing measures.

Gottschaldt Figures

Another aspect of cognitive functioning is measured by the embedded figures test, which involves the ability to restructure a perceptual field so as to discover a simple geometrical figure concealed within a complex figure. This task was originally devised by Gottschaldt (1926) as a demonstration of the classical Gestalt theory of visual perception. It has since been found to relate to a number of aspects of cognitive and personality function; it has been used by Witkin (Witkin, Dyk, Faterson, Goodenough, & Karp, 1962), for instance, as a measure of "field independence," and has been found to be an excellent measure of the "adaptive flexibility" factor in studies of creativity (Barron, Guilford, Christensen, Berger, & Kettner, 1957). It is also found consistently to load highly on the factor of spatial ability in factorial studies of mental abilities in children as well as adults (Vernon, 1970). The version used in this project was the Crutchfield revision. The subject is given 20 problems, all of them involving locating a simple geometrical figure embedded or camouflaged in a more complex design. The score is the number of correct solutions. This test was administered to the subjects, along with a battery of creativity measures, in 1965.

The results obtained from this test are shown in Table 4-4. Each of the comparisons between the three cities is significant at the .01 level. As with the Raven, the Rome group has the highest mean score, but the ordering for Boston and Palermo is reversed—the mean score for Boston is the lowest of the three and Palermo is intermediate. The Italian–American group is, on the average, least able to break perceptual set, whereas the Rome boys are superior in this ability,

TABLE 4-4

GOTTSCHALDT FIGURE COMPARISON

	Comparison of Groups			Comparison of Means		
	N	Mean	SD		t	p
Boston	95	10.24	3.65	Boston-Rome	9.18	<.01
Rome	123	13.81	2.31	Rome-Palermo	6.05	<.01
Palermo	120	11.73	3.14	Boston-Palermo	3.34	<.01

although their superiority to the Palermo group may partly be accounted for by the significant difference between these groups in intelligence as measured by the Raven. Correlations with the Raven are: Boston, $r = .44$; Rome, .18; Palermo, .48.

Should we conclude from these findings that the Boston sample is, on the average, more conventional in their thinking and more field-dependent than the Italian groups? The findings from the parent interviews (see Chapter 2) of earlier independence training and greater permissiveness of the Boston families would make such a conclusion somewhat surprising. Interpretation of this finding and those on creativity in the next section must await examination of the intercorrelations of these measures with the various measures of personality and family relations.

It is also of some interest that while the Gottschaldt test is only very slightly correlated with digit ordering in Boston and Rome (r's run from .07 to .20, and only the one for digit ordering, first minute, in Rome is significant at the .05 level), the correlations in Palermo are first minute, $r = .17$; second minute, .31; third to tenth minutes, .34; the latter two correlations being significant at the .01 level. Thus Gottschaldt figures and digit ordering in Palermo seem to tap some common aspects of cognitive functioning, perhaps related to anxiety in the face of relatively novel tasks.

Creativity

Divergent ability, or creativity, has been found by a number of investigators to be a factor of cognitive functioning somewhat independent of convergent ability, or the more usual measures of general intelligence (see Kagan & Kogan, 1970). A wide variety of psychological tests designed to measure aspects of creative thinking have been developed (Barron, 1968). The factorial structure of the domain represented by these tests has been investigated exhaustively by J. P. Guilford and his associates at the University of Southern California (Guilford, 1968). Some of the tests, or revisions of previous tests, constructed at the Institute of Personality Assessment and Research of the University of California at Berkeley have been analyzed in conjunction with the Guilford tests and have been shown to be appropriate as marker variables for certain factors (Barron, *et al.*, 1957). Their validity as measures of creativity has been supported in a number of studies on American samples (Barron, 1955).

The measures used in this project were chosen and scored under the supervision of Professor Frank Barron. In addition to the Gottschaldt figures, which he designates a measure of adaptive flexibility, three other factors were represented.

Ideational Fluency This factor reflects an individual's ability to produce a large number of ideas quickly, irrespective of quality. Two well-established measures of this factor are (*a*)   *Alternate uses*   This test calls upon the respondent to list six possible uses to which each of several common objects can be put. This test is closely timed, and most respondents cannot think of six uses for each object in the time allotted. Score is the number of acceptable uses suggested.

(*b*)   *Categories*   This test presents the respondent with a list of objects and calls upon him to classify them in as many ways as he can within the time limit. Score is simply the number of acceptable categories suggested.

Originality   This factor reflects an individual's ability to think in a divergent or unusual manner. Ideas that are both unusual and meet the requirements of the problem are considered original. Tests for this factor were

(*a*)   *Consequences B*   In this test the respondent is asked to write down what would happen if certain changes were suddenly to take place. Remote or nonobvious consequences are considered original. Score is the average rating on originality assigned to the individual's responses.

(*b*)   *Plot Titles B*   Two story plots are presented, and the respondent is asked to write as many titles as he can think of for each plot. Each suggested title is rated for cleverness, and the average cleverness rating is the score for originality.

(*c*)   *Cartoons*   A cartoon showing a situation with possible comic value is displayed and the respondent is asked to think up a caption for the cartoon. The captions are rated for their wit or cleverness, and the average cleverness rating is the score for originality.

Preference for Complex Displays   The Barron–Welsh Art Scale (Barron & Welsh, 1952) was used to measure the subjects' preferences for complex versus simple phenomenal fields. This measure did not prove differentiating in this study and will not be further discussed.

In order to ensure objectivity in scoring, the verbal test responses of the Rome group were translated into English, and culturally idiosyncratic expressions were removed from both sets of protocols. Ratings were done from typed protocols, with order among the groups randomized. Expert raters were employed to judge the degree of originality of responses to Consequences, Plot Titles, and Cartoons. Interrater agreement ranged from .38 to .78, with a mean correlation of .61. Cartoons were the least reliably rated; the correlation between judges fell below the .50 level, which we have considered minimally acceptable. The responses of the Palermo subjects were not available when the original ratings were done on the responses of the other two groups. They were scored later by members of the project staff who also rescored the other two sets of protocols. Since the overall results on the two groups originally scored agree so closely with the first set of ratings, we have felt justified in using the staff ratings on all three groups, but the reader should bear in mind the degree of subjectivity involved in these scores. Alternate Uses was scored by the staff psychometrician on the basis of the Guilford manual and norms, and presents no problems in judgment.

The comparisons of group means on the various creativity measures are shown in Table 4-5. Cartoons, the least reliable measure, does not differentiate between any of the groups. On three of the other measures, Categories, Consequences, and Plot Titles, the Rome subjects are scored significantly more original or creative in their responses than the members of the other two groups. On the fifth measure, Alternate Uses, the mean score for Palermo is significantly lower than those for both Rome and Boston, which do not differ from each other. In general, it seems that the Rome gorup of boys responded to this set of tasks with greater fluency and originality, while the Palermo subjects tended on the whole to be the least creative.

Since these differences parallel the group differences in performance on the Raven test, and since measures of divergent ability tend to be correlated with general intelligence in heterogeneous samples, we might be tempted to conclude that the differences in creativity simply reflect differences in general intelligence. The actual correlations of these measures with the Raven and the Gottschaldt (see Table 4-6) cast some doubt on this interpretation. In Boston, the Gottschaldt test is closely related to the creativity measures, and both correlate positively with the Raven. Three of the measures, Plot Titles, Alternate Uses, and Cartoons, correlate significantly with the Raven. In Palermo, while there are several significant correlations (at the .05 level), their magnitude is generally much lower, and there is no consistent association in Rome. Thus it would seem that measures of divergent and of convergent intellectual functioning are much less closely as-

TABLE 4-5

COMPARISON OF BOSTON, ROME, AND PALERMO GROUPS
ON TESTS OF CREATIVITY

Creative Factors	Boston			Rome			Palermo			Comparison of Means		
	N	Mean	SD	N	Mean	SD	N	Mean	SD	Boston-Rome	Rome-Palermo	Boston-Palermo
Ideational Fluency												
(a) Alternate Uses	93	12.28	7.41	123	12.24	6.07	120	10.55	4.70	t= .05 NS	t=2.46 p< .05	t=2.14 p< .05
(b) Categories	93	43.04	14.66	125	48.02	13.46	120	42.20	12.35	t=2.66 p< .01	t=3.57 p< .01	t= .47 NS
Originality												
(a) Consequences	94	3.70	3.49	125	5.46	3.69	120	2.82	2.69	t=2.65 p< .01	t=3.57 p< .01	t= .47 NS
(b) Plot Titles	93	3.06	1.45	123	3.72	1.20	120	3.19	1.10	t=3.74 p< .01	t=3.67 p< .01	t= .75 NS
(c) Cartoons	93	3.48	1.14	124	3.51	1.16	120	3.27	1.33	t= .16 NS	t=1.55 NS	t=1.30 NS

TABLE 4-6

INTERCORRELATIONS OF COGNITIVE MEASURES

	Boston		Rome		Palermo	
	Raven	Gottschaldt	Raven	Gottschaldt	Raven	Gottschaldt
Creativity	19	20	19	20	19	20
Ideational Fluency 99	.19	.41+	-.04	-.06	.07	.09
Consequences 100	.17	.30+	.03	-.03	-.03	.21+
Plot Titles 101	.33+	.36+	.11	-.11	-.04	.14
Alternate Uses 102	.35+	.50+	.19+	.01	.29+	.17
Cartoons 103	.34+	.23+	-.08	-.15	.27+	.21+

sociated among Italian than among American–Italian (and generally among American) adolescents, and may well reflect somewhat different social and emotional determinants.

PERSONALITY, SOCIAL, AND EMOTIONAL DEVELOPMENT

Between 1958 and 1960, when the boys were on the average 14–16 years old, information was collected on a number of aspects of their social development, emotional adjustment, and personality organization. The findings to be reported here come from several sources: interviews with the boys, responses to a specially adapted measure of thematic fantasy, and several standardized questionnaires. These last included the High School Personality Questionnaire devised by Cattell (1958), the S–R Inventory of anxiety developed by Endler, Hunt, and Rosenstein (1962), and the EV 3—an instrument devised by Schircks to tap attitudes toward theft.

The Interview

Two rounds of interviews, lasting from 20 to 40 min on each occasion, were conducted with the boys themselves in 1958–1959 and 1959–1960. The interviews were, for the most part, conducted by different staff members (a pediatric psychiatrist in Rome, psychologists in both Boston and Palermo) from the social workers who interviewed the parents. In the small proportion of cases where the social worker also interviewed the boy, the occasions were at least a year apart, so that the possibility of contamination of correlations between the two sets of data by interviewer halo effects are minimal. Some checks on reliability were carried out by the principal investigator. Judgments on a number of categories referring to the boy's personality, adjustment, relations with parents, etc., were made at the time of the interview and the answers to other questions were recorded for later coding. Since many of the codes were categorical rather than continuous, only a few variables lent themselves to comparisons of means and correlational analyses. In most cases we compared frequencies of the different categories of response in the three cities; these findings are now summarized.

Interests   The boys in all three groups showed a healthy interest in amusement and adventure. When asked what they like most in life, they mentioned amusement and adventure to an equal extent. Adventure novels were preferred by all groups, but especially in Palermo (91%); these boys were least likely to prefer books about sports and serious subjects. There were some minor differences in their preference for films, probably related to availability: the Boston group especially liked mysteries, the Rome group liked romances and thrillers, the Palermo group liked westerns. Sports were listed as their most important interest by about 50% of the boys in all locations, but there are evidences that this was a stronger interest in Boston. The Boston group was somewhat more likely to mention a sporting figure as their most admired person, they were more likely to read books about sports, and 30% of them mentioned sports as "what I like most in life." In response to this last question, more subjects in Palermo mentioned happy personal and family relationships, whereas the Rome boys were more likely to mention studies or work. Telling jokes was most popular in Boston, least so in Palermo. The Boston subjects would rather tell jokes than listen to them, and some of their other interests seem a bit more active: mechanics and constructions versus collections, which apparently were popular among Italian boys. About a third of all groups mentioned some historical figure as their most admired person. In addition to admiring sports figures, the Boston subjects tended to admire living politicians, whereas the Italian boys more often mentioned singers and actors. An interesting sidelight on political attitudes: *none* of the Palermo subjects mentioned a living politician. Asked about places they would like to travel, 59% of the Boston subjects chose Italy, whereas the choices of most of the Italian boys are equally divided between the United States and Europe.

Vocational Aspirations   When asked about career plans, about 50% of all groups expressed aspirations in the highest category—professional and managerial jobs. The Boston subjects, however, were more likely than the Italian boys to pick skilled manual jobs (21% versus 3% and 1%), and the Italian subjects (40% in Palermo and 32% in Rome versus 15% in Boston) were more likely to pick "white-collar" jobs—skilled clerical or technical. Somewhat fewer of the Boston sample expressed no preference, an indication that their vocational goals may have been a bit more mature. The responses to the question about most-preferred occupations parallel those for vocational plans: the Italian boys chose very heavily according to status, whereas the Boston boys distributed their choices pretty evenly between professional and skilled manual jobs. When they were asked about occupations they disliked, however, things were turned around; the Boston subjects rejected more low-status jobs more frequently. Most boys in all groups indicated liking the conditions and type of work as the main reason for preferring a given occupation, but the Boston subjects were somewhat more likely to choose a job because it seemed interesting, whereas the Rome boys were more likely to indicate that their choice was based on feeling capable of doing the work. Most boys in all groups stated that they would decide their own careers, but this was especially true in Boston (83%), whereas in Rome 26% said that the father or both parents would decide. More of the boys in Palermo indicated that their parents' choice of career for them was different from their own.

Family Relations   In line with our parent interview findings, the Boston subjects seemed to feel somewhat more freedom from parental control with respect to choice of career and mode of dress; there was no difference between the groups on choice of friends. The difference between Rome and Palermo is slight and inconsistent; more subjects in Rome said their parents would choose their career, but more in Palermo said they were not free to dress as they pleased. In all three groups, over half the subjects reported that the father is the more severe parent, but more of the boys in Rome were likely to report both parents as equally severe (21%). Almost twice as many Italians as Boston subjects said that the father was the most important member of the family; 31% in Boston picked the mother, and another 22% said that both parents are equally important. One gets the impression of a trend away from patriarchal and toward egalitarian family life in Boston, at least as the boys see it. Perhaps as a consequence the boys in Boston seem closer to their fathers. Thirty-five percent of Boston subjects said they preferred to spend time with their father or their older brothers (21%), whereas a greater percentage of Italian boys chose to spend time with the mother. All three groups said that they would entrust a secret to their father to about the same extent; the Boston subjects were more likely to pick the mother to confide in, whereas the Italian boys tended to pick a friend rather than a family member. In other ways, the Boston subjects seemed to experience more positive relations with parents; 73% of them felt that adults usually understood them, whereas only about half of the Italian boys felt this way; 25% of the Palermo subjects felt they were *never* understood by adults. When asked about occasions when they were praised, 42% of the boys in Palermo and 29% in Rome could not remember any, whereas practically all Boston subjects reported some instance of praise. In all three groups, the boys were most often praised for good school performance, but a fair number of those in Boston also received praise for good deeds and nonscholastic accomplishments. Perhaps wistfully, almost all in Palermo said they liked praise, whereas a few in Rome and a fair number in Boston had some reservations about it.

The greatest number of subjects in Palermo (37%) said that unity is the most important quality to be respected in family life, and they were also most likely to report quarreling with other family members as the thing they were most afraid to do in front of their parents. It is interesting that these responses run counter to the estimates of family cohesiveness based on the parent interviews. One gets the impression of a good deal of suppression of aggression within the family in Palermo. Boston subjects stressed both unity and affection as important in family life, whereas the boys in Rome emphasized respect or faith and parental authority; all three groups mentioned obedience about equally. Italian boys also mentioned neglecting their school work as something they were afraid to do in front of their parents, whereas Boston subjects did not. The Boston boys most frequently mentioned swearing and smoking in this connection, perhaps another sign of emerging masculinity. All three groups said that family quarrels usually began over differences of opinion, but the Boston subjects mentioned children and money—perhaps an indication of greater awareness of economic stress. More of the Palermo subjects (22%) said they had received *more* unjust treatment than others, whereas the boys in Boston were most likely to say they had received less.

Aggression with Peers   Most of the boys in all groups said that if a school friend hit them they would hit him back, but a fair number (27%) of the Boston subjects said that they would handle the situation verbally, and a similar proportion said that their parents would expect such behavior of them. However, more of the Boston boys said that their parents would expect them to hit back, whereas more of the Italian boys said that their parents would expect them to ignore the aggression. These responses tend to confirm the impression we gained from the parents themselves of greater permissiveness toward aggression in Boston. Very few of the boys in any groups said that they would be expected to appeal to adult authority (the highest frequency [18%] occurred in Palermo), and none said they would do so. In general, the boys in all three groups seemed aware that their parents, while expecting them to handle such problems themselves, would favor a less aggressive response. The Boston subjects showed signs of a somewhat greater social sophistication, whereas the Palermo subjects were perhaps the least mature.

Affiliation   The responses to the group of questions about friendships suggested that the American boys were more wholeheartedly and indiscriminately sociable than their Italian counterparts. Almost all of the Boston subjects (96%) said they liked to have many friends, whereas about a third of the Italian boys preferred to have a few friends. The Bostonians also claimed more friends; 39% of them said they had more than 10 real friends. About 20% of the Italian boys said they had no friends or only one, whereas only 2% of the Boston boys gave such a response. Over half of the Boston group (57%) would not have liked to eliminate any of the members of their class, whereas two-thirds of the Italian boys would have liked to eliminate at least one or two. Most of the boys in all three groups said they preferred to play with friends; only in Palermo did an appreciable number (16%) say they preferred to play alone, and 8% of the Palermo subjects as against almost none in the other groups indicated that their parents would prefer them not to have friends. It may be that the Italian boys were freer to reject peers, as well as less sociable.

In general, the reports of the boys themselves tend to confirm our impression that the Italian–American parents, as compared to their Italian counterparts, placed more emphasis on sociability and granted their sons more freedom in peer relations, and that their sons picked up these values with enthusiasm.

Emotional Adjustment   Boston subjects were more likely to report concrete sources of fear (harm to self, animals), whereas Italian boys mentioned failure or moral lapses more. There were no differences between the groups in reported feelings of guilt, however. The Rome subjects were more likely to deny specific fears, but they reported somewhat more somatic signs of anxiety than did either the Boston or Palermo samples. The Palermo subjects were somewhat more likely to say they felt worried or nervous, whereas the Boston subjects reported more changeable moods and were more likely to say they felt tired rather than serene when they woke up in the morning. There were no differences in reporting unpleasant early memories, but the Boston subjects were twice as likely to report pleasant ones. This latter difference may be a function of their somewhat more positive family relations. There may be some slight evidence of greater neuroticism among the Italian boys, but certainly the differences are not striking. There are no differences on the items reflecting self-concept, except with respect to feelings of unjust treatment, reported above in connection with family relations.

The remainder of the interview codes represented judgments of the interviewer, rather than responses of the boys themselves. These items are as likely to reflect differences in the interviewer's frames of reference or cultural biases as real differences among the groups. While they are useful for internal analysis of correlations with other measures on a particular group, the group comparisons listed here should be viewed with caution:

Fewer boys in Palermo judged laconic
More in Boston judged restless
More in Rome judged timid
Fewer in Boston seemed embarrassed
Independence: Palermo highest, Rome lowest
Capacity to solve practical problems: Boston highest
Capacity to solve emotional problems: Rome lowest
Open and affectionate with family: Rome lower, Boston higher

Open and affectionate outside family: Rome lower, Boston higher
Support from his home: Rome lower, Boston higher
Support he gives his home: Rome lower, Boston higher
Responsibility toward the community: Boston higher, Palermo lower
Aggressive toward others: Rome lower, Palermo highest
Logical capacity to reason: Boston lower, Palermo highest
Capacity to work with others: Boston highest, Palermo lowest

These differences do tend to reinforce the impression that the Italian–American boys seemed more sociable, expressive, active, self-confident, and socially responsible than the Italian boys, and that they experienced more positive family relations.

The Imagination Test

The main projective measure of personality employed in the project was a verbally presented story-completion test, suggested by David McClelland and based on the pictorial methods used by McClelland, Atkinson, and their collaborators (see Atkinson, 1958) in the assessment of various motives. The subject was asked to make up and write down a series of stories in response to each of the following eight situations, followed by four probes: (a) What is happening? (b) What has led up to this situation; that is, what has happened in the past? (c) What is being thought? What is wanted by whom? (d) What will happen? The seven story stems were

1. A mother and her son; they look worried
2. A boy sitting in a schoolroom with an open book in front of him
3. A boy and a girl walking together
4. Two men in a workshop standing by a machine; one is older
5. A young man alone at night
6. A father and son talking
7. Two small children, a boy and a girl, walking together
8. Any situation you choose; please write title

The subject was given 5 min to write each story. The test was administered in Rome and Palermo in 1958–59 and in all three cities in 1959–60.

The three main motives that the verbally presented situations were designed to elicit were Achievement, Affiliation, and Power. The eight stories told by each subject were scored for these needs in two ways: by simply tallying whether a relevant theme occurs in the story, and by a more differentiated method (as suggested by McClelland *et al.* for Achievement, Heyns *et al.* for Affiliation, and Veroff for Power; see Atkinson, 1958) that takes into account different elements in the story. (Since it is possible for the scoring scheme for Achievement to yield negative scores, a constant of 8 was added to the Achievement total scores for IBM punching and analysis.) In general these total scores yield better differentiation between individuals and groups and more significant relationships to other variables. The means for the three samples are presented in Table 4-7.

Of the possible comparisons, Boston is significantly higher than Palermo on n-Achievement and Boston and Palermo are both significantly higher than Rome on both n-Affiliation and n-Power.

By combining some categories that were originally scored separately, scores were obtained on 11 other variables: n-Aggressions, n-Autonomy, n-Succorance, p-Nurturance, p-Dominance, Positive Self-Concepts, Negative Self-Concepts, p-Fear-Worry, n-Sex Affiliation, n-Sex Activity, n-Civic-mindedness. Scores on these variables are simply the number of stories in which relevant content appeared. Theoretically, individual subjects' scores can very between 0 and 8, but in actuality the maximum is 6 and there are many 0's. Comparisons by means of χ^2 of the distributions for the three cities yielded the following significant differences:

n-Aggression: Boston > Palermo (Rome in between)
n-Autonomy: Rome > Boston (Palermo in between)
Negative Self-Concepts: Boston > Rome (Palermo in between and almost identical to Boston)
p-Fear-Worry: Rome > Boston, Palermo > Boston
n-Sex Affiliation: Boston > Rome, Boston > Palermo
n-Sex Activity: Boston > Palermo (Rome in between)
n-Civic-mindedness: Boston > Palermo, Rome > Palermo

Considered all together, these differences suggest that the Boston subjects, as compared to the Italian group as a whole, felt more free to express impulses, both sexual and aggressive, and were lower in anxiety. This would seem to be a reflection of the more premissive family atmosphere which this group had experienced, as already noteu in our discussion of the interview material. The Boston group also seemed to hold higher standards for their own behavior—they scored higher in n-Achievement and gave more responses that suggest self-criticism. We cannot know, of course, whether to interpret this last set of differences as evidence of acculturation to the Protestant ethic or as a result of the

TABLE 4-7

	Achievement Total	Affiliation Total	Power Total
Boston	6.37	7.64	4.70
Rome	5.27	5.64	3.56
Palermo	4.51	7.26	4.38

much greater social and economic mobility which the emigration of these families brought with it.

The Rome boys seem, as a group, lower in motivation toward interpersonal interaction (both Affiliation and Power). They also express more needs for Autonomy, a finding which seems to agree with the indications in the interviews that these boys experience tighter parental control than the other groups.

Finally, the Palermo sample is notably low in evidences of achievement standards and an interest in the broader community. They are also less likely than the other groups to express impulses, especially aggressive ones, in fantasy. Paradoxically, they are more likely to be rated aggressive by the interviewer. We noted that they were also somewhat more likely than the boys in the other groups to say that if a school friend hit them they would hit him back. This discrepancy between expression of aggression in fantasy and in overt behavior may perhaps be explained if we assume that the Sicilian family is particularly likely to prohibit expression of aggression within the family but tends to condone aggressive behavior outside of the home. We found some support for this hypothesis in the interviews: the subjects in Palermo were much more likely than those in the other groups to say that they were most afraid to quarrel with other family members in their parents' presence. We wish we had more complete information on parents' handling of aggression.

In addition to the inferences we can draw from the fantasy responses themselves, it is of interest to examine possible differences between the three groups in the relations of fantasy to self-reports and observer judgments obtained in the interview with the subject. Of the Imagination Test Variables, only Achievement, Affiliation, Power, and Aggression scores are sufficiently well distributed to justify such a correlational analysis, and Aggression does not yield any significant relationships. Among the rest of the variables, we have examined only those that yielded more than the chance number of significant correlations. It is interesting to note that many more relationships appear for the Rome subjects than for the other two groups. No obvious explanation offers itself, other than the somewhat larger n in Rome, since the Rome subjects as a group were not notably more expressive in fantasy (the Boston group gave slightly more responses), but their responses may have been a more direct reflection of their feelings. Table 4-8 shows the correlates, both within the projective material and in the interview, of n-Achievement, n-Affiliation, and n-Power.

The correlates of n-Achievement for the Boston sample form a coherent picture and one in line with theoretical expectations. The boys who expressed higher Achievement motivation in fantasy also gave evidences of more positive self-concepts (both in fantasy and in the interview) and higher vocational aspirations and described themselves as relatively less anxious (at least by the criterion of "butterflies in the stomach"). They were also more civic-minded. The interviewer apparently agreed with their estimate of their own intelligence, rating

TABLE 4-8

INTERVIEW CORRELATES OF THREE MAIN VARIABLES
FROM THE IMAGINATION TEST

Variable	Boston		Rome		Palermo	
n-Achievement	Positive Self-Concepts	+.31	n-Affiliation	+.18	n-Aggression	-.28
	Civic-mindedness	+.24	p-Nurturance	+.18		
	Status Professions Pref.	+.23	Anxiety with teacher	+.18		
	Butterflies in stomach	-.23	Butterflies in stomach	+.18		
	Self-rating, Intell.	+.30	Self-rating, Intell.	-.24		
	Ability Reason Log.	+.23	Unjust Treatment	+.20	Unjust Treatment	-.28
			Support from home	+.18	Ability solve practical problems	+.26
			Aggression	-.19		
n-Affiliation	Sex Affiliation	+.47	n-Achievement	+.18	n-Aggression	+.19
	Sex Activity	+.36	Sex Activity	+.19	p-Nurturance	+.24
	Mother more severe	+.21	Parents pleased has friends	-.21	Sex Affiliation	+.49
	Support from home	-.22	Guilt feelings	-.18	Ability Reason Log.	+.27
n-Power	n-Autonomy	+.36	n-Autonomy	+.28	n-Autonomy	+.33
	p-Dominance	+.51	n-Succorance	-.18		
	Sex Activity	+.22	p-Dominance	+.35	p-Dominance	+.38
	Civic-mindedness	-.22	Sex Activity	-.20		
	Timid in Interview	+.23	Status Professions Preferred	-.20	Ability solve emotional problems	-.27
			Status Professions Rejected	-.20	Affection outside family	-.23
			Anxiety with teacher	-.24	Ability Reason Log.	-.30
					Ability work with others	-.22

them as more able to reason logically. We can say, then, that in these Italian–American subjects, high fantasy n-Achievement is associated with self-confident, ambitious, well-organized personality, and with strong evidence of a mature interest in the broader community.

In Palermo, the correlates of n-Achievement are sparse. Apparently it tends to be associated with a somewhat aggressive approach in the interview, but with low fantasy aggression. The high n-Achievement subjects take a positive view of their treatment at home and are seen by the interviewer as capable in solving practical problems. The implication is of direct self-assertion and interpersonal bravado rather than of amibition for the future, as in the Boston group.

The greatest contrast is in Rome. Here high n-Achievement is related to the expression of dependency needs in fantasy, to high anxiety, to negative self-concepts, to a feeling of unjust treatment, and to interviewer judgments of low aggressiveness and lack of support from home. In short, the pattern is the opposite of those found both in Boston and in Palermo, with the additional emphasis on high dependency needs perhaps related to some actual emotional deprivation. These differences are reminiscent of the different theoretical points of view about the sources of achievement motivation. There are those who, like Crandall (1963), consider achievement striving as ultimately a substitutive form of dependency behavior, a more mature and socially acceptable way of seeking adult approval. Other theorists, like White (1959), see achievement motivation as derived from intrinsic needs for exploration, competence, and mastery. The

Boston and perhaps the Palermo subjects would appear to conform to the latter view, whereas the former formulation certainly fits the data from Rome.

Motivation for Affiliation seems to be associated with sexual fantasy in all three groups; probably this is a product of the scoring system, since a score on Sex Affiliation or Sex Activity automatically implies seeking positive association with others. For the Palermo subjects, n-Affiliation is associated with both nurturance and aggression in fantasy—perhaps evidencing a generally extraverted pattern. That this is not an especially immature pattern for these boys is attested by the interviewer's judgment of their ability to reason logically. In Rome, there is some evidence that affiliation fantasies are associated with parental interference with actual peer contacts and with denial of guilt. In Boston, fantasies of affiliation seem to have a compensatory function, in that they are associated with an interviewer judgment of lack of support from home. These boys (those high in n-Affiliation) also tended to see their mothers as more severe than their fathers, a pattern often associated with passivity and feminization in males.

Evidence of need for power in the Imagination Test is associated with need for autonomy and a feeling of being dominated by parents in all three cities. This is, again, probably a function of the way the variables were defined. The variable n-Power, then, is an expression of a wish to gain control rather than being controlled in interpersonal situations. That these are compensatory, wish-fulfilling fantasies in these early adolescent boys is evident in both Palermo and Boston. In Palermo, high n-Power is correlated with generally unfavorable interviewer ratings, especially as regards capacity for more mature interpersonal relations. (We shall see that n-Power and p-Dominance tended to be higher in lower class boys in Palermo, and this may account in part for the unfavorable ratings.) In Boston it is associated with lack of civic-mindedness and with timidity in the interview. In Rome, the picture is less clear. Need for power is associated with low expression of need for succorance, denial of anxiety, and lower status of professions both preferred and rejected. Perhaps fantasies of power are related to a denial of dependency, vulnerability, and needs for future status.

As has been noted, few of the other Imagination Test variables yielded more than the chance number of significant correlates in Boston and Palermo, and all correlations are of small magnitude. In Boston, the two variables that did appear significant were Positive and Negative Self-Concept (see Table 4-9). They were related, respectively, to status of preferred professions and expressiveness in the interview (positive self-concepts) and to denial of desire for friends and admission of anxiety (negative self-concepts). These findings, while certainly not startling, seem sensible. It is of some interest that a statement of desiring few or no friends seems to be a sign in Boston of low self-evaluation, whereas in Rome it seems to have just the opposite implication, being associated with positive self-concepts.

TABLE 4-9

OTHER IMAGINATION TEST VARIABLES WITH > CHANCE NUMBER
OF CORRELATES IN THE INTERVIEW

Boston

12. Pos. Self-Concepts	Status of preferred professions	+.27
	Expressiveness in the interview	+.28
13. Neg. Self-Concepts	Wants few or no friends	+.29
	Butterflies in stomach	+.24

Rome

9. n-Succorance	Status of professions rejected	+.23
	Anxiety with teacher	+.22
10. p-Nurturance	Mother more severe than father	+.20
	Embarrassed vs. impolite in intervies	+.22
	Aggression interviewer rating	-.19
11. p-Dominance	Talkative in interview	-.28
	Ability to solve emotional problems	-.18
	Support from home	-.20
	Capacity to reason logically	-.21
12. Pos. Self-Concepts	Wants few or no friends	+.22
	Capacity to reason logically	+.24
14. Fear-Worry	Capacity to solve emotional problems	+.20
	Low support from home	-.21
15. Sex-Affiliation	Anxiety with teacher	+.22
	Talkative in interview	+.22
	Active in interview	+.26
	Aggression interview rating	+.20
16. Sex-Activity	Active in interview	+.20
	Affection with family	-.18
	Capacity to reason logically	-.28

Palermo

11. p-Dominance	Free to choose friends	-.22
	No. of classmates like to eliminate	+.19
	Unjust treatment	+.19
	Affection outside family	-.22
14. Fear-Worry	Capacity to solve practical problems	-.22
	Capacity to solve emotional problems	-.19
	Ability to reason logically	-.26

112

In Palermo, indices of anxiety expressed in fantasy are, as one might expect, associated with unfavorable ratings of adjustment by the interviewer—low capacity to solve emotional problems, to solve practical problems, and to reason logically. The correlates of p-Dominance are somewhat confusing. It is related to a feeling of unjust treatment, but also to the report that the boy's parents have left him free to choose his own friends. Apparently the boys high in p-Dominance would choose to exercise this right by eliminating several of their classmates, and the interviewer judged them as expressing less affection outside the family. It may be that their feeling of being pressured and restricted originated outside the family, or that in the interview situation they tended to displace these feelings away from parents to figures outside the home.

The correlates of p-Dominance in Rome are more coherent. It is associated with a lack of expressiveness in the interview, unfavorable judgments by the interviewer of capacity to solve emotional problems and to reason logically, and a low rating of support from the home. One infers that in this population at least, p-Dominance is a sign of maladjustment. The expression of anxiety in fantasy, however, apparently is not. It is also associated with an interviewer judgment of low support from the home, but with a favorable rating on capacity to solve emotional problems—just the opposite of the judgment for Palermo. The expression of sexual fantasy, which is much less frequent among the Rome than the Boston sample, seems to be associated with an unusually active and assertive interpersonal approach and a general lack of inhibitions. The boys who gave thematic responses portraying sexual activity may also have been seen by the interviewer as somewhat lacking in judgment and as low in affection to the family. Perhaps they were beginning to turn away from object relations within the family. Finally, the expression of dependency needs in fantasy (n-Succorance, p-Nurturance) seems related for these Rome boys to a generally passive interpersonal orientation and to a report, as we might expect, that the mother is more severe than the father.

It is difficult to summarize these findings and, since most of the correlations are small, we might simply attribute them to the workings of chance. They do seem to provide an illustration, however, of the different cultural contexts. Not only may some themes appear much more frequently in the fantasies of one group than in another, but when they do appear they may predict quite different patterns of conscious self-report or of overt interpersonal behavior.

Anxiety

A short form of the Children's Manifest Anxiety Scale (CMAS) (Castaneda, McCandless, & Palermo, 1956) developed by Levy (1958) was administered in 1960. The CMAS is itself based on the Taylor Manifest Anxiety Scale, a self-report instrument developed for use with adults. The ten items of the Levy version, which according to his data from a sample of Rhode Island fourth, fifth, and sixth graders, yield a score that correlates highly with total CMAS score and is free from age and sex differences, are as follows:

1. I get nervous when someone watches me work.
2. Others seem to do things easier than I can.
3. I feel alone even when there are people around me.
4. I get nervous when things do not go the right way for me.
5. I worry about what my parents will say to me.
6. I have trouble swallowing.
7. I worry about what is going to happen.
8. I worry when I go to bed at night.
9. I often do things I wish I had never done.
10. I often worry about what could happen to my parents.

The results of the overall comparisons between the three groups on this measure are given Table 4-10. These differences indicate that the Boston subjects report feeling less anxious than the two Italian groups. We cannot tell, of course, whether they actually experience less anxiety, or whether they are simply reflecting the influence of the taboo in American culture against expressions of emotionality by adolescent males. It should be noted that these items as a group refer either to generalized feelings of anxiety or to anxiety in interpersonal contexts, especially in relation to parents. The meaning of this result will perhaps be clearer when we can compare it to the results from another anxiety measure, with more concrete and specific content, administered to the subjects 2–3 years later, and to other measures of motivation and adjustment.

TABLE 4-10

	Mean	Standard Deviation
Boston	3.9	1.73
Rome	5.1	1.68
Palermo	5.2	1.55

The High School Personality Questionnaire

At the time that the first major round of personality measures was administered to our subjects, two possible choices of personality inventory presented themselves: the California Personality Inventory (CPI) of Gough (see Chapter 6) and the High School Personality Questionnaire (HSPQ) of R. B. Cattell (1958). The latter was chosen, primarily because of its considerably shorter length and convenience of administration, and because the Italian version of the CPI was then only in the process of development. In retrospect, this choice seems somewhat unfortunate since, at a later stage of the project (1968–1969) when the subjects were young adults, the CPI seemed clearly the preferable instrument for a variety of reasons, especially its use in previous longitudinal studies at the Institute of Human Development at Berkeley. Thus we do not have direct longitudinal comparisons on either instrument, although the associations of each with other measures collected at earlier and later stages of the research are of some interest from a longitudinal point of view. Both inventories have been used in numerous other cross-cultural studies and are thus of interest from a comparative perspective.

An Italian translation of the HSPQ was carried out for the purposes of this project and standardized on a sample of 778 boys attending Italian secondary schools. Only the results of the standardization study for Form A are available, and it is this form of the HSPQ that was used throughout. The Italian version was developed in collaboration with the Psychological Division of the National Research Council in Rome and was published in 1958 by the Organizzazioni Speciali in Florence. In order to satisfy themselves further that the instrument was truly equivalent in the original English and in the Italian versions, the research staff applied it to several bilingual and bicultural children, comparing their responses item by item as well as factor for factor. Inconsistencies between the two language versions and between Forms A and B of the test were discussed at length with the subjects and among the staff. Resultant revisions were incorporated in the final version of Form A which appears in the Italian manual and which was used in the longitudinal study.

The HSPQ was administered in Rome and Palermo in 1958–1959 and in Boston in 1959–1960.

It yielded scores ranging from 0 to 10 on 14 independent factors, labeled by the author as follows:

A Schizothymia versus Cyclothymia
B Mental Defect versus General Intelligence
C Dissatisfied Emotional Instability versus Ego Strength
D Phlegmatic Temperament versus Excitability
E Submissiveness versus Dominance
F Desurgency versus Surgency
G Lack of Rigid Internal Standards versus Superego Strength
H Threctia versus Parmia
I Harria versus Premsia
J Dynamic Simplicity versus Neurasthenic Self-Critical Tendency
O Confident Adequacy versus Guilt-Proneness
Q_2 Group Dependency versus Self-Sufficiency
Q_3 Poor Self-Sentiment Formation versus High Strength of Self-Sentiment
Q_4 Low Ergic Tension versus High Ergic Tension

Various of the individual factors can also be combined to yield two composite scores, said to be indicative of Anxiety or General Neuroticism and of Extraversion–Introversion, respectively.

Table 4-11 lists the mean raw scores for our three groups on each of the 14 factors. The mean sten scores based on the American and the Italian norms, respectively, are also listed in Table 4-11. However, raw scores have been used to compare the three groups in our study, since we are interested in part in the exploration of cultural differences, and the use of sten scores based on the different norms for each culture would automatically cancel out those differences between Boston and the two Italian cities. The t's for the comparisons of the raw score means of each city with each of the others on each of the factors are given in Table 4-11. Subsequent intercorrelational analyses of associations between the HSPQ and other measures are based on sten scores since their use automatically produces approximately normal distributions.

Based on the mean raw score comparisons, the Boston subjects as contrasted to both of the Italian groups would be characterized as warmer, more sociable, more good-natured, easygoing, and adaptable, having a greater liking for group action, more self-confident, cheerful, and resilient, but also more lax and uncontrolled (lower in self-sentiment). The subjects in Rome, compared as a group to those in Boston, would appear to be more cool, aloof, critical, suspicious, and rigid, also more individualistic, fastidious, and self-sufficient, more anxious, insecure, depressed, and sensitive but also more controlled and exacting, possessing greater willpower. As compared to the Palermo group, however, the Rome subjects would seem to be more sociable, easy-going, warm and adaptable, more intelligent, more self-assertive, demanding and attention-getting, more enthusiastic, cheerful and expressive, tougher, more realistic and self-reliant, and having a greater liking for group action. The Palermo subjects, on the other hand, as compared to both of the other groups, seem more aloof, critical and suspicious, less intelligent, more stodgy and self-effacing, more individualistic, self-sufficient, and fastidious. As compared to the boys in Rome, they are seen as also more glum, sober, introspective and brooding, more esthetically sensitive, gentle, imaginative, and intuitive. Finally, as compared specifically to the Boston group, the Palermo subjects are seen as more emotionally immature, excitable, changeable and worrying, more anxious, depressed, sensitive and fussy, and more controlled and exacting.

While expressed in somewhat value-laden and perhaps inappropriately psychopathological terms, these thumbnail descriptions derived from the HSPQ have considerable correspondence with the other findings reported in earlier sections of this chapter and with one's stereotypes of modal personality differences between American and Italian adolescents and between Romans and Sicilians. When we examine the sten scores, it becomes evident that when Italian norms are applied to the two Italian groups, most of the differences become

TABLE 4-11

H.S.P.Q. BOSTON, ROME, PALERMO — RAW SCORES

Variable		Boston		Rome		Palermo		t	p
A	N:	91		121		118	B-R	2.08	.05
	Mean:	5.58	4.9	5.25	4.85	4.58	R-P	3.56	.01
	SD:	1.75		1.74		1.79	B-P	5.385	.01
	Sten:	6.75		6.16		5.46			
B	N:	91		122		118	B-R	1.019	NS
	Mean:	6.89	6.7	7.08	7.37	6.27	R-P	5.728	.01
	SD:	2.05		1.55		1.59	B-P	3.2821	.01
	Sten:	5.96		5.13		4.19			
C	N:	91		122		118	B-R	1.8836	NS
	Mean:	5.77	5.4	5.43	5.22	5.18	R-P	1.6490	NS
	SD:	1.73		1.72		1.63	B-P	3.3637	.01
	Sten:	5.77		5.65		5.37			
D	N:	91		122		117	B-R	0.2922	NS
	Mean:	4.83	5.0	4.78	5.12	4.46	R-P	2.1724	.05
	SD:	1.61		1.65		1.61	B-P	2.1958	.05
	Sten:	5.02		4.89		4.52			
E	N:	91		122		118	B-R	.7790	NS
	Mean:	4.85	5.0	4.71	4.87	4.44	R-P	1.7728	NS
	SD:	1.76		1.68		1.69	B-P	2.2757	.05
	Sten:	5.85		5.68		5.33			
F	N:	91		122		118	B-R	.2977	NS
	Mean:	5.51	5.4	5.56	5.25	5.24	R-P	2.0163	.05
	SD:	1.55		1.64		1.87	B-P	1.4343	NS
	Sten:	5.52		5.67		5.38			
G	N:	91		122		118	B-R	.8153	NS
	Mean:	5.78	6.0	5.92	5.95	6.05	R-P	.9193	NS
	SD:	1.79		1.52		1.61	B-P	1.5237	NS
	Sten:	4.94		5.26		5.48			
H	N:	91		122		118	B-R	1.3296	NS
	Mean:	5.66	4.7	6.28	5.25	5.91	R-P	.9647	NS
	SD:	1.83		5.66		1.84	B-P	1.300	NS
	Sten:	6.35		5.94		6.13			
I	N:	88		120		116	B-R	1.5057	NS
	Mean	4.06	4.2	3.77	3.60	4.41	R-P	3.9776	.01
	SD:	1.91		1.73		1.80	B-P	1.775	NS
	Sten:	4.90		5.67		6.32			
J	N:	91		122		118	B-R	3.0075	.01
	Mean:	4.54	5.1	5.02	5.00	5.34	R-P	2.6868	.01
	SD:	1.81		1.27		1.37	B-P	4.8426	.01
	Sten:	5.87		5.66		6.08			
O	N:	91		122		118	B-R	6.2736	.01
	Mean:	4.54	5.0	5.70	6.09	5.35	R-P	.1555	NS
	SD:	1.81		1.73		1.71	B-P	5.0248	.01
	Sten:	4.74		5.09		4.64			
Q_2	N:	91		122		118	B-R	.1646	NS
	Mean:	6.07	5.5	6.17	6.22	5.98	R-P	1.2960	NS
	SD:	1.55		1.59		1.65	B-P	.5350	NS
	Sten:	6.05		5.35		5.17			
Q_3	N:	91		122		118	B-R	2.9496	.01
	Mean:	4.48	4.9	4.99	4.71	4.93	R-P	.4243	NS
	SD:	1.78		1.55		1.58	B-P	2.5728	.02
	Sten:	4.92		5.94		5.87			
Q_4	N:	87		121		118	B-R	1.6772	NS
	Mean:	4.51	4.5	4.80	4.82	4.796	R-P	.0265	NS
	SD:	1.62		1.61		1.71	B-P	1.6192	NS
	Sten:	5.32		5.68		5.70			

relatively slight and that the profiles are overall rather similar and generally within the range of sten scores of 5 and 6 which Cattell characterizes as ''normal.'' Exceptions are the relatively high average sten in Boston on Factor A (warm, sociable, adaptable) and Factor H (adventurous, active, friendly, overt interest in the opposite sex). Palermo, on the other hand, is slightly elevated on Factor I (esthetically sensitive, gentle, dependent) and has markedly lower scores on Factor B (indicative of lower intelligence) and to some extent on Factor D (phlegmatic temperament).

The composite scores were not derived for individual subjects, but may be calculated for the groups as a whole on the basis of the mean sten scores on the individual factors. This yields overall indices of anxiety of 52.20 for Boston, 51.85 for Rome, and 50.48 for Palermo, very little different from each other and all a bit below the "average" score of 55. The indices of Extraversion–Introversion similarly derived run 42.49 for Boston, 41.19 for Rome, and 39.77 for Palermo, placing all three groups slightly in the extraverted direction (a score of 38.5 is presumed to be average), Boston being the highest, as we might expect from the separate factors scores.

Moral Judgments[1]

Differences in judgments concerning the moral appropriateness of various instances of behavior among members of different subcultures and at different points of time can be related to a number of different causal sources. Moral judgments may differ as a function of the particular nature of the behavior and the context in which it occurs. Second, judgments may differ as a function of the prevailing moral ethos characteristic of the particular culture. Third, judgments may change from one point in time to another as a function of either sociohistorical changes in the culture or changes in the individual resulting from psychological development. Further, of course, differences in moral judgment may be a function of various combinations of the preceding factors and other factors not listed. Much of our understanding of moral development comes from work by Piaget (1932) and Freud (1930/1955). Piaget has presented evidence that evolution of moral values is a stage process involving cognitive development. Freud and his followers, on the other hand, have been concerned to associate moral values with early personality development and, in particular, with the concepts of superego identification and guilt. Summaries of research in this field have been published by Hoffman (1963; 1970, pp. 261–360) and Kohlberg (1963, 1964). In general, Piaget's approach suggests that moral judgments show a developmental progression from "judging on the basis of immediate external physical consequences to judging in terms of subjective or internal purposes, norms, or values [Kohlberg, 1964, p. 399]." Kohlberg has noted, however, that some aspects of moral development suggested by Piaget, do not appear to be general, universal dimensions, but rather are subject to age reversals and the influence of culture, class, intelligence, and situational factors (see Kohlberg, 1964). In particular,

---

[1]We are much indebted to Irving Torgoff for his review of issues in moral development as they apply to Italian and Italian–American immigrant youth, and for his analyses of the data on moral judgments and on social attitudes reported here and in Chapter 7.

Kohlberg points to such dimensions, among others, as "modification of obedience to rules or authority because of situational demands or human needs; maintaining peer loyalty demands as opposed to obedience to authority [p. 399]." While there are a number of institutional sources of moral authority (law, government, family, peer group), Kohlberg believes that they present the same basic moral rules, regardless of the individual's particular position in society. The child's interpretation of these institutions and rules, however, are determined to a large extent by his position in society. "Law and government are perceived quite differently by the child if he feels a sense of potential participation in the social order than if he does not [p. 407]." With increasing age, one might expect changes in the child's perception of the potential for such participation. Further, cultural differences in such perception would also affect interpretation of moral rules and consequent moral judgments.

It is interesting in this regard to note Tarrow's comment (1967) that

> the values that lead to cynicism and corruption are really functional in terms of the basic relationships that dominate southern Italian society. The state of mind engendered is less akin to the *anomie* (normlessness) described by Durkheim than the *ressentiment* described by Scheler. One rejects the authenticity of the institutions that dominate the society, but one continues to operate within their framework. Such is the real meaning of Banfield's *The Moral Basis of a Backward Society,* (1958), a documentation of the distrust, disaffection, and cynicism rife in southern Italian society [p. 59].

Tarrow further makes the observation that, while southern Italians are highly politically conscious, the nature of the social structure is such that individual participation in political life takes the form of *clientilismo,* in which the "individual is linked to the authority structure through personal ties of obligation and loyalty, rather than through the merger of his interests with others of the same social group, or ideological persuasion." ". . . the clientele system links a distinct chain of individual and personal interests through the benefits of patronage [p. 74]." "One 'reaches' the structure of authority, not by merging one's demands with the parallel demands of others, but by linking one's self to a hierarchical chain of personal acquaintance that reaches power holders at the higher level [p. 75]."

Previous cross-cultural investigations of the moral orientation of Italian and American youth involved comparisons of data collected in Italy (Grasso, 1961) with the results obtained at an earlier point in time by another investigator (Rettig & Pasamanick, 1959) from American students, or, as in the participant observation study conducted by Gans (1962) during 1957–1958, with concepts derived from a participant-observation study conducted earlier in southern Italy (Banfield, 1958).

Rettig and Pasamanick (1959) factor analyzed a large number of moral judgments by American students to reveal six different subtypes of morality: basic, religious, family, puritanical, predelinquent, and economical. Taking their work as a point of departure, Grasso (1961) obtained moral judgments on the same fifty items from Italian students, both boys and girls, from public and from church schools. He found that the American students revealed a general tendency to greater severity of moral judgment than did the Italians. Within the Italian groups, the girls were more severe in judgment than the boys, and subjects from church schools were harsher in judgment than students in public schools.

For purposes of this research, the inquiry was simplified by narrowing the topic of antisocial behavior to the crime of stealing. Furthermore, instead of trying to establish gradations in the culpable behavior described to the subjects, the anecdotes or stories of the test were varied by including extenuating circumstances that provided differing probabilities that the delinquent act might be judged justified or inadmissible.

The scale used to measure moral judgments, the EV 3, was developed by Schircks while at the Harvard–Florence Project. It consists of 11 items, in each of which the protagonist steals an identical sum of money (1000 lire in Italian currency, then worth $1.60 at normal exchange rate, and $3 in American money, a comparable amount—having the same appeal value to the subjects in both cultures when the differing ways of life are considered). The conditions in which the protagonist steals (degree of distress), from whom he steals (family, acquaintance, institution), and for whom he steals (family, self, friends, strangers) vary, however, from story to story. The subjects were asked to respond to each item by indicating whether the action seems "justified" (a score of 1), "almost justified" (score of 2), "almost inadmissable" (score of 3), or "inadmissable" (score of 4). The items were as follows:

1. After the death of his father, Albert, in order to help his sick mother, started working as a shoeshine boy. One day when he had no customers, in order to come home with the little money on which his mother counted, he stole three dollars.
2. Mark took three dollars from his sister's purse, which she had left lying open.
3. Henry, hungry for 3 days and out of work, decides to steal three dollars.
4. William, on his way home from school, is accosted by someone he doesn't know who says he is desperate, and indeed seems so, and asks William for help. William says he is sorry he has nothing now, but will try to help him tomorrow. The next day he steals three dollars and gives it to the man.
5. John sees three dollars fall out of Ernest's pocket. Remembering that Ernest had never returned the borrowed ball he had lost, John picked up the bills and stuffed them into his pocket.
6. Ronald, who had not eaten for two days, stole three dollars in order to have a good meal.

7. Joseph stole three dollars to help his friend Ben who, playing football in the street, broke a window and didn't want his sick father to find out.

8. Bernard reached the railway station at the last minute. In order not to miss the train to Providence he didn't stop to buy a ticket. The train was just arriving in Providence when the conductor started walking down the aisle. Instead of telling him the situation, Bernard slipped into the lavatory (men's room) and locked the door.

9. Paul stole three dollars because he hadn't had lunch and was hungry and wanted to eat something good before the evening.

10. It was Joan's birthday. Frank didn't have the money to buy her a present, but being very fond of her, he stole three dollars to buy something for her.

11. John stole three dollars to buy some candy to which he was much addicted.

Prior to its use in the longitudinal study, the EV 3 was administered to a total of 1067 subjects, both male and female, in Florence and Boston. They were secondary school students, ranging from age 11 to 17. It was evident that severity of moral judgment differed by sex and as between adolescents in the two cultures, as would be predicted on the basis of previous research. The American subjects rendered more severe moral judgments than did the Florentines. In Boston, the order of severity was girls, boys in parochial schools, and boys in public schools. In Florence girls were more severe than boys.

The EV 3 was administered to the subjects in the longitudinal study in 1960 and again in 1965. It is thus possible to examine both the cultural differences between the three groups and changes over time within each locale, although in interpreting the latter it will be important to remember that developmental changes in the subjects are necessarily confounded with historical changes in the social conditions in Italy and America during this 5-year period. The analysis of the longitudinal data is reserved for Chapter 7 on outcomes in early maturity. Here we shall consider only the results of the first administration, when the boys were on the average about 15.

The total scale showed good internal consistency, as estimated from the average intercorrelations of all 11 items with each other: Boston, $r = .76$; Rome, .64; Palermo, .57. Scores on the individual items were added to derive two summary scores, one based on items 1, 4, 7, and 10, and a total score based on all 11 items. The separate score for the four items mentioned appeared justified since, in each of these items, extenuating circumstances for the theft are described which involve the needs and feelings of others; thus less severe judgments on these items as a group might be considered to reflect what Hoffmann has termed "humanistic" as opposed to "conventional" moral values.

The differences between our three groups of subjects in average severity of judgment, for the subscore and the total score, are presented in Table 4-12. For both the subscore and the total score, the mean differences between Boston and the two Italian cities are significant at $p < .001$. Thus the subjects in the longitudinal study conform to the general finding that American adolescents render more severe moral judgments than do Italians. There are no differences between the central and southern Italian groups, as represented by Rome and Palermo.

We also examined the correlations of the EV 3 with the other personality measures. In Boston, it is associated with HSPQ Factor A+ (warm, sociable, $r = .22$) and with p-Fear-Worry ($r = .31$) and low n-Affiliation ($r = -.24$) and n-Power ($r = -.23$) in the Imagination Test. In Rome, it is related only to the interview variables of status of profession preferred ($r = .24$) and interviewer judgments of support to home ($r = .21$) and capacity to work with others ($r = .20$). In Palermo, it relates to *high* n-Affiliation in the Imagination Test ($r = .21$) and to the interviewer's judgment of openness and affection outside the family ($r = .23$).

Thus severity of moral judgment shows some indication of being related to warmth and outgoingness in social relations, but correlates in opposite directions with the fantasy measure of motivation for affiliation in Boston and Palermo. This may not be as inconsistent as it appears, since we saw earlier that n-Affiliation seems to be inversely related to overt measures of social integration in Boston and more directly related to socially outgoing behavior in Palermo.

INTERRELATIONS OF SOCIALIZATION, PERSONALITY, AND COGNITIVE DEVELOPMENT

Family Characteristics, Socialization, and Personality

In this section we shall examine the associations between family characteristics and socialization attitudes, as assessed by the social inquiry and previously discussed in Chapter 2, and the various measures of personality discussed in the preceding section. We have already seen that these variables, although measured as much as possible by means of equivalent instruments, seem in many instances to have differing implications in the three cultural settings. This impression will be reinforced as we inspect the differeing sets of intercorrelations. The basic data are presented inTables 4-13a–c. Only those correlations that reach at least the .05 level of significance are shown.

Socioeconomic Status

In Boston   Predicts only HSPQ Factor B, intelligence.

In Rome   Correlates positively with n-Autonomy in the Imagination Test, also positively with status of professions both preferred and rejected, but nega-

TABLE 4-12

EV 3 — FIRST ADMINISTRATION

		Boston		Rome		Palermo
Sum Items 1, 4, 7, 10	N	87	N	119	N	109
	Mean	13.36	Mean	11.18	Mean	11.30
	SD	2.24	SD	2.78	SD	2.50
Total Score	N	87	N	119	N	109
	Mean	36.26	Mean	33.53	Mean	33.53
	SD	5.46	SD	5.10	SD	4.40

tively with interviewer's rating of independence. As in Boston, predicts Factor B in the HSPQ and also H+, adventurous.

In Palermo Again predicts status of professions chosen and rejected, the self-rating of intelligence in the interview, and the interviewer's judgments of the boy's independence (positively, this time), of his ability to solve both practical and emotional problems, and of openness and affectionateness in the family. Again, is positively related to Factor B in the HSPQ.

The HSPQ factor designed to measure intelligence correlates with SES in all three cities, another indication that is both cross-culturally valid and tends to reflect the social components of measured "intelligence." The additional correlations in the two Italian cities suggest that the socioeconomic position of the family into which one is born tends to have a greater influence, perhaps set tighter limits, on one's aspirations and self-perceptions in Italian culture. (One must add that the findings, particularly in Palermo, might also be interpreted as a function of interviewer bias, since the interviewers were certainly aware of the subject's general socioeconomic position.) There is some indication that in Rome, where parents tended on the whole to be the most controlling, the boys of higher SES were more likely to wish for more independence.

Relations with Parents

In Boston The overall rating derived from the social inquiry of the amount of affection the boy received from his family predicts higher scores on p-Fear-Worry and Sex Affiliation from the Imagination Test, status of the boy's choice of profession, and the interviewer ratings of talkativeness and openness and affection towards the family. This picture seems reasonable except for the higher scores on Fear-Worry; however, we shall see this particular fantasy measure tending in Boston to be consistently associated with more positive social characteristics, as if boys who are more comfortable and more self-confident can

TABLE 4-13a

CORRELATES OF FAMILY VARIABLES WITH PERSONALITY MEASURES -- BOSTON

Personality Measures	Family Variables												
	SES B5	Rela-tion w Father B51	Rela-tion w Mother B52	Resp. in Home C17	Ag-gres-sion C38	Affec-tion C46	Free-dom of Exp. E7	Co-he-sion E11	Sex Rest. E15	Con-trol E19	Peer rela-tions E23	Indul-gence E31	Acad. Pres-sure E35
Imagination Test													
X12 Achievement					-.27								
X18 Power										-.24			
X20 Aggression		.24	.27										
X21 Autonomy							.40						
X24 Dominance													.27
X27 Fear-Worry				.22		.22							-.36
X28 Sex Affiliation		-.20			-.22	.26							
Interview													
D20 Prof.-1st Choice						.21	.23				.24	.23	
D38 #Would Eliminate			.21										
D54 Heart Beats Faster													-.27
D61 Intelligent (More Than Others)												.30	-.30
D63 Unjust Treatment						.26							
D64 Loved										.21			
D65 Talkative						.31							
D66 Restless												-.22	-.25
D67 Aggression								.25		.23	.29	.27	
D69 Independence								.21					
D70 Practical Problems				.21									
D72 Affection in Family						.23							
D74 Support from Home		.20					-.27						
D75 Support to Home								-.22					
D77 Aggression										.22	-.23		
D78 Reason Log.			.27										
EV3													
E47 Total					-.23								

124

TABLE 4-13a (continued)

Personality Measures		Family Variables												
	SES B5	Rela-tion w Father B51	Rela-tion w Mother B52	Resp. in Home C17	Ag-gres-sion C38	Affec-tion C46	Free-dom of Exp. E7	Co-he-sion E11	Sex Rest. E15	Con-trol E19	Peer Rela-tions E23	Indul-gence E31	Acad. Pres-sure E35
HSPQ													
45 A											.55	.30	
47 B	-.33										.41	.28	-.24
49 C							.25				.38	.30	
51 D											.20	.23	.27
53 E					-.22						.25	.21	
55 F							.22				.45	.23	
57 G							.28				.26		
59 H											.42	.35	
61 I							.40					.39	
63 J							.21				.36	.26	
65 O					-.24		.23				.24		
67 Q2				.24			.34				.32	.30	
69 Q3													.21
71 Q4							.27				.27	.25	
CMAS													
73 Taylor Anxiety												.25	

feel freer to reveal anxieties in their fantasy productions. Poor relations with both parents are related to aggressive, hostile fantasies in the Imagination Test. A relatively poor relation with father predicts lower sexual fantasy, but paradoxically is related to a higher interviewer rating of support from the home. A relatively poor relation with mother correlates with the number of friends the boy would choose to eliminate but also with the rating of capacity to reason logically.

In Rome   The overall rating of affection from family predicts only the interviewer's rating of ability to solve practical problems. A relatively poor relation with father relates, reasonably enough, to the boy's judgment that the father is the more severe parent and to HSPQ Factor O (guilt proneness, insecurity). A relatively poor relation with mother relates to *high* sexual fantasy, and to interviewer ratings of restlessness and of low support to the home. Here we see that sexual fantasies seem to have a very different meaning in Rome and in Boston, which we might predict from the different attitudes of the two groups of parents toward sexual expression. While in Boston they are an expression of social integration and of positive identification with the father; in Rome they seem to

TABLE 4-13b

CORRELATIONS OF FAMILY VARIABLES WITH PERSONALITY MEASURES - ROME

Personality Measures	Family Variables												
	SES B5	Rela-tion w Father B51	Rela-tion w Mother B52	Resp. in Home C17	Ag-gres-sion C38	Affec-tion C46	Free-dom of Exp. E7	Co-he-sion E11	Sex Rest. E15	Con-trol E19	Peer Rela-tions E23	Indul-gence E31	Acad. Pres-sure E35
Imagination													
X12 Achievement							-.23						
X18 Power									-.21				
X20 Aggression									-.26				
X21 Autonomy	-.19								.26				
X23 Nurturance									-.21				
X28 Sex Affiliation			.30		.20							-.53	
Interview													
D20 Prof. 1st Choice	-.24									-.19			
D23 Prof. Rejected	-.19												
D36 Parents Pleased										.19			
D37 Free to Choose									.22				
D45 Parent More Severe			-.29				-.21			-.21			
D56 Guilt									-.18				
D61 Intelligent (More Than Others)												-.20	-.22
D62 Strength (More Than Others)									.34				
D63 Unjust Treatment							-.26	-.18					
D64 Loved									-.19			-.18	
D66 Restless			.18									.20	
D67 Aggression									.24	-.19			
D69 Independence	.18				-.28								-.19
D70 Practical Problems						.24							
D71 Emotional Problems					-.21								
D75 Support to Home			-.19										
D77 Aggression									.18				

arise out of compensatory needs in the context of a sense of rejection by the mother—the Freudian interpretation would be Oedipal fixation.

In Palermo Overall affection from the family relates to low n-Autonomy in the Imagination Test, and conversely poor relations with both parents predict higher n-Autonomy; in this group of subjects, themes of autonomy in fantasy

TABLE 4-13b (continued)

Personality Measures	Family Variables												
	SES B5	Relation w Father B51	Relation w Mother B52	Resp. in Home C17	Aggression C38	Affection C46	Freedom of Exp. E7	Cohesion E11	Sex Rest. E15	Control E19	Peer Relations E23	Indulgence E31	Acad. Pressure E35
HPSQ													
47 B	-.22				-.22					-.20			
49 C							-.19						-.19
51 D													.21
55 F										-.20		-.26	
59 H	-.19												
61 I					-.20								
63 J								-.18					.23
65 O			-.23		-.26								.20
67 Q2							-.19						

would appear to represent escape from unhappy relations with parents. A relatively poor relation with the father is associated with the boy's report that his parents are not pleased at the number of his friends and with a lower interviewer rating of the capacity to solve emotional problems, also to HSPQ Factor Q2 (group dependency). There are no correlates here of relation with mother, perhaps a reflection of the more central position of the father in the Sicilian family.

A published analysis by Mussen, Young, Gaddini, and Morante (1963) of interview and Imagination Test variables associated with differences in reported paternal affection yielded findings generally consonant with those reported here. The rating (from the social inquiry) of paternal affection was not distributed in a manner which would justify correlational analysis, but the authors divided the boys in each location into those who had received sufficient or insufficient paternal affection and compared these two groups with respect to a number of self-report, fantasy, and interviewer rating variables. With some minor group differences (one being the same association of sexual fantasy with a positive paternal relation we have just noted as characteristic of the Boston subjects but not of the Italian boys), which the authors attributed mainly to the more authoritarian structure of the southern Italian family, the findings in all three groups indicate that boys who had experienced "insufficient" paternal affection were less oriented to social relations, more poorly adjusted socially, less secure and self-confident, more unhappy, and less calm and relaxed. They tended to feel distant from their fathers, whom they regarded as dominating, and in addition

TABLE 4-13c

CORRELATIONS OF FAMILY VARIABLES WITH PERSONALITY MEASURES - PALERMO

Personality Measures	SES B5	Rela-tion w Father B51	Rela-tion w Mother B52	Resp. in Home C17	Ag-gres-sion C38	Affec-tion C46	Free-dom of Exp. E7	Co-he-sion E11	Sex Rest. E15	Con-trol E19	Peer Rela-tions E23	Indul-gence E31	Acad. Pres-sure E35
Imagination Test													
X20 Aggression									-.32				
X21 Autonomy		.24	.19			-.23							
X23 Nurturance							-.25						
X24 Dominance					-.25								
X27 Fear-Worry								.33					
Interview													
D20 Prof. 1st Choice	-.25					.19							
D23 Prof. Rejected	-.19												
D36 Parents Pleased			.23										
D38 #Would Eliminate									-.25	-.22			
D54 Heart Beats Faster											-.19		
D61 Intelligent (More Than Others)	-.21												
D65 Talkative													.21
D66 Restless											.21		
D69 Independence	-.19												.22
D70 Practical Problems	-.22		-.20									-.22	
D71 Emotional Problems	-.26									-.24			
D72 Affection in Family	-.19												
D74 Support from Home					-.20								
D76 Community Resp.													.22
D78 Reason Log.									-.23				
D79 Work with Others													.20
EV 3													
45 1, 4, 7, 10												-.23	
47 Total													-.28

TABLE 4-13c (continued)

Personality Measures	Family Variables												
	SES B5	Rela-tion w Father B51	Rela-tion w Mother B52	Resp. in Home C11	Ag-gres-sion C38	Affec-tion C46	Free-dom of Exp. E7	Co-he-sion E11	Sex Rest. E15	Con-trol E19	Peer rela-tions E23	Indul-gence E31	Acad. Pres-sure E35
HSPQ													
45 A											-.19		
47 B	-.21							-.20					
51 D					-.26								
53 E										-.30			
63 J												-.24	
65 O					-.21	-.29							
67 Q2			-.17							-.19			-.22
69 Q3												-.20	

were relatively less likely to show affection toward their families or others outside their home. Their achievement needs were weak but their power needs (interpreted as a need to manipulate others) were strong. The findings were interpreted as generally supportive of the cross-cultural validity of developmental and role-taking theories of identification.

Responsibility in the Home

In Boston   The extent to which the parents reported that the boy was expected to carry out responsibilities at home was negatively correlated with p-Fear-Worry in the Imagination Test, with the interviewer's judgment of his ability to solve practical problems and also related to lower scores on HSPQ Q2 (self-sufficiency).

In Rome   Positively related to the interviewer's rating of independence and ability to solve emotional problems.

In Palermo   Positively related to p-Dominance in the Imagination Test and to interviewer's rating of support from the home; also related to HSPQ Factor O+ (guilt-proneness and insecurity).

Clearly this variable has different implications in the different cultural settings, which we do not have enough information to clarify; we can only speculate that in both Boston and Palermo being given much domestic responsibility may be a reflection of family stresses and be sex-role inappropriate.

Parental Attitudes toward Aggression

In Boston   Parental encouragement of an aggressive response to an attack from a peer relates to higher n-Achievement and higher Sex Affiliation fantasies, to more severe moral judgments on the EV 3, and to HSPQ Factors E+ (dominance, ascendance) and O+ (guilt-proneness).

In Rome   Encouraging aggression predicts *lower* sexual fantasies, HSPQ Factors E+ (intelligence), I+ (esthetic sensitivity, imaginativeness), and O+ (guilt-proneness).

In Palermo   Also predicts HSPQ O+ and D+ (excitability, attention-getting).

The consistent association in all three cities with the "guilt-proneness" factor on the HSPQ, reinforced with higher EV 3 scores in Boston, suggests the psychoanalytic interpretation of conscience as related to identification with the aggressor.

Beyond this common association with evidences of conscience, the pattern of correlates in the three cities is quite different—in Boston, encouragement of aggression relates to assertiveness and freer expression of sexual fantasies, in Rome on the other hand to less expression of sexual fantasy but greater intellectuality and imaginativeness, and in Palermo to excitability and attention-getting tendencies. Perhaps each of these patterns is syntonic with conscience formation in each of the three different cultural settings, or perhaps we simply have another illustration of the culturally diverse meanings of a given parental attitude (encouragement of aggression), which as we have seen tends to be much more characteristic of the Italian–American group of parents.

Freedom of Expression

In Boston   Parental reports of encouraging freedom of expression are negatively related to wishes for autonomy expressed in fantasy, are positively related to status of the boy's preferred profession and to interviewer's judgments of support from the home, and are associated with the majority of the HSPQ Factors—C (emotional immaturity), F (desurgency), G (lack of rigid internal standards), I (realistic, self-reliant), J (liking group action), O (self-confidence), Q2 (group dependency), and Q4 (relaxed, composed)—a pattern suggesting a realistic, self-confident and socially well-integrated orientation, but also some degree of emotional lability, perhaps partly a function of greater emotional expressiveness.

In Rome   Freedom of expression relates positively to n-Achievement, relates also to the boy's report that the mother is the more severe parent (perhaps an indication of milder paternal authority) and to feeling less unjustly treated. Relates also to HSPQ Factors C+ (ego strength, emotional maturity) and Q2+ (self-sufficiency).

In Palermo   Correlates only with p-Nurturance in the Imagination Test.

Cohesiveness of the Family

In Boston   Relates to interviewer ratings of less independence and more support to the home.

In Rome   Relates to high n-Aggression, low n-Autonomy, and high p-Nurturance; relates to less sense of unjust treatment reported in the interview, and to HSPQ J+ (fastidious individualism).

In Palermo   Correlates negatively with p-Fear-Worry, positively with the number of friends the boy would choose to eliminate, with the interviewer rating of capacity to reason logically, and with HSPQ B+ (intelligence). The latter two correlates one might expect from the close association of cohesiveness and SES in Palermo.

With the exception of the association with fantasy aggression in Rome, these rather sparse correlates suggest a boy who is rather content with his position in a close family system.

Restrictive Attitudes toward Sexuality

In Boston   Related to lower n-Power, higher interviewer ratings of aggressiveness both in the interview and outside the family.

In Rome   Also relates to lower n-Power and higher ratings of aggressiveness from the interview. Also relates to the boy's report that he is less free to choose his friends, that he has a higher sense of guilt, and that he judges himself stronger but less loved than others.

In Palermo   Related to lower aggressive fantasy, the boy's statement that he would choose to eliminate relatively few friends, and the interviewer's judgment that he is relatively less able to solve emotional problems.

Whereas restrictive attitudes toward sexuality are likely to lead to a more passive, repressive reaction in Palermo, where they are most likely to be characteristic, they seem to generate a more aggressive reaction in both Boston and Rome, combined in Rome with a strong sense of guilt and perhaps of rejection. Perhaps the aggression may be interpreted as a counterphobic reaction to an underlying feeling of being relatively powerless and perhaps emasculated.

Control

In Boston   Relatively strict parental control is positively related to status of preferred profession, feeling more loved than others, and being rated less aggressive toward others.

In Rome   *Negatively* correlated with status of preferred profession, associated with parents not being pleased at the number of the boy's friends, the boy viewing his father as the more severe parent, being rated less aggressive in the interview, and with HSPQ F− (desurgency, depression).

In Palermo   Relates to the boys's report that his heart is likely to beat faster when a teacher asks him a question, correlates with being rated restless in the interview and with HSPQ E− (submissiveness) and Q2 (group dependency).

Strict parental control is less typical in Boston than among the Italian parents, tends to be associated with higher SES and with parental affection, and seems to lead to, or at least be associated with, a positive identification with parental standards, and perhaps a suppression of aggression (there is an almost significant positive correlation with fantasy aggression). Perhaps in Boston the Control variable indexes what Baumrind (1967) would label "authoritative" rather than "authoritarian" parental attitudes. For the Italian boys, however, where it seems to be associated especially in Rome with an authoritarian father, parental restrictiveness predicts passivity, depression, anxiety, and dependent submissiveness.

Intervention in Peer Relations

In Boston   Is positively related to status of preferred profession, the self-rating of intelligence, and the interviewer's rating of aggressiveness. It predicts HSPQ A+ (warm, sociable), B+ (intelligence), C+ (ego strength, emotional maturity), D+ (excitability, attention-getting), E+ (dominance, ascendance), F+ (surgency, talkative, cheerful), G+ (superego strength), H+ (adventurous, friendly), J+ (individualism, self-sufficiency), O+ (guilt-proneness), Q2+ (self-sufficiency), and Q4+ (ergic tension).

In Rome   Nothing.

In Palermo   Negatively correlated with the interviewer's rating of ability to solve practical problems, negatively correlated with severity of moral judgment in situations where extenuating circumstances involving the needs of others are involved and slightly related to HSPQ A− (social withdrawal).

Clearly parental intervention in peer relations has far-reaching implications among Italian–Americans for the boy's social development, and seems to be associated with an extraverted, assertive, friendly, independent, and generally both socially and intellectually effective pattern of functioning. Perhaps among the Boston parents, intervention in the boy's social life is primarily of a support-ive kind, and we have seen that it tends to be associated with the parents having a rather gregarious pattern themselves. Clearly, this variable does not have the same implications for the Italian family, and in Palermo seems to be associated with a rather shy and ineffectual approach to others, although perhaps also with some sensitivity to their needs. It is possible, of course, that in Palermo the parent who intervenes in her son's social relations is reacting to his need for support in this area rather than "causing" his withdrawal.

Indulgence

In Boston Boys whose parents tended to socialize them at later ages and generally more indulgently were judged less restless and more aggressive in the interview. Indulgence was also associated with a large number of the HSPQ factors: A+ (warm, sociable), B+ (intelligence), C+ (ego strength), D+ (ex-citability), E+ (dominance), F+ (surgency), H+ (adventurous), I+ (esthetically sensitive, demanding, subjective), J+ (individualistic), Q2+ (self-sufficiency), Q4+ (ergic tension), and with somewhat higher scores on the CMAS.

In Rome Highly negatively correlated with sex affiliation fantasies, as-sociated with lower self-ratings of intelligence and a sense of being less loved than others, and with being judged more restless. Also relates to HSPQ F− (desurgency, depression).

In Palermo Related to HSPQ J− (liking for group action) and Q3− (poor self-sentiment, uncontrolled, lax).

Indulgent early socialization tends to be much more typical of the Italian parents, and where carried to extremes seems to have an infantilizing effect. The very high negative correlation with sexual fantasies in Rome may be an expres-sion of a general social immaturity associated with parental indulgence, or might be more dynamically interpreted as a repression of sexuality related to prolonga-tion of the habit of sleeping with the parents, which tends to be part of the indulgent pattern in Italian families. In Boston, on the other hand, where most of the parents have been influenced by American norms of earlier habit-training and demands for maturity, the more indulgent pattern may represent closer adherence to the family's cultural origins. Where indulgence has been retained among the Italian–American families, its effect seems to be much more positive, leading to a generally extraverted, cheerful, assertive pattern of social relations, high ego strength and intellectual effectiveness, and also more sensitivity and emotion-ality. In fact, this sounds very much like the friendly, expressive, ebullient social behavior one often tends stereotypically to ascribe to Italian–Americans con-trasted with other ethnic groups within the United States.

Academic Pressure

In Boston   Negatively related to p-Dominance and p-Fear-Worry in the Imagination Test, associated with reports of the heart beating faster when a teacher asks a question and to feeling less intelligent than others. Related to HSPQ B− (low intelligence), D+ (excitability), and Q3+ (high sentiment).

In Rome   Negatively related to the self-rating of intelligence and to the interviewer rating of independence. Related to HSPQ C− (emotional instability, immaturity), D+ (excitability), J+ (fastidious individualism), and O+ (guilt-proneness, worrying, anxious, depressed).

In Palermo   Associated with being rated more talkative, more independent, higher in community responsibility, more able to work with others, less severe moral judgments, and HSPQ Q2− (group dependent).

Here we see considerable similarity in the patterns for Boston and Rome, and a somewhat different set of correlates in Palermo. It may be that in Palermo parental concern with the boy's school work is experienced by him as a manifestation of positive interest and support. In the other two groups, it is clearly related to lowered self-esteem in relation to intellectual performance and to indications of anxiety and emotional disturbance. Here we have the usual chicken-and-egg problem in interpretation of this kind of correlational picture; the parent's concern and pressure may well be a reaction to the boy's academic ineffectiveness rather than the cause of lowered self-esteem, but in any case it is not experienced by the son as helpful or supportive. We may be able to sort out these relations better in the light of later information about educational attainment.

Relations between Cognitive and Personality Functioning

We turn now to a consideration of the degree to which cognitive performance in our three groups of subjects may be a function of differences in personality; or conversely differences in emotional and interpersonal behavior may reflect differences in intelligence and patterning of abilities. The correlations between the two sets of measures that reach the .05 level of significance are presented for each city separately in Table 4-14a–c.

The Raven

In Boston   Raven scores correlate positively with n-Achievement, n-Power, p-Nurturance, and p-Dominance on the Imagination Test. They also relate to the subject's report that his heart is less likely to beat faster when a teacher asks him a question, to higher self-ratings of intelligence, to HSPQ factors B+ (intelligence) and Q4+ (ergic tension).

TABLE 4-14a

CORRELATIONS OF COGNITIVE MEASURES WITH PERSONALITY NEEDS - BOSTON

Personality Measures	Cognitive Measures									
	Raven	Gott-schaldt	Creativity					Digits		
	Test 1 C7	C15	Idea-tional Fluency 9-10	Conseq. Remote 9-12	Plot Titles 9-18	Alter-nate Uses 9-20	Car-toons 9-22	Min 1 L104	Min 2 L105	Min 3 L106
Imagination Test										
X12 Achievement	.27	.25	.25			.30	.27	.32	.32	.37
X15 Affiliation								.24		.25
X18 Power	.20							.26		
X21 Autonomy		-.26	-.42			-.46				
X23 Nurturance	.24	.30								
X24 Dominance	.25									
X27 Fear-Worry					.31					
X28 Sex Affiliation								.27		
Interview										
D38 #Would Eliminate				.37				.39		.35
D54 Heart Beats Faster	.24	.27				.27				
D61 Intelligent (More Than Others)	.30	.37				.31	.22			
D62 Strength (More Than Others)								.29	.24	.22
D63 Unjust Treatment					.35		.22			
D65 Talkative			.24		.21					
D67 Aggression				-.23					.21	.22
D70 Practical Problems		.25								
D71 Emotional Problems		.22								
D73 Affection Outside						-.30				
D77 Aggression						.23				
HPSQ										
47 B	.51	.37	.32	.26	.40	.45	.30			
49 C									.27	
51 D					-.33	-.24				
57 G		.21	.26			.31				
59 H									.27	
61 I		.21	-.31		.21					
71 Q4	.20									

135

TABLE 4-14b

CORRELATIONS OF COGNITIVE MEASURES WITH PERSONALITY MEASURES - ROME

Personality Measures	Raven Test 1 C7	Gott-schaldt C15	Ideational Fluency 9-10	Conseq. Remote 9-12	Plot Titles 9-18	Alternate Uses 9-20	Cartoons 9-22	Min 1 L104	Min 2 L105	Min 3 L106
Imagination Test										
X20 Aggression		.20								
X23 Nurturance							.22			
Interview										
D20 Prof. 1st Choice								.18		
D23 Prof. Rejected								.53	.49	.53
D34 # Of Friends		-.20								
D36 Parents Pleased		.64						-.20	-.22	-.19
D37 Free to Choose							-.18			
D56 Guilt								.19	.20	.19
D61 Intelligent (More Than Others)	.19						.23	.25	.29	.29
D65 Talkative			.34	.20	.45	.25	.26			
D67 Aggression			.29							
D70 Practical Problems			.26	.29	.30	.30	.19			
D71 Emotional Problems			.19							
D72 Affection in Family			.20							
D73 Affection Outside		-.21								
D76 Community Resp.	.22		.18			.20				
D77 Aggression			.21							
D78 Reason Log.	.28				.33	.24				
D79 Work with Others	.18									
EV 3										
45 1, 4, 7, 10	.24									
47 Total	.25									
HPSQ										
47 B	.35						.22	.35	.31	.37
61 I								-.18		
65 O			-.24			-.29				
67 Q2				.19						
71 Q4					.18					

136

TABLE 4-14c

CORRELATIONS OF COGNITIVE MEASURES WITH PERSONALITY MEASURES - PALERMO

Personality Measures	Raven Test 1 C7	Gott-schaldt C15	Creativity					Digits		
			Idea-tional Fluency 9-10	Conseq. Remote 9-12	Plot Titles 9-18	Alter-nate Uses 9-20	Car-toons 9-22	Min 1 L104	Min 2 L105	Min 3 L106
Imagination Test										
X12 Achievement		.25			.27					
X18 Power							.22			-.33
X20 Aggression								-.25		-.34
X23 Nurturance							.34			
Interview										
D34 # of Friends				-.23						
D37 Free to Choose						-.22				
D56 Guilt		.22								
D61 Intelligent (More than others)									-.19	-.20
D63 Unjust Treatment	-.26					-.38				
D65 Talkative					.27				-.19	
D66 Restless				.22					-.22	-.30
D67 Aggression		.20				.20				
D70 Practical Problems		.20								
D72 Affection in Family										-.24
D73 Affection Outside						-.22	-.21			
D76 Community Resp.									.26	
EV 3										
45 1, 4, 7, 10								-.31		
47 Total							*	-.24		

In Rome Correlates positively with the self-rating of intelligence, with the interviewer's judgment of sense of community responsibility and of capacity to reason logically and to work with others, with severity of moral judgment on the EV 3, and with HSPQ B+ (intelligence).

In Palermo Relates to a sense of unjust treatment and to HSPQ Factors A+ (warm, sociable), B+, I− (tough, realistic), and to Q2+ (self-sufficiency).

In general, these correlations provide encouraging evidence of the validity of the self-report measures of intelligence.

TABLE 4-14c (continued)

Personality Measures	Raven Test 1 C7	Gott- schaldt C15	Creativity					Digits		
			Idea- tional Fluency 9-10	Conseq. Remote 9-12	Plot Titles 9-18	Alter- nate Uses 9-20	Car- toons 9-22	Min 1 L104	Min 2 L105	Min 3 L106
HSPQ										
45 A	.24				-.22					
47 B	.23						.33			
51 D					.27					
53 E					.24					
59 F								.19		
61 I	-.22							-.19	-.22	-.23
63 J		.24								
67 Q2	.23									
69 Q3								(-.17)	-.25	-.21
CMAS										
73 Taylor Anxiety							-.22			

Gottschaldt Figures

In Boston Is associated with high n-Achievement, and p-Dominance and low n-Autonomy on the Imagination Test, with the self-rating of intelligence and with reporting that the subject's heart is less likely to beat faster when a teacher asks him a question, and with interviewer ratings of capacity to solve both practical and emotional problems. Also associated with HSPQ B+, G+ (superego strength), and I+ (esthetic sensitivity, imaginativeness).

In Rome Associated with Aggressive fantasy, with low number of reported friends, with parents not being pleased at the number of friends, and with being judged less open and affectionate outside the family.

In Palermo Correlates with high n-Achievement, with low sense of guilt reported in the interview, with interviewer ratings of aggressiveness and ability to solve practical problems, and with HSPQ J+ (individualism, self-sufficiency).

Creativity

In Boston Higher scores on the creativity measures are associated with high n-Achievement, low n-Autonomy, and higher Fear-Worry scores (in one case). Creativity is also related to the number of friends the boy would choose to eliminate, reporting his heart unlikely to beat faster when a teacher asks him a question, to the self-rating of intelligence, to less feeling of unjust treatment, to being judged more talkative and less aggressive in the interview, and less affectionate and more aggressive outside the family. It is also associated with HSPQ Factors B+ (intelligence), D− (Phlegmatic, stodgy, self-sufficient), G+ (superego strength), and inconsistently to Factor I (toughness versus esthetic sensitivity).

In Rome   Creativity scores are associated with p-Nurturance, the boy's report that he is not free to choose his friends, a higher self-rating of intelligence, and to being rated talkative (very consistently), aggressive, able to solve practical problems (also very consistently), able to solve emotional problems, being open and affectionate in the family, community responsibility, aggressiveness (slight), and ability to reason logically. There is also a slight relation to HSPQ Factor B+, and relations to O− (self-confidence, adequacy), Q2+ (self-sufficiency), and Q4+ (ergic tension).

In Palermo   There are some correlations with n-Achievement, n-Power, and p-Nurturance in the Imagination Test. One or another of the creativity measures is also associated with reporting fewer friends but also with being judged restless, talkative, and aggressive in the interview and less open and affectionate outside the family. There are also relations with HSPQ A− (social withdrawal), B+, D+ (excitability), and E+ (dominance, ascendance) and with lower scores on the anxiety scale.

Digit Ordering

In Boston   Is positively correlated with n-Achievement and n-Affiliation and slightly so with n-Power and with Sex Affiliation. Correlates also with the number of friends the boy would choose to eliminate, his self-rating of strength, and being rated aggressive in the interview. Better performance on digits is also associated with HSPQ C+ (ego strength, emotional maturity) and H+ (adventurous).

In Rome   Better performance on the digits task is associated with status of preferred profession and of profession rejected, the boy's report that his parents are pleased at the number of his friends, and self-reports of seldom feeling guilty and feeling relatively more intelligent than others. Is also associated with HSPQ B+ and slightly with I− (tough, realistic).

In Palermo   Better scores on the digits task tend to be associated with low n-Power, low n-Aggression on the Imagination Test, low self-ratings of intelligence, and being judged by the interviewer to be less talkative, less restless, less affectionate in the family but higher in community responsibility. Digit ordering is also associated with less severe moral standards on the EV 3, and with HSPQ

Factors H+ (adventurous, thick-skinned), I− (tough, realistic), and Q3 (poor self-sentiment, uncontrolled).

Overall, there is more communality in Boston than in the Italian groups among the correlates of the cognitive measures, as we would expect since the cognitive variables are more closely intercorrelated there. In general they are associated with self-confidence, ambition and assertiveness, and realistically positive estimates of the subject's own abilities. More specific to the creativity measures, as contrasted with the measures of more convergent abilities, are indications of some conflict in interpersonal relations. Torrance (1963) and others have reported similar findings that suggest that highly creative children may often be somewhat hard to get along with.

In the two Italian groups we find more specificity in the correlates of the different cognitive measures, and there are also some differences between the two cities. In Rome high scores on the Raven relate to a pattern of success through conformity and internalization of societal standards. Subjects who score higher on the digit-reordering task, on the other hand, which is more novel in this culture, tend to be self-sufficient, tough, realistic, and less likely to experience guilt. Higher creative subjects in this group appear to be more aggressive and expressive as well as self-sufficient. When we come to the correlates of superior performance on the Gottschaldt, we find this more aggressive and self-sufficient orientation carried to the point of hostility, supporting the interpretation of this task as a measure of "field-independence" or "differentiation."

In Palermo, not only the measures of more divergent abilities (creativity, the Gottschaldt) but also performance on the Raven and, in a somewhat different way, the digits task seem to be related to some disarticulation with the social order, rejection of conventional morality, a sense of being unfairly treated, and a tough and somewhat cynical self-sufficiency. Perhaps brightness and independence of mind, in this traditional and relatively authoritarian cultural setting, is likely to be associated with a tendency to question the social order and a need to "go it alone." Barzini (1964) describes cynicism as typical of the Sicilian view of life, so perhaps these brighter boys are simply reflecting earlier the attitudes which are likely to characterize them as adults. Here performance on the digits task, which has been interpreted as reflecting relative freedom from anxiety, especially in the face of a novel or challenging situation, is related to more relaxed moral judgments and a generally rather "devil-may-care" pattern of emotional and interpersonal functioning.

Socialization and Cognitive Functioning

Tables 4-15a–c display the correlations with each of the four aspects of cognitive functioning of our selected set of variables reflecting family characteristics, parent–child relations, and child-rearing attitudes.

TABLE 4-15a

CORRELATIONS OF COGNITIVE MEASURES WITH FAMILY VARIABLES - BOSTON

Family Variables		Cognitive Measures									
		Raven Test 1 C7	Gottschaldt C15	Creativity					Digits		
				Ideational Fluency 9-10	Conseq. Remote 9-12	Plot Titles 9-18	Alternate Uses 9-20	Cartoons 9-22	Min 1 L104	Min 2 L105	Min 3 L106
B5	SES	-.26	-.25			-.27	-.23				
B52	Relation with Mother					-.22					
C38	Aggression	-.25						-.26	-.31	-.26	-.30
E7	Freedom of Expression								.21		.21
E23	Int. Peer Relations	.22						.29	.31	.32	.36
E31	Indulgence			-.28	-.22				.30	.30	.31

TABLE 4-15b

CORRELATIONS OF COGNITIVE MEASURES WITH FAMILY VARIABLES - ROME

Family Variables		Cognitive Measures									
		Raven Test 1 C7	Gottschaldt C15	Creativity					Digits		
				Ideational Fluency 9-10	Conseq. Remote 9-12	Plot Titles 9-18	Alternate Uses 9-20	Cartoons 9-22	Min 1 L104	Min 2 L105	Min 3 L106
B5	SES	-.20	-.28	.20					-.24		-.21
C17	Resp. in Home				-.25						
E11	Cohesion			.21							
E15	Sex Restrictiveness		-.23						-.22	-.22	-.22
E35	Academic Pressure			-.18						-.19	-.18

TABLE 4-15c

CORRELATIONS OF COGNITIVE MEASURES WITH FAMILY VARIABLES - PALERMO

Family Variables	Cognitive Measures									
			Creativity					Digits		
	Raven Test 1 C7	Gott-schaldt C15	Idea-tional Fluency 9-10	Conseq. Remote 9-12	Plot Titles 9-18	Alter-nate Uses 9-20	Car-toons 9-22	Min 1 L104	Min 2 L105	Min 3 L106
B5 SES	-.32	-.22						-.27		
C17 Resp. in Home						-.20	-.25			
C38 Aggression		-.26								
E7 Freedom of Expression							-.19			
E35 Academic Pressure										-.21

The Raven

As we would expect from the analysis of variance presented early in this chapter, performance on the Raven is associated with socioeconomic status in all three cities, the correlation being highest in Palermo. The Raven does not correlate with any of the socialization measures in either of the Italian cities, but does correlate with parental encouragement of an aggressive response to an attack from a peer and with intervention in peer relations in Boston. In general, there seems to be a somewhat closer association between socialization experiences and cognitive functioning for the Italian–American boys, and this may again reflect the somewhat greater significance placed on social relations in the American culture.

Gottschaldt Figures

Performance on the embedded figures test, on the other hand, correlates only with SES in Boston (we would predict this correlation from the relatively high correlation between Gottschaldt and Raven in Boston), whereas in Rome it is associated with more permissive parental attitudes toward sex and in Palermo with encouraging counteraggression toward peers.

Creativity

The measures of divergent ability tend to be associated with higher SES in Boston, as we would again expect from the relatively high correlations there with the Raven, but this association does not occur in either of the Italian cities; in fact, in Rome one of the measures, Ideational Fluency, tends to be associated with lower SES. In Boston, Ideational Fluency and Consequences are both negatively correlated with indulgence, performance on Plot Titles is associated with a better relationship with the mother, and Cartoons is positively correlated with encouraging aggression and with intervention in peer relations, again to about the same extent as the Raven.

In Rome, Ideational Fluency is associated with low family cohesiveness and low academic pressure and Consequences is associated with being given much responsibility in the home. In Palermo, both Alternate Uses and Cartoons are associated with responsibility in the home, and Cartoons is also slightly correlated with freedom of expression. Thus in the two Italian cities higher divergent ability tends to be associated with a family environment that combines permissiveness for self-expression with relatively high expectations of responsibility. This seems consonant with the findings reported in the previous section which suggest that creativity among Italian boys is associated with more aggressive, expressive, and self-sufficient interpersonal attitudes.

Digit Ordering

In Boston, better performance on this task is associated, even more strongly than the Raven, with parental encouragement of aggression and intervention in peer relations. It is associated also with lower freedom of expression and with indulgent early socialization. In the two Italian cities, higher scores on digits tend to be associated with higher SES and with lower academic pressure, and in Rome digits is consistently correlated with more permissive attitudes toward sexuality, as is the Gottschaldt.

In summary, better cognitive functioning in Boston is consistently associated with parental encouragement of sociable and appropriately aggressive interactions with peers. This is true for measures of divergent as well as convergent abilities, the only addition being that divergent ability also seems to be related to more indulgent early socialization and a particularly positive relation with the mother, factors that might well fit with the psychodynamic interpretation of creativity as an expression of capacity for "regression in the service of the ego."

Again, as we find with the personality variables, measures of cognitive functioning seem to be more discrete from each other and more diversely related to socialization variables for the Italian subjects, and there are overall fewer significant correlations. Attitudes of Italian parents toward their adolescent sons which appear to facilitate intellectual functioning are characterized by freedom from academic pressure and more permissiveness for impulse expression. (One should not ignore the possibility of a reverse direction of effect, namely that parents of brighter boys react to them more permissively and feel less need to press for academic achievement.) In Palermo, encouragement of appropriate aggression toward peers seems to be of special significance, as it is also in Boston, whereas in Rome it is the more open and permissive attitudes toward sex that seem to be of critical significance. Again, we are reminded of the psychoanalytic hypothesis that repression of sexual impulses often carries with it an inhibition of curiosity and thus of ability to function on intellectual tasks, especially those that are novel or which, like the Gottschaldt, involve restructuring of visual stimuli. On the other hand, especially where the southern Italian culture has come under American influence, parental encouragement of appropriately aggressive peer interaction is likely to be supportive of masculine sex-role development and thus syntonic with academic as well as social functioning, especially in nonverbal tasks.

Cultural Differences in Cognitive Style

A further note on differences between the Italian and the Italian–American groups in the area of cognitive style comes from a more projective situation devised by Wartegg (1957). We have not included these findings with our main analyses since they are based on a sample of only 59 of the Boston subjects and 59 of the Italian subjects, mainly from the Rome group. (Originally 120 subjects took this test, but one in each group had to be dropped because the protocol did not provide sufficient material for analysis.) The Wartegg Test was originally conceived for adults and consists of a single page, providing eight separate "windows"; each of these windows contains some small configuration that the subject must elaborate into some larger drawing of his own imaginative designing. Thus we have for each subject eight spontaneous drawings, each elicited by the initial small configuration within the window in response to the instructions to exercise his own imaginative resources. The test was administered when the subjects were on the average 14.

The analysis of these productions was carried out by Robert H. Knapp. He elected to analyze each drawing on the basis of considerations of both content and style, without any special reference to the nature of the original configuration. Eventually three aspects of style and four aspects of content were selected for rating, although others were explored. With respect to style, the following three variables proved measurable and consistent. These were, first, *precision,* a term that is largely self-explanatory but that defines the degree of accuracy of delineation, clearness of the termination of lines, definiteness of angles or features when represented, and similar qualities. Second was the stylistic component of *expansion versus constriction.* This was defined simply by whether or not the subject used the full area or the smaller part of each window in general for their imaginative construction. Expansive persons tended to use a larger area; constrictive persons tended to use a smaller area. A secondary aspect of this feature, of course, consisted in their tendency to define outer boundaries or not to define them. Third was the dimension of *rotundity versus angularity,* or the tendency to use round or curvilinear forms as opposed to linear–angular forms.

In estimating the content of the drawings, four categories emerged, the first being the most general. This category consisted of rating each drawing for its *intelligibility;* that is to say, did it represent an identifiable object from the objective world? Our second category of contents consisted of *architectural* motifs so far as they could be recognized. These included, naturally, the drawings of buildings and gross architectural structures, but it also included details of architecture such as staircases and the like. Our third content category consisted of *human figures* in any form whatever, including both full-length figures and human faces, or, more rarely, other parts of the anatomy. Finally, we had a category that included the representation of *mechanical devices* such as wheels, implements, vehicles, and many other such identifiable contrivances. This class actually proved to be fairly small for both groups.

In order to evaluate the productions of our Italian and American boys, we enlisted the aid of three members of the staff of the Institute for Esthetics in Paris.[2] Each of them rated all drawings from our 118 subjects on the seven variables we have described. Average interjudge reliabilities ranged from .79 to .96 on the seven variables; the uncorrected reliability coefficients exceed +.90 in the case of all the content categories, representing a clear consensus among the judges on the nature of the stimulus properties.

The comparative performance of the two groups with respect to our seven rating variables may be seen in Table 4-16. Each variable is measured by the sum of the rankings of our three judges. It can be clearly seen that five out of our seven rating scales yielded incisive differences between the two groups. Only in the case of Mechanical Motifs and the production of Intelligible Objects did the two groups not differ significantly. Most strikingly, they differed in that the Italian children much preferred the production of architectural motifs as compared with the Americans who preferred the production of human subject matter. An analysis of the intercorrelations among the stylistic qualities reflected in our first three dimensions of precision, angularity, and expansion are largely to be thought of as a consequence of this subject matter preference.

Precision shows a conspicuous positive correlation with Architectural Motifs, Intelligibility, Angularity, and Mechanical Motifs. It bears a negative relation, however, to the production of human figures. The Expansion tendency is negatively related to Angularity, positively to Intelligible Objects, and somewhat positively to Human and Mechanical Motifs. In short, there is a general tendency, more striking in Americans than Italians, to use a fuller area when they produce an intelligible production of whatever sort. Those drawing Human Motifs, predominantly our American subjects, tend to be low in Angularity ratings, high in Intelligibility, and somewhat high in Expansion. In contrast, those drawing Architectural Motifs (principally the Italian subjects) show a posi-

[2]We are indebted to Mmes. de Lambilly, Carlier, and Svobodny.

TABLE 4-16

COMPARISON OF GROUPS ON WARTEGG VARIABLES

	American-Italians		Italian-Italians			
	Mean	SD	Mean	SD	t	p
Precision	10.2	4.9	14.3	4.5	4.0	.001
Expansion	14.8	5.1	11.2	4.9	3.9	.001
Angularity	10.2	4.2	14.2	3.6	6.6	.001
Intelligibility	12.3	5.5	13.2	6.3	.86	N.S.
Architectural Motif	1.9	2.0	3.8	2.9	4.2	.001
Human Motif	6.2	4.0	4.0	3.4	3.2	.01
Mechanical Motif	3.2	3.3	3.4	3.3	.43	N.S.

tive correlation with Angularity and an equally positive correlation with Intelligible Objects, but a somewhat negative correlation with Mechanical Motifs. Thus our foremost finding is related to the different subject matter selected by the two groups and differences in the stylistic qualities of Precision, Angularity, and Expansion follow from this. Only in the case of Expansion could it be argued that temperamental considerations in the immediate sense, and not the subject matter involved, may be a differentiating variable between the two groups.

Because of the limited samples involved, we have not attempted further to analyze the Wartegg productions in relation to other measures on our subjects. Certainly these findings, however, are consonant with the general implications of our measures of interpersonal relations and family life as they differentiate the Italian–American from the Italian, especially the Rome subjects. Both the boys in Boston and their parents place much more positive emphasis on social relations, and appear to be much more gregarious and more engaged in group activities. We have also seen that in Boston the boy's assertiveness and sociability, and his parents' support of peer relations, are likely to be significantly related to cognitive functioning to a greater extent than among the Italian subjects.

The nature of the Wartegg stimulus material probably has fairly high pull for architectural themes, but this type of content was much more characteristic of the Italian subjects. Italians' culture places a premium, as it justly might, upon architecture as a cultural art form revered within their national history and contemporary civilization. This simple cultural fact may well account for the much greater prevalence of this choice of subject matter among the Rome boys, who live surrounded by the great monuments of over 2000 years. Besides the specific content differences, the stylistic differences also would seem to justify a somewhat more general interpretation of differences in the disposition of the two groups to expansiveness and constriction. The bulk of our observations certainly convince us that both in family life and even more surely in the school environment the American community favors greater freedom of expression and spontaneity, the Italian environment stressing greater obedience and conformity, especially for early adolescents. It might be argued, therefore, that the relative expansiveness of the American boys and the constrictiveness of the Italians in dealing with this projective task, while by no means an overhwhelming difference, reflects in a general way these contrasting attitudes toward social discipline.

SUMMARY

In this chapter we have reported the comparisons between our three subject groups on measures of cognitive development, interests, motives, personality indices, and measures of social and emotional development.

With respect to intelligence, the superior performance of the Rome sample on the Raven Progressive Matrices probably reflects an original selection bias. Raven scores vary similarly with SES in all three groups but show long-term stability only in Boston. The subjects in Palermo did less well than the other two groups on the digit-reordering task. The Rome group was superior to the other two on the Gottschaldt figures and Boston scored significantly lower than both Italian groups. The Roman subjects also performed consistently better than the other two groups on several measures of creativity. Measures of divergent and convergent intellectual functioning seem less closely related among the Italian than among the American subjects.

Overall, the three groups of boys showed fairly similar patterns of interests and aspirations in early adolescence, with those in Boston being more interested in sports and politics than those in Italy. The Italian–American subjects reported more positive and more egalitarian relations with parents than did the Italians, and more sociability and assertiveness with peers. (Generally, the interviews with the subjects themselves supported the conclusions from parent interviews.) On a verbal projective measure (the Imagination Test), the average score on need Achievement was highest in Boston; Rome scored lowest on both Affiliation and Power motives. The Boston subjects were also more likely to express aggressive and sexual impulses than were the Italian boys. The data provide an illustration of the different meanings of fantasy themes in different cultural contexts.

The Boston subjects as a group scored lower on a self-report measure of anxiety than did the Italians. Their group profile on the Cattell HSPQ also suggested that they were more socially outgoing and relaxed. The Roman subjects as a group were more aloof and individualistic, more critical and self-reliant, but also more anxious and sensitive than the other two groups. The Sicilians appear especially suspicious, introspective, and emotional. On the whole, however, profile differences between the groups were small. The Boston subjects rendered more severe moral judgments than did either of the two Italian groups.

Generally higher correlations between personality measures and SES in Palermo than in the other two cities suggested that in the traditional South the family's socioeconomic status may have a more decisive impact on motives and interpersonal relations. In all three groups, lack of paternal affection was associated with poorer emotional adjustment. Parental encouragement of aggression was associated with assertiveness in Boston but with emotionality in Italy. Parental control and indulgence also seemed to have differing consequences in the two cultural settings; in Boston, closer adherence to traditional Italian child-rearing patterns seemed to be associated with greater emotional security within the family.

Examination of the intercorrelations of personality and cognitive variables yielded a number of findings that tend to support the validity of both sets of measures. In Boston, superior cognitive performance was generally associated with self-confidence and assertiveness, and with parental encouragement of sociability and self-assertion. Among the Italian subjects, specific cognitive measures tended to show more diverse patterns of correlates. In Rome, the Raven scores related to success through conformity while divergent ability was associated with greater assertiveness and self-sufficiency. Among the Italian subjects divergent ability was also associated with greater freedom of expression and higher expectations of responsibility in the home—a somewhat atypical pattern of family relations in Italy. We have also reported on some differences in cognitive style as reflected in performance on the Wartegg figure drawing test; the American subjects' productions were more expansive.

CHAPTER 5

Interrelations of Physical and Psychological Development

SOME PSYCHOLOGICAL, SOCIAL, AND CULTURAL VARIABLES ASSOCIATED WITH DIFFERENTIAL PATTERNS OF GROWTH AND BEHAVIOR

We turn now to some associations between differential patterns of growth and sexual development in adolescence, on the one hand, and psychological variables and the social environment, on the other. The assumed connection between body type and temperament represents an old tradition within the study of individual development (e.g., Sheldon, 1954) which fell into some disrepute as a result of the overwhelming environmental bias reflected in American psychological theories of personality and even of intellectual development. Critics of the assumption that physique determines personality were quick to point out that, where relationships are found, they may well be a function of differing social stereotypes about individuals of different physique, and also, particularly in adolescence, of the very real social advantages that superior size, strength, health, and energy level may confer on the individual.

More recently, investigators of early development and its continuities into later life (see, e.g., Thomas, Birch, Chess, Hertzig, & Korn, 1963) have rediscovered temperament, at least under the guise of neonatal differences in patterns of reactivity, as a set of congenitally given and possibly genetically determined characteristics that may in important ways shape the course of early mother–infant interaction and thus have a determining influence on social and emotional development. Studies of psychosomatic disorders, including obesity, have also pointed out the possible influences of emotional and interpersonal factors on growth, body type, and patterns of health and disease in a wide range of organ systems. The possibility of influence between psychology and physiology thus runs in both directions, and we are dealing as usual with a very complex set of interactive relationships.

This study provides a rich source of information on individual differences in patterns of growth and health, as well as on differences in psychological development and social influences. We shall appraise some of the possible connections between these two realms of development. At the same time, the cross-cultural character of our subject population allowed us to examine the extent to which connections between physical and psychological development might be specific to a particular cultural setting, and thus perhaps a product of social stereotypes, dietary patterns, or other environmental influences prevalent in that setting. To what degree may any associations between physical growth and personality or intellect found in the southern Italian population have been altered by migration to Rome or to Boston? Since we are dealing with correlational data, we cannot provide any definitive answers to such questions, but especially where the longitudinal nature of the study allows us to discover predictive relationships, let us say, between rate of growth in early adolescence and social adjustments or interpersonal attitudes in early maturity, we might uncover intriguing leads for future research.

Rate of Puberal Maturing and Personality

At an earlier stage of the project, the principal investigator, in collaboration with Paul Mussen, compared a number of personality characteristics of early and late maturers within this subject population. The results of these comparisons have been published in detail elsewhere (Mussen & Young, 1964). This study was an attempt to replicate the investigation of Mussen and Jones (1957), based on data from the Berkeley longitudinal samples, in which they found that late maturers were

> more likely to have negative self-conceptions, feelings of inadequacy, strong feelings of being rejected and dominated, prolonged dependency needs, and rebellious attitudes toward parents. In contrast, the early-maturing boys presented a much more favorable psychological picture during adolescence. Relatively few of them felt inadequate, rejected, dominated, or rebellious toward their families. More of them appeared to be self-confident, independent, and capable of playing an adult role in interpersonal relationships [p. 255].

These correlations between rate of physical maturing, on the one hand, and social status, personality structure, and adjustment, on the other, might be attributed, at least in part, to the American cultural emphasis on motives such as competence, achievement, and competition. Consequently, personal characteristics such as "maturity" and "independence" and greater size and strength are highly valued, especially for males. When the boy attains mature size and strength, he is likely to be regarded and treated as a young man, and if he reaches this stage earlier than most of his peers, he will enjoy some of the advantages, privileges, benefits, and rewards associated with the status of manhood before the others do. As a result, this boy is likely to become self-assured, independent, and generally better adjusted socially and emotionally. In contrast, his peers who mature slowly are more likely to lack self-confidence and to feel inadequate, dependent, and rejected.

It seems reasonable to assume that rate of physical growth might not have the same influence on personality in cultures with different values—for example, in a culture in which the child's situation is extremely comfortable and secure, where parents attempt to foster and to prolong the child's dependence, and where social status has little or no relationship to physique. These have been often described, traditional characteristics of Italian culture. We have seen that the Italian boys are more likely to be indulged and protected as small children and that fewer maturity demands are made on them. Independence is not such a highly esteemed characteristic as in America, and parents enjoy and encourage their children's dependence on them, doing relatively little to stimulate the development of autonomy and independence (Campisi, 1953, pp. 126–137; Ianni, 1961). Moreover, in evaluating others, Italians pay much less attention to physical size and strength than do Americans.

For this particular study, the Rome and Palermo groups were combined with 150 boys from Florence who had also been given complete physical examinations and interviewed with the same schedule used in the longitudinal study. (However, the Imagination Test was not given to the Florence sample, so that the comparisons of fantasy variables involve only Rome and Palermo, contrasted with Boston.) Early- and late-maturing boys were selected in the following way: Distributions of the maturity ratings of each age group (e.g., 12, 13, etc.) were constructed separately for each research site. All boys who *at any time during adolescence* were rated above or below the modal rating for the group, i.e., who were not at the stage of maturity most characteristic of boys their own age in their own community, were considered either accelerated or retarded in development. These were the subjects of the study. The numbers of early maturers and late maturers, respectively, in the four research sites were as follows: 35 and 22 in Florence, 17 and 28 in Rome, 17 and 16 in Palermo, a total of 69 early maturers and 66 late maturers in Italy; and 25 early and 17 late maturers in Boston.

Mussen and Young found that, among the Boston subjects, the early maturers generally held more favorable self-concepts (considered themselves more intelligent, more loved, and to have more friends) than the late maturers, whereas among their Italian subjects the only difference in self-perception indicated that the Italian early maturers were somewhat less likely to feel misunderstood by adults than the late maturers. They conclude that early maturing carries much greater social advantages for American than for Italian adolescent boys, and that the Italian–American adolescents in this study have been influenced by these cultural differences in peer-group values. With respect to more underlying self-conceptions as assessed by the Imagination Test, Italian late maturers tended to have more negative self-concepts than the early-maturing Italian comparison group. (This comparison involves early maturers from both Rome and Palermo contrasted with the late maturers from those two groups.) With respect to motivations expressed in fantasy, neither Italian nor Italian–American late-maturing boys differed from early maturers in their own cultures in dependency motivation, as measured by the Imagination Test. Like the American groups studied, however, a significantly greater proportion of physically retarded than of physically accelerated Italian adolescent boys displayed strong autonomy needs—specifically, motivations to escape from or to defy their parents. This cross-cultural finding might be interpreted to mean that late-maturing adolescents in both these cultures are regarded, and treated, as immature children. The boys, aware that they were becoming mature—albeit at a slow rate—probably resented these parental attitudes and kinds of treatment and, in their fantasies at least, rebelled against their parents. (Incidentally, these stories of escape and defiance were often of a childish sort, probably indicative of emotional immaturity.)

Among the Italian–American subjects, the difference was reversed: strong autonomy needs were manifested by more early- than late-maturing boys. This difference might be interpreted in terms of another difference between the two groups that will be discussed in the next section; namely, early-maturers of this cultural background tend to feel more dominated by their parents. Actually their elders, imbued with traditional Italian attitudes, probably did not allow these boys the degree of freedom and independence enjoyed by mature American boys, who undoubtedly served as the Italian–American boys' reference group. The strong autonomy needs may therefore be viewed as reactions against what they regard as inordinately strong parental domination. By contrast, the late-maturing Italian–American boys, perhaps comparing their situations with those of other late-maturing American boys who also tend to be restricted and treated as children, do not feel unusually strongly dominated, and consequently they react less rebelliously.

Another difference between the two Italian–American groups, consistent with this last-mentioned difference, involved the motivation for power—to control and to manipulate others. In this variable too, early maturers of this cultural background scored higher than their late-maturing peers, probably again reflecting this group's resentment at being (in their view) unduly restricted, dominated, and controlled by their parents while other American boys their age were allowed greater independence. Consequently, in their fantasies, they reversed the real situation, controlling others as they felt they had been controlled.

American late maturers showed stronger motivations for heterosexual affiliation in their Thematic Apperception Test (TAT) protocols (stories involving love, romance, dating, and marriage) than did their early-maturing peers. This finding was explained in terms of their stronger needs for affiliation and greater orientation toward social activity, often of an immature sort. This explanation seems reasonable in the light of other data—based on the research staff's observations of social behavior—that indicated that late maturers had *less* overt interest in girls and probably fewer successful and rewarding experiences with them. In contrast, those more physically accelerated among both Italian and Italian–American boys gave evidence of strong needs for heterosexual affiliation. Boys who are physically mature are undoubtedly, for many reasons, more responsive—and more attractive—to the opposite sex and probably have more successful relations with girls than those who are immature. Late and early maturers from these two cultures—as opposed to those from middle-class American culture—did *not* differ in needs for affiliation and social interaction.

To summarize the contrasts with the Berkeley findings, more late-maturing than early-maturing American boys have negative and rebellious attitudes toward their families and more feelings of parental rejection and dominance. The direction of the difference was reversed for the Italian–American groups. According to their Imagination Test stories, more of the late maturers regarded their parents as highly nurturant and helpful; fewer of them felt dominated or rebellious. It seemed likely that the parents of these boys had retained the traditional values of Italian culture, enjoyed their sons' dependence on them and encouraged it, and that the late maturers were less likely to rebel against this somewhat infantilizing parental treatment.

The physically accelerated Italian–American adolescent is more likely to view his parents as restrictive and dominating. He is likely to resist their ''babying'' him, and their preventing him from achieving the independent status to which he feels entitled. Hence, he is more likely to become rebellious.

More of the early- than of the late-maturing Italian subjects also felt dominated by their parents, whom they perceived as highly restrictive. Undoubtedly the rapidly maturing Italian boys felt that they were almost adults and should be granted some adult privileges and greater independence. Their parents may share this realization but have conflicts about it, for at the same time they wish to prolong their sons' dependence and childlike status. As a result, they may become sterner disciplinarians with their early-maturing sons who then feel dominated by their parents.

In spite of the fact that Italian early maturers felt their parents to be dominating and restrictive, they, like American early maturers, seemed to have generally good relations and close ties with their familes and positive attitudes toward them.

Correlates of Somatic Variables in Early Adolescence

With more complete longitudinal data now available, it was possible to examine the intercorrelations of 106 selected psychological and social variables (including most of those used in the earlier Mussen and Young study) with a number of somatic variables measured at successive ages through the course of adolescent development. It was also possible to examine *predictive* relations in the longitudinal sense, i.e., the correlations between somatic status in early adolescence and psychological and social outcomes assessed in early maturity (and discussed in more detail in the final section of this volume). For this correlational analysis we chose to examine the somatic measures taken at age 14, since they presented the best dispersions of scores, especially on the measure of pubertal maturity, and were also contemporaneous with most of the data on family background and psychological characteristics collected in early adolescence. Five of the somatic variables were chosen as best representing the following components of growth: body height (linear growth), puberal age (developmental measure of sexual development), bone-muscle (body mass), and two fat measurements (skin folds of biceps and subscapular). Weight was avoided as being too complex a variable to represent body mass. The correlates of these selected somatic variables are shown in Table 5-1a–c.

Boston: Age 14   There were some positive correlations between puberal maturity, height and bone muscle, and intellectual performance—Raven, Digits, HSPQ B; boys who are bigger and more mature do somewhat better on tests of intellectual effectiveness.

This cluster of measures—puberal maturity, height, and bone muscle—is also associated with low n-Autonomy, higher surgency (F) on the HSPQ, and higher interviewer ratings of aggressiveness and independence. In other words, smaller and less mature boys are perceived as more passive, are less optimistic, and express more wishes for autonomy in fantasy. There is little in the socialization variables to suggest that these correlations are a function of different parental attitudes and relationships, except that height is negatively correlated with parental control and puberal age is positively related to encouragement of peer relations. Perhaps the parents of the taller, more mature boys grant them somewhat more freedom. More probably, however, these correlations reflect the social advantages of the more mature boy and his greater self-confidence with peers and in relation to academic tasks.

The fat measures tend to be associated with some of the same variables as the height and maturity measures (lower n-Autonomy, higher aggressiveness), as

TABLE 5-1a

BOSTON: CORRELATES OF SOMATIC VARIABLES AT AGE 14

	Height 108	Dyna-mometer 114	Puberal Age 115	Fat 117	Fat 118	Bone Muscle 120
Number of children		.24				
Freedom of expression				-.21	-.21	
Control	-.21					
Intervention--Peer relations			.22			
Need achievement		-.25				
Need autonomy	-.48		-.42	-.39	-.37	-.48
Peer dominance					.28	
# Friends would eliminate				.32		
Unjust treatment (-)		-.26				
Aggression	.24			.24		.25
Independence						.22
Support from home					.30	
Support to home				-.22		
Aggression	.25		.24			.28
HSPQ B			.21			
HSPQ F			.23			
HSPQ G		-.22				
Raven			.22			
Creativity: Cartoons		-.23				
Digits - 1st		-.23				
Digits - 2nd	.27		.26			.28
Digits - 3rd-10th	.25		.21			.27
Torgoff Achievement				-.24		
		-.26				
EV3		-.24				
Time perspective		.28				

one would expect from the high intercorrelations of all these somatic variables. However, there are some other psychological variables more specifically related to the fat measures. They are associated with higher interviewer ratings of support *from* the home and lower ratings of support *to* the home—perhaps a reflection of a somewhat passive adjustment to a relatively traditional pattern of family life, reflected in feelings of being dominated by parents. The correlation with the number of classmates the boy said he would like to eliminate is perhaps a reflection of the tendency for fat boys, in American culture, to be teased by their

TABLE 5-1b

ROME: CORRELATES OF SOMATIC VARIABLES AT AGE 14

	Height 108	Dyno-mometer 114	Puberal Age 115	Fat 117	Fat 118	Bone Muscle 120
Number of children			-.18		-.19	-.17
Ordinal position	-.17		-.22		-.18	-.19
Bad relationship with father	.22	.19	.23			.22
Parental permission of aggression		-.23				
Sex restraint	-.22					
Restrictiveness				.21	.22	
Age of socialization		.20				
Indulgence		.22				
Academic pressure		.22				
Need autonomy			.25			
Status of professions rejected.	.19		.19	.24	.20	.20
Number of friends						-.20
Guilt (-)	.18	.18	.19			
Aggression				-.18	-.18	
HSPQ E		.24				.18
Raven	-.18	-.19				
Gottschaldt		.21				
EV3-II	.25	.23	.26		.20	.24
Live with parents (No)		.25	.22			

peers. One of the fat measures in early adolescence also predicts lower scores on the Torgoff achievement scale (discussed in Chapter 7), a lower sense of mastery over the environment as a young adult.

Rome: Age 14   In Rome, all of the size, maturity, and strength variables tend to be related to status of profession rejected, to having a poor relationship with father (and in the case of some subjects, to having fewer friends) and to lower guilt scores. They were also associated with parental reports that the boy enjoyed good health. Strength and bone muscle also correlate with dominance (HSPQ).

It should be noted that taller and stronger boys, among the Rome sample, had a slight tendency to score lower on the Raven but higher on the Gottschaldt. Thus greater size and maturity in early adolescence, for this group, were not clearly positively related to intellectual functioning as they were in Boston.

Size, sexual maturity, and strength in early adolescence, for the Rome group, were predictive of more severe moral judgment in early maturity (higher EV 3-II, see Chapter 7) and a tendency to live away from home. The latter correlation may be a reflection of the poorer relationship with father and more self-assertive tendencies evident in early adolescence. Puberal maturity at that period was also positively correlated with n-Autonomy expressed in the Imagination Test. It should also be noted that height was associated with less restrictive parental attitudes toward sexuality, so that at least in this respect the parents of the taller boys tended to be more permissive.

Fatness, which was less prevalent in Rome than in Boston, also showed a less distinct pattern of correlates. It did tend to be associated, in the Rome families, with the pattern of indulgence in early childhood and greater control in adolescence that we have found to be more characteristic in general of the Italian parents. Thus it is possible that fatter boys, in Rome, have been somewhat infantilized. They were also seen as less aggressive in the interview.

TABLE 5-1c

PALERMO: CORRELATES OF SOMATIC VARIABLES AT AGE 14

	Height 108	Dyno- mometer 114	Puberal Age 115	Fat 117	Fat 118	Bone Muscle 120
Cuddled	.20			.20		.20
Power	-.24					-.25
Autonomy					.32	
Succorance				.47		
Nurturance				.30	.25	
Mother more severe	.28	.28			.25	
Strength greater than others		.28			.26	.31
Can solve emotional problems					-.21	-.21
Affection in family	-.24	-.25	-.28			-.22
Support from home	.25	-.23				
Solve emotional problems	-.22					
Self-sufficiency					.19	
HSPQ - Ergic tension				.24	.20	
Raven	-.23					
Ideational fluency	-.21	-.20				-.20
Time perspective					-.20	
Years in school	-.35	-.32		-.24		-.34

Palermo: Age 14   Height, bone muscle, and strength were negatively related to ideational fluency and (in the case of height) to the Raven, and also predict fewer years in school. Thus, as in Rome, bigger boys were somewhat less likely to score well on intellectual measures and they were also likely to drop out of school earlier. (It should be noted that, since the size measures are unrelated to SES, this association is independent of the tendency for education to be related to a family's socioeconomic level.)

Here there are no socialization measures that relate to the somatic variables, except for the parents' tendency to report that the bigger boys were cuddled more in infancy. It thus seems curious that these boys tended to see the mother as the more severe parent. The boys in Palermo who had more bone muscle and were more mature sexually saw themselves, realistically, as stronger than others. They were also perceived by the interviewers as expressing less affection in the family, receiving less support from the home, and having a lower capacity to solve emotional problems. Perhaps there is some connection between these interpersonal variables and their lower creativity and educational attainment.

Fatness, in Palermo, is related to higher fantasies of nurturance and succorance and to lower need for autonomy, but to higher self-sufficiency and ergic tension on the HSPQ. Fatness is also predictive of lower scores on the Jessor measure of time perspective (see Chapter 6). Perhaps especially in the southern Italian environment, where economic privations are a more pressing social reality, being physically well-nourished brings with it feelings of psychological nurturance and support and is associated with a more optimistic approach to life, but also with a tendency to live in the present and to let tomorrow take care of itself.

Although our comparisons of the patterns of correlations between growth and personality in the three groups must necessarily be post hoc and highly speculative, we note that this method of analysis does not entirely sustain the conclusions of the Mussen and Young study. That study was based on a different sampling of the subjects and on the comparison of small groups of "early" and "late" maturers, rather than on correlational findings based on the total range of maturational rates. It is only the findings on the Boston group that are close to those reported for earlier studies of American adolescents, which suggest that early maturers tend to be socially advantaged and late maturers may feel dominated by parents and express stronger rebellious needs in fantasy.

LATERAL DOMINANCE: EFFECTS OF CULTURAL PRESSURES

We classified the subjects in the longitudinal study (and an additional sample gathered from the school population in Florence) with respect to laterality, using a set of measures developed by Clark (1957) and described in the following, as strong or moderate right-dominant, ambidextrous, or strong or moderate left-dominant. Table 5-2 shows the prevalence of left-dominance in the four research centers. While these figures may reflect a genetic shift in Rome, further in the direction of right-dominance, it is slight. It should be noted that the prevalence of left-footedness (less likely to reflect cultural pressures than handedness) was identical (10%) in all three of the longitudinal samples of southern Italian origin, while it was 7% in Florence. Thus, while the groups of boys resident in Italy and in America seem to have been drawn from a genetically equivalent population with respect to laterality, the situation with respect to hand usage was very different. While all of the left-dominant Boston subjects used the left hand in writing, *not one* southern Italian subject was a left-handed writer, although we would have expected the same prevalence (10%) in both groups.

The problem of the effects of forced change was thus presented to us and our investigation of this issue has been reported in part in an earlier publication (Young & Knapp, 1966). Up to 1961 the entire population of Italian resident left-handers (of whom we discovered 48 boys in a total sample of 724) were obliged to convert to the right side. In America no opprobrium attaches to left-handedness, children are not required to "convert," and this quality is even often considered an advantage in various sports. The left-handed person in America suffers few penalties, if any. In Italy, traditionally, it was otherwise. Left-handedness was considered both a moral and personal defect and regarded with widespread suspicion. The term "sinister" means both "left" and "dangerous" in Italian. As a result of this, the left-handed in Italy were subject to a peculiar and frequently painful personal experience not shared by their American counterparts. We were drawn to explore possible differential effects upon their development in their differing circumstances.

Throughout recent western history there has been a distrust of left-handers, although there seems to have been no opprobrium attached to Leonardo da Vinci, a well-known representative. Perhaps as western society became more complex during the past 500 years, there was an accompanying distrust by the organizers

TABLE 5-2

City	Total N	Left Lateral Dominant	
		N	%
Boston	95	11	12
Rome	127	10	8
Palermo	108	11	10
Florence	489	27	6
Total	819	59	7

of society of the probability of holding it together as a working unit. In this way anomalies would be frowned upon and efforts made to convert the "renegades," as until quite recently western society tried to convert or "cure" homosexuals.

Prejudice against left-handers has been expressed in the words *sinister, awkward, clumsy, ill-omened, wicked.* More recently it has been shown that they are neither more clumsy, less intelligent, nor lower achievers (Clark, 1957; Ihinger, 1963, pp. 70–74). Among those with reading disability there is not, as has been supposed, a higher proportion of this minority (Belmont & Birch, 1965). Could they be more imaginative or original? As yet we have no evidence on this point. It is an overall impression that left lateral dominants do not differ from right-handers, at least in tolerant cultures. This is a contrast to evidence that ambilaterality may be associated with poor ego strength and more maladjustment (Palmer, 1963).

An amusing historical review of left-handedness has been written by Barsley (1966). Up to the mid-twenties of this century there were determined efforts in all western cultures to convert left-dominants to the use of the right side; attention was directed to the hand and not to the foot, although the two are highly correlated ($r = .79$). In 1969–1970 our research group examined a socially stratified sample of 1058 Arab Tunisian school boys aged from 11 to 16 years, by use of the methods later described, and found that 5.9% were left lateral dominant when the hand alone was considered but that this proportion increased to 10.2% when the foot was considered. Use of the right hand for writing and other activities has been strictly enforced in most Arab countries and thus the true left prevalence is possibly closer to 10%, the same proportion we found in our smaller sample in Sicily, just 200 km away.

This prevalence is supported by some objective methods applied to more than 7000 school children in California primary schools (Hardyck, Goldman, & Petrinovich, 1975), although the methodology was somewhat confused by the introduction of "eye dominance" rather than fields of vision. (The more recent paper in *Science* (Teng, Lee, Yang, & Chang, 1976) on the prevalance of left lateral dominance in Taiwan children may be criticized because of its reliance upon self-reports by the subjects and a less than adequate review of the literature.)

In order to assess basic lateral dominance (in contrast to hand usage for writing, eating, etc.) Clark's (1957) tests of laterality were employed in our study sample.

(*a*) *Handedness* was determined from three tests.   (1) Clark No. 18, Throwing—A small box was placed on a chair. The boy stood at about 2 yards distance with the ball on the table in front of him. He was requested to pick up the ball and to throw it into the box. (2) Clark No. 12, Reaching—The boy was seated with his arms hanging down. The tester stood behind him holding a cylinder over his head almost out of reach but in an equally favorable position for either side. The boy was asked to reach up and take the tube. (3) Clark No. 1, Manual rotation—Here a small screw-top bottle, filled with colored counters, was used. The task was to remove the top, take the counters, arrange them, put them back, and then replace the top. The task was performed on three occasions and note was made of which hand was used for manipulation of the top and the counters.

(*b*) *Foot* preference was based on three tasks. (1) Clark No. 5, Kicking—A rubber ball was placed 3 yards from a chair. The boy was asked to kick the ball between the legs of the chair. (2) Clark No. 17, Hopping—The boy stood with his back against the wall and his feet together. He was instructed on command to commence hopping to the far side of the room (3) Clark No. 8, Stepping—The boy stood with his back against the wall and his heels touching it. On the command, ''go,'' he was to take two steps out from the wall.

Each of the preceding tests was performed three times. Subjects were not informed that these were tests for lateral dominance and were left with the impression that the examiner was interested in motor skills and agility. Three tests for ear dominance and four for eye dominance were also performed, but these will not be reported here since eye and ear dimensions are not subject to coercive correction in Italy.

In order to adhere to Clark's findings as to the relative importance of these tests, a double weighting was accorded to throwing and kicking. Subjects were then classified as marked right (R2), moderate right (R1), ambidextrous (0), moderate left (L1), and marked left (L2). In each of the three longitudinal groups (Boston, Palermo, Rome) and in Florence, where a sample of boys of equivalent age, education, and social status was used, available left-handers were selected. A control group of right-handers, in every instance twice the number of left-handers, was selected from the remaining subjects in each city. In all three cities the right-handed control group was selected in such a fashion that their average Raven Progressive Matrix score (Raven, 1956; Young & Tesi, 1962b) was equated with that of the left-handed subjects. The subjects had all taken the High School Personality Questionnaire (Cattell & Beloff, 1957; Cattell, Beloff, & Coan, 1961).

The composite score for lateral dimensions for the hand and foot tests yielded a Pearson correlation of 0.79 among the boys included in this study. Table 5-3 gives the mean raw scores for each factor of the High School Personality Questionnaire for right- and left-handed boys in each center. Between right- and left-handers there are no significant differences in Boston. A significant difference on Factor A (Schizothymia vs Cyclothymia) for Palermo (left-handers are more schizothymic) is not sustained in Rome or Florence. A significant difference on Factor C (ego strength) for Palermo (left-handers have less ego strength) is not sustained in Rome or Florence. On Factor E (Submissiveness vs

TABLE 5-3

RAW FACTOR SCORES ON THE HSPQ FOR RIGHT AND LEFT HANDERS IN FOUR CITIES

City		N	A	B	C	D	E	F	G	H	I	J	O	Q^2	Q^3	Q^4
Boston	L	11	5.5	6.7	6.1	4.7	4.8	5.4	5.9	5.3	3.8	5.6	4.5	6.6	4.9	4.3
	R	22	5.8	6.6	5.2 NS	5.0	5.2	5.5	6.0	5.7	4.0	5.3	4.2	5.2 NS	5.0	4.1
Palermo	L	11	3.9	6.3	4.2	4.8	5.3	4.6	6.0	6.2	4.8	5.1	5.9	5.6	4.2	4.6
	R	22	4.9	6.4	5.8	4.1	4.5	6.2	6.1	6.2	3.4	5.2	4.9	6.0	4.5	4.9
			p=.05		p<.01			p<.02					p<.10 .05			
Rome	L	10	4.7	7.6	5.5	4.2	5.2	5.9	6.2	5.4	4.6	4.6	5.8	6.7	5.0	4.9
	R	20	5.2	6.7	5.8	4.5	4.7	5.6	6.4	6.1	3.3 p<.10 .05	4.9	5.3	6.6	5.0	4.8
Florence	L	27	5.4	8.4	5.3	4.3	4.2	5.6	5.9	5.4	4.1	5.2	5.8	6.4	4.8	5.0
	R	49	5.5	7.6	5.5	5.1	5.3 p<.01	5.4	5.5	5.2	3.0 p<.02	5.1	5.9	6.2	4.3	4.9

Dominance) the Florence left-handers are significantly more submissive, but there is a reverse trend (neither significant) in Palermo and Rome. On Factor F (Desurgency vs Surgency) the left-handed Palermo subjects are significantly less enthusiastic and happy-go-lucky, but this is not sustained in the other two Italian centers. Only on Factor I (Harria vs Premsia) is there a marked consistent trend in all three centers. The left-handers scored consistently more "premsic"; that is, more demanding, impatient, subjective, dependent, hypochondriacal. Thus only Factor I yields consistent differences in all three Italian cities between right- and left-handers. The differences on Factors A, C, and F observed in the Palermo sample are not sustained in the other two cities. There is reason to believe that the cultures of Sicily and southern Italy imposed greater penalties upon the left-handed child than those of central and, especially, of northern Italy. But we shall not attempt here to advance any conclusive explanation of the special findings applying to the Palermo sample.

An analysis of variance confirmed the overall significant association of left lateral dominance with a high score on Factor I (significant beyond the .001 level of confidence) among Italian subjects.

The interpretation of these findings is not entirely clear. It is tempting to attribute this difference to the forced conversion; but apart from such conversion there is still the relatively more hostile environment to assess.

It is our impression that since World War II much of the opprobrium associated with left-handedness has dissolved, at least among the upper social classes in Italy. On the other hand, it still remained until recently the practice to require left-handed children to convert in school to right-handedness in writing. Were opprobrium and not conversion the prime source of elevation on Factor I, we might expect this factor to be lower among subjects from higher social classes. This proves on inspection not to be the case, suggesting that the duress of faced conversion in school may be the primary determinant of our finding.

Factor I is regarded by Cattell as having an association with neuroticism but not with anxiety. There is evidence that it is associated with over-protective treatment in early childhood, and also of association with insecurity in the child (Cattell, 1965). Cattell considers this factor as being strongly affected by the environment. It is clear, in any event, that the personal qualities associated with this factor must be related to hypersensitivity and heightened self-preoccupation. It was striking that the separation of right- and left-handed subjects on Factor I, so incisive in Italy, was not confirmed in our sample of adolescents in Boston, where left-handers had not been forced to convert.

Clark (1957) has presented suggestive evidence that subjects who had been forcibly converted from left to right did less well on achievement tests than right-handers paired for intelligence. Sielicka, Bodganowicz, Dilling-Ostowska, Szelozynska, and Kaczenska (1963) have observed a high proportion of neurotic symptoms in 83 left-handed children who had been forcibly converted. It must be concluded that attention should be given to the psychological fate of left-handed children, especially in those cultures that, through opprobrium or forced conversion in school, force them to abandon their natural disposition or to face the disadvantage of social penalties.

The organization of social systems may not always be appropriate to human biology. It seems that more should be known about basic human needs and that social organization should be tailored to accommodate them, rather than the reverse—a situation in which a sizable biological minority has been oppressed by the social system.

SUMMARY

Longitudinal studies of American adolescents have demonstrated an association between earlier puberal maturing and more favorable personal attributes. Mussen and Young examined the cross-cultural generality of these findings using the data from the present study. They found early maturing related to more favorable self-concepts only among the Italian–American boys, and they argued that reaching maximal physical growth and sexual maturity at an early age does not confer the same social advantages in Italian as in American culture. More early- than late-maturing Italian and Italian–American adolescents expressed strong needs for autonomy and showed signs of resenting parental control—a reversal of the pattern previously found among American youth. Correlational data based on a more complete set of variables largely confirmed these conclusions, although none of the associations was very strong. Boston subjects who were larger and more mature sexually at age 14 were also more intellectually effective, self-confident, and assertive. Fatter subjects in this group appeared more passive, especially in relation to the family, and expressed more negative feelings toward peers. Early maturing Roman adolescents scored higher in fantasy dominance, were cognitively less field-dependent, although not generally more intelligent, showed more resentment of paternal authority, and indeed tended to move away from home earlier. In Palermo, early-maturing adolescents who were large and strong physically tended to be less successful academically than later maturers. Fatness among Italian adolescents appeared to be associated with parental indulgence and did not seem to have the same negative social connotations as among American teenagers.

Lateral dominance is another area in which cultural standards may interact with physical predispositions. Much stronger traditional sanctions in southern Italy against the use of the left hand were manifested among our subjects; *all* of the southern Italian boys used the right hand in writing, although the prevalence of left lateral dominance, as assessed by a number of measures, was the same (about 10%) in all three groups. (Most of the Italian–American boys who were basically left-handed also wrote with the left hand as did two who were basically right-handed.) The possibly stressful effects of the forced conversion experienced by the Italian left-handers were evident in higher scores on HSPQ scales indicative of neuroticism.

PART III

Outcomes in Early Maturity

CHAPTER 6

Attainments, Personal and Social Adjustments

The bulk of our information on the family life of our subjects and their socialization experiences was gathered in 1957 to 1959, when they were just entering adolescence. Most of the data on cognitive functioning and on social and emotional development dates from this same period of the study. Physical examinations continued for each subject until his growth was complete—the final examination occurring between 18 and 23 years of age. Since that time no systematic data on growth or health have been collected. A number of social scientists have, however, visited the project in more recent years (since 1965). They were interested in comparing our three groups of subjects, by then well into their twenties, with respect to their personal, educational, and vocational attainments, emerging patterns of adjustment and orientation to life, values and personal philosophies. Thus we can begin to discern some differences between our Italian and Italian-American young men in early maturity in ways of coping with social realities and the consolidation of personal identity, as well as many similarities among them. These more recent data also provide us with a number of rich possibilities, unique in the literature of longitudinal research, of gaining a cross-cultural perspective on the relations between socialization and psychological functioning in early adolescence and individual outcomes in early maturity.

PERCEIVED OPPORTUNITY, ALIENATION, AND
DRINKING BEHAVIOR

In 1966, Richard Jessor took advantage of a stay in Florence to extend his previous work on the personal and ethnic determinants of patterns of alcohol usage. Lolli (1958) had observed that in Italian culture no emphasis is placed on any "psychological" or "escape-providing" qualities of wine. Rather wine is considered a regular part of the diet, and while alcohol consumption (almost invariably in the form of wine) may have some ceremonial significance and may be associated with hospitality and the occasions of family life, it is not institutionalized in Italian culture as a way of providing relief from personal stress or release from normal cultural restrictions.

The study of Jessor, Young, Young, & Tesi (1970) represented "an effort to examine empirically the differential consequences of Italian and American socialization and institutionalization of the use of alcohol [p. 216]." He hypothesized that the Italian–American group of young men would be closer to the typical American patterns of alcohol usage than the Italian groups, and would show a significant relationship between drinking behavior and aspects of personality reflecting frustration, failure of goal attainment, and the expectation of limited future opportunity. The findings of this study have been reported in more detail elsewhere (Jessor *et al.*, 1970); they will be summarized here, and we will go on to examine the relations of the personality measures developed and collected by Jessor to some of our other data on differential socialization and psychological development.

The information was collected by means of a questionnaire designed by Jessor and carefully pretested after translation and backtranslation to ensure comparability of the American and Italian versions. The questionnaire was mailed out to all three groups of subjects (on the average, 21 years of age at this time) and returned by 83% in Boston, 81% in Rome, and 91% in Palermo; these percentages are high enough to merit some confidence in the representativeness of the data. A check of the SES of respondents as compared to nonrespondents revealed no differences. The questionnaire contained a variety of questions about the learning and context of drinking as well as a number of other measures relevant to the main hypothesis. Three key measures of personality attributes were included. The first of these was a 17-item measure of *expectations of goal attainment* (perceived opportunity) in a variety of need areas (such as affection and achievement), and in a variety of life areas (such as family, work, and friendships). The second was a 13-item Likert-type measure of *alienation* patterned after the Srole scale and emphasizing feelings of social isolation and lack of meaning in daily role activities. The third personality measure was a 12-item forced-choice scale assessing the degree to which a subject felt he had *internal control* over his future and over the outcomes of his behavior. The main measures of drinking behavior were two: a *quantity-frequency* measure of intake, based on the average quantity (ounces) of absolute alcohol consumed per day; and a measure of the reported frequency of occasions of *drunkenness* during the preceding year. All of these or related measures are described in greater detail elsewhere (Jessor, Graves, Hanson, & Jessor, 1968).

An additional focus of the questionnaire was on the meanings or psychological functions attributed by the subjects to their own use of alcohol.

The resulting descriptions of the socialization of our subjects' drinking behavior reveal that the Italian samples, as expected, had wine most frequently for their first drink, more than twice as often as the Boston sample (Boston = 29%, Rome = 75%, Palermo = 64%); for the Boston sample, beer was the most frequent beverage for the first drink (Boston = 56%, Rome = 6%, Palermo = 15%). For the Italian samples, parents or family were present at the first drink in a significantly larger proportion of the cases than for the Boston sample (Boston = 56%, Rome = 88%, Palermo = 78%; x^2 = 21.59, $p < .001$). The Italian samples also began more or less regular drinking at a significantly younger age than the Boston sample (Boston = 17.7, Rome = 14.9, Palermo 14.7; $p < .01$). These data tend to corroborate the apparent differential institutionalization of drinking in Italian and American culture.

Turning to the drinking measures of immediate concern to this study—the quantity–frequency index of alcohol intake, and the frequency of reported drunkenness in the past year—the data show, as expected, that both Italian samples had a significantly higher intake of wine than the Boston sample (Boston wine quantity–frequency was .17; Rome wine quantity–frequency, .84; Palermo wine quantity–frequency, .72; $p < .01$). However, with respect to *overall* alcohol intake, that is, a quantity–frequency index based on beer, wine, and liquor together, there is no difference between the groups, overall quantity–frequency indexes being similar in Boston, Rome, and Palermo (Boston overall quantity–frequency was 1.2; Rome overall quantity–frequency, 1.4; Palermo overall quantity–frequency, 1.4; NS).

Despite this similarity in overall intake, there is a marked difference in frequency of reported drunkenness between Boston and the two Italian samples. Fifty-two percent of the Rome drinkers and 58% of the Palermo drinkers reported *no* occasions of being "drunk or pretty high" in the last year; only 24% of the Boston sample could say the same thing. On the other hand, 30% of the Boston drinkers reported having been drunk four or more times during the preceding year, whereas only 9% of the Rome youth and 10% of the Palermo youth could say the same thing. The difference in the distribution of drunkenness frequencies between the Boston and the Italian samples is highly significant (x^2 = 24.39, $p < .001$), with more frequent drunkenness in the American sample.

These differences in drunkenness are also to be expected as a function of the differential institutionalization of drinking, and the present findings are entirely consistent with previous studies of Italian drinking (Lolli, 1958) and with the similar analysis of the role and context of drinking among Jews (Snyder, 1958). Additional data in the present study with respect to the occurrence of physical upsets associated with the use of alcohol, for example, headaches, nausea, stomach upset are also consistent with the drunkenness differences between Americans and Italians. Significantly more frequent physical upsets were reported in the Boston sample than in either of the two Italian samples ($x^2 = 9.82$, $p < .01$).

In each of the three samples, the personality measures included in the Jessor questionnaire evidenced similar psychometric properties, suggesting that they were being responded to by the three samples in a similar way. The expectations measure showed good internal consistency (Scott's homogeneity ratio) and reliability (Cronbach's alpha) in each of the samples; homogeneity and reliability were lower but still adequate for the alienation measure; they were lower than desirable for the measure of internal control. In each sample the product-moment correlation between expectations and alienation was strongest ($-.51$, Boston; $-.49$, Rome; $-.37$, Palermo), followed by the correlation between expectations and internal control ($.30$, Boston; $.38$, Rome; $.28$, Palermo), and then by the correlation between alienation and internal control ($-.20$, Boston; $-.17$, Rome; $-.11$, Palermo). The magnitude of these correlations indicates adequate independence among these three measures; the direction of the correlations supports the validity of the measures.

The data in Table 6-1 indicate that the Boston sample had significantly *higher* expectations for goal attainment than either the Rome or Palermo groups, the latter being identical in mean scores. The Boston youth were also *less* alienated than either of the Italian samples, although the difference is short of statistical significance in regard to Rome. Finally, the Boston subjects scored significantly *higher* on internal control than both the Rome and Palermo subjects. In general, then, the personality data show the Boston youth to have been experiencing less frustration or dissatisfaction than the Italian youth; the scores of the two Italian samples were similar, with the exception that the Palermo subjects expressed significantly greater alienation than did those in Rome. This finding is in line with the observations of many writers on southern Italian culture who emphasize the fatalism and lack of confidence in the individual's own ability to control the environment. We shall see this finding echoed in our next two chapters on differences in values, personal philosophy, and political attitudes.

With respect to the main hypothesis of the Jessor study, the findings confirm the expectation that the personality measures would relate to drinking behavior specifically in Boston and not among the Italian subjects. In Boston, the quantity–frequency measure of drinking was found to correlate $-.27$ with expectations of future goal attainment and $-.45$ with internal control, while reports of drunkenness correlate positively ($.25$) with alienation, all significant at the .05

TABLE 6-1

MEAN SCORES ON PERSONALITY ATTRIBUTES

Attribute	Boston (n=79)	Rome (n=94)	Palermo (n=108)	p-values		
				B vs. R	B vs. P	R vs. P
Expectations	51.0	46.3	46.3	<.01	<.01	NS
Alienation	27.9	29.1	31.0	.10	<.01	<.01
Internal Control	18.4	15.4	15.2	<.01	<.01	NS

level or better. In Rome and Palermo, most correlations between drinking behavior and the personality variables are close to zero. There is a slight *positive* correlation between expectations of future goal attainment and quantity-frequency (.22 in Rome, significant at the .05 level), suggesting that alcohol consumption in the Italian culture may be associated with a more optimistic outlook on life rather than with frustration, as in the American culture. As further support for the notion that alcohol usage is related to personal frustration and is a means of relieving stress among the Boston subjects, Jessor examined the associations of the personality variables on the one hand and alcohol usage on the other with a measure of the "personal effects functions" of alcohol. This was derived from a 10-item scale asking the subject to report the extent to which he used alcohol for reasons such as "to get my mind off failures," "helps you forget you're not the kind of person you'd like to be," or "makes the future seem brighter." Only in Boston did this measure of personal effects yield significant correlations in the expected directions with both personality measures and alcohol usage measures, thus supporting the hypothesis that the linkage between alcohol usage and personal frustration in American culture is mediated by the psychophysiological effects attributed to alcohol. There are no correlations among the Roman subjects significantly different from zero, and in Palermo personal effects functions are somewhat positively associated with alcohol usage but show no association with the personality measures. Thus while southern Italian young men show evidences of being significantly more frustrated and alienated than their American and even their northern Italian counterparts, they show no inclination to relieve these feelings through increased alcohol usage. On the other hand, there is strong evidence that two or three generations of residence in Boston have had the effect of shifting the Italian–American young men in a direction that diverges from the more benign Italian pattern of alcohol usage in the direction of more typical American patterns, in which alcohol is used as a drug to seek relief from stress and to escape from personal frustrations.

It is also possible for us to examine the associations between the personality measures collected by Jessor and the current life status of our subjects and their earlier socialization histories and personal dispositions. The somewhat different patterns of relationships that emerge for the three groups are of some interest. In Boston, internal locus of control and the associated measure of future time perspective are positively correlated with indices of achievement motivation. Future time perspective in Boston is also associated with earlier parental demands for maturity (less indulgent early socialization) while internal control is associated with lower creativity. In Rome, on the other hand, both of these variables and also expectations of future goal attainment seem to be associated with a pattern suggestive of "middle-class morality." They are significantly positively correlated with paternal income and occupational status, the status of the boy's own choice in early adolescence of future occupation, positively correlated with the Raven but negatively with performance on the digits test and some measures of creativity. They are positively correlated with a number of indices of morality and responsibility and quite highly negatively correlated with aggressive fantasies as expressed in the Imagination test (r's are .42 for future time perspective, .33 for internal control, and −.34 for expectations of future goal attainment). Thus there is some evidence of association of these variables as measured in early maturity with earlier suppression of aggression and conscience development in the Roman group. In Palermo, internal locus of control also seems to be associated with lower aggression fantasy, but rather than being associated with responsibility and morality seems to be a reflection of a family pattern in which the mother is the primary source of affection and discipline. Boys higher on these variables tended to be rated by the interviewers as less logical and resourceful when they were adolescents. We have seen that future time perspective and positive expectations of goal attainment tend to be less characteristic of the young men in Palermo, and when they do occur may reflect a less realistic orientation. Feelings of alienation, generally more prevalent in Palermo, are associated with feeling more intelligent than others, but with lower achievement motivation and a somewhat lower family income. In Boston, feelings of alienation may be a reflection of frustration, since they correlate −.32 with status of occupation among those subjects who are employed rather than still in school, but they are also associated with lower creativity scores and with a number of HSPQ variables suggestive of a generally pessimistic and somewhat schizoid personality orientation. In Rome, on the other hand, feelings of alienation correlate *positively* (.39) with status of subject's current occupation and of father's occupation (measured earlier), with indices of conscience and social responsibility, and with higher need Succorance as well as lower need Aggression in the Imagination Test. This suggests a much more socially integrated pattern than the correlates for the Boston subjects, although we do find the same association with lower creativity. We should not attempt any definitive conclusions from these scattered correlational findings, but they do once again suggest the rather different meanings and antecedents that such self-report measures of personality dispositions may have in different cultural contexts. Certainly it is considered much more socially acceptable and much more realistic in Italy than in America to express feelings of cynicism about one's relation to authority and to society at large, and about one's future prospects and certainly in the south fatalistic attitudes are the norm. We shall see very similar trends when we consider political attitudes in a later section.

PERSONAL CIRCUMSTANCES IN EARLY MATURITY

The year following the Jessor study, the project staff decided to collect information from as many of the subjects as possible about their current life circumstances and personal attainments. At the same time we also asked them to complete the California Personality Inventory, as described in the next section. A brief personal questionnaire, inquiring about marital status and plans, current living situation and amount of contact with relatives, years of school completed and future educational plans, occupational status and plans, relations with friends, participation in sports and other interests, was mailed out to all subjects in late 1967, with a follow-up letter in the summer of 1968. Most subjects returned the questionnaire in early 1968, when the average age of the group was 23. Rates of return were 68% in Boston, 65% in Rome, and 64% in Palermo. While somewhat lower than would have been desirable, the rates of response are at least comparable in the three locations, and no significant selective biases were evident when these subjects were compared to the total sample.

Education

There was a tendency for a few of the Italian boys to have dropped out of school very early, whereas all of the Boston subjects completed at least 8 years. Only half of the Boston subjects continued beyond 12 years, whereas 72% in Rome and 87% in Palermo did. However, only 42% in Rome and 45% in Palermo continued beyond 14 years, so the main difference here may be attributed to the structure of the two school systems and the number of years required to complete secondary school. Somewhat more of the Italian boys (85% vs 64% in Boston) planned to get a university degree, but at this point very similar percentages in the three cities had completed more than 16 years of school (about 8%). In general, except for the small proportion of early dropouts, education continued longer for the Italian boys, but about the same proportion of the Italian and the American subjects were obtaining a college education.

Given the similarity of overall educational attainment in the three groups, it is of some interest to examine the correlates of number of years of schooling for the three groups of young men. Among the Roman subjects, the amount of schooling completed shows a modest degree of association with indices of the parents' socioeconomic status and with achievement motivation. It is also associated with frequent visits to relatives currently, with earlier indices of family cohesiveness and of a positive relation between the boy and his mother, and with slightly higher need for affiliation. There are fewer significant correlations in Palermo, but they point in the same direction—the boy who continues longer in school is likely still to be a member of a warm and supportive as well as a somewhat higher status family system. In Boston, on the other hand, greater amounts of schooling would seem to be a function of more personal aspirations and achievement strivings and more closely associated with occupational goals. Years of school completed correlates .48 with status of occupation, for those of our subjects who are already working, and there are also significant correlations with both the boy's and the parents' reports of vocational aspirations in adolescence. There are also positive correlations with measures of achievement motivation and of intellectual performance—the Raven, the Gottschaldt, and one of the creativity measures. There is also a significant negative correlation ($-.38$) with parents' pressure for academic performance when the boy was an adolescent. These findings would seem to be in line with the American ethos, which views advanced education as a route to be followed by the individual in pursuit of a higher status occupation and general social mobility. The boys who continued longer in school gave evidence in early adolescence of such internalized aspirations and the intellectual resources to achieve them. Continued education in Italy is not nearly so clearly linked to vocation aspirations nor to internalized achievement motivation, and may be related to a continued comfortable dependence on the family.

Work

Many more of the Boston respondents had worked (50 versus only 28 in Rome and 15 in Palermo), and they also reported having held more jobs. The majority of the Italian subjects who had worked had only one job, whereas 71% in Boston had at least two, and 19% had four or more. The jobs of the Italian subjects who were working tended to be of higher status. Sixty-four percent in Palermo, 53% in Rome, and only 40% in Boston had jobs coded 7 (clerical or technical) or above on the occupation scale. However, the Boston subjects were earning much more: 44% of them made over $500 a month, whereas only 19% did in Rome, and none in Palermo. In mentioning aspects of their jobs they liked and disliked, the Boston subjects were somewhat more likely to mention relations with others. The Italian subjects were more likely to mention the conditions of the work, whereas the Boston subjects were more likely, paradoxically, to express dissatisfaction with salary. The subjects in Palermo were much more likely than the other groups to say they like the general purpose of their work; only in Boston was this mentioned as a source of dissatisfaction.

Among those respondents who were employed in Boston, status of occupation was related, as we have seen, to the amount of school completed and also quite highly correlated with the vocational aspirations expressed by the parents when the boys were early adolescents and with less restrictive parental attitudes, particularly about sexual behavior. There are also modest correlations with indices of the boy's own achievement motivation and intelligence, but significant correlations with fantasies of nurturance in the Imagination Test, with external rather than internal locus of control and with excitability (D−) in the HSPQ. A rather different set of correlates is manifest among the Roman respondents who are employed. Here status of occupation is highly positively correlated (.49) with internal locus of control, with expectations of future goal attainment (.36), but also with alienation (.39). It is also associated with earlier scores on the HSPQ (factors C and E), indicative of dominance and ego strength. There are also correlations of lesser magnitude with earlier interviewer ratings suggesting assertiveness and practical ability, with lower fantasies of nurturance, and the young men with higher status occupations are slightly more likely to be living away from parents and to plan to marry soon, altogether a much more independent orientation than seems to be associated in Boston with early occupational success. Among the very few young men in Palermo who were employed at this time, the correlates of occupational status are different again—it is *negatively* correlated with all of the indices of the family's socioeconomic status, is slightly associated with achievement fantasies in adolescence. Occupational status is associated with higher expectations of future goal attainment (.40), with less current sociability (−.40) with frequency of meeting friends, a somewhat schizoid orientation in adolescence (.45 with HSPQ factor A), and with higher creativity (.39 with alternate uses). Thus for a young man in his early twenties in Palermo to achieve relatively high occupational status may imply a highly independent turn of mind and a sharp break with his family's social and economic position—probably a fairly rare event in the economically depressed and traditional South.

Interests

The Rome subjects reported much more active participation in sports than the other two groups; this is a continuation of the pattern noted when they were adolescents and is closely associated with the subject reporting that he has no plans to marry. However, the Boston subjects were more likely to mention sports as an interest. The Italian subjects reported they read more than did the American boys (a reversal of the pattern noted for their parents), but this may be because more of them were still in school. Both Boston and Rome reported more passive patterns of interests (reading, movies, etc.), as was noted when they were younger. On the whole, however, except for the amount of reading reported, the patterns of interests in the three groups were overall pretty similar.

Family Relations

The most striking difference between the Italian and American subjects was in the rate of marriage. Of those responding (65 in Boston, 82 in Rome, and 72 in Palermo), 19 in Boston were married and none was in either of the two Italian groups. Another 19 in Boston planned to marry within the next 2 years, whereas 84% of the Italian subjects had no plans to marry. The Boston respondents who stated that they did *not* plan to marry soon gave evidences in adolescence of greater self-confidence and intellectual effectiveness (correlations of .43 with HSPQ factor B, and of .41 with one of the creativity measures, for instance) and also had slightly higher scores on a measure of "amoral familism" (see Chapter 7). The same association with creativity appears among the Roman respondents, among whom a lack of any immediate thoughts of marriage is closely associated with continuing to live with parents. Later marriage, as many observers have noted, is the norm among Italian men, especially in the South. Where this pattern seemed to persist among our Boston subjects, it may have been to some extent a reflection of adherence to traditional family values, but seemed much more clearly a reflection of individual characteristics of self-confidence and originality.

Fewer of the Boston subjects lived with their parents (65% vs 85% in Rome, and 90% in Palermo). Not surprisingly, they saw them somewhat less often, although the percentages of subjects who saw their parents every day were about the same. It is the Rome group, however, who saw other relatives the least often. Only 25% in Rome visited relatives as often as once a month, as against 50% in Boston and 55% in Palermo. As we noted in Chapter 2, the Boston group has retained the pattern of frequent contact with the extended family to a greater extent than the Rome group, many of whose relatives still live in the South and thus can be visited less frequently; these differences seem to be persisting among our subjects at least into their early adult years.

Among the Boston subjects, living away from parents and infrequent visits to relatives tend to be associated with higher vocational aspirations expressed by the parents when the boys were early adolescents, a more cohesive nuclear family at that time, more nurturance expressed in fantasy, lower academic pressure, higher intelligence, lower anxiety (correlations of −.32 and −.34 with the DMAS), and more social independence. These associations do not appear for the Italian young men, for whom living at home remains the norm. Apparently early separation from parents is a reflection of the value placed on autonomy as an indication of personal effectiveness in the American culture.

Friendships

In contrast to the marked differences in sociability in early adolescence, there was now no significant difference in reported friendships. The Boston subjects still showed a slight tendency to report a greater number of close friends, but they indicated that they met them less often than did the Italians—perhaps some indication that the friendships in Boston were a bit less intense. The Boston subjects who report a large number of friends and meeting them often tend to have slightly higher achievement motivation, but lower scores on the measures of internal control and expectations of future goal attainment. Not surprisingly they also have lower scores on alienation. They tend to come from families characterized when they were adolescents by high control but low affection and large numbers of siblings. Perhaps a very gregarious pattern in one's early twenties represents, among the Italian–American young men, an escape from an overly restrictive and crowded home, and an orientation toward immediate gratification. No such pattern appears for the Italian subjects, although there are slight indications that spending much time with friends may be related to strained family relations, especially with the mother. Thus while reported patterns of friendship may not differ a great deal between Boston and the Italian cities, as they did earlier when all of the subjects were schoolboys and under parental supervision, their meaning may still differ considerably, with friendship in Boston representing to some extent a mode of self-enhancement as well as a source of personal intimacy.

PERSONALITY PATTERNS

In addition to obtaining information about the life circumstances of our three groups of subjects in early maturity, we wished to gain a comparative picture of patterns of personality. While retesting with the Cattell questionnaire used when the subjects were adolescents might have been desirable from the point of view of obtaining comparable longitudinal data, neither that instrument nor others available from Cattell's laboratory seemed truly suitable at this point in the study. On the other hand, the California Personality Inventory (CPI) developed by Harrison Gough had in the meantime been applied in a number of cross-cultural studies including Italian groups (e.g., Gough 1964, 1966a,b) and had yielded interesting comparative findings. We thus had considerable assurance of the applicability of this instrument in both its American and Italian versions to our study population. A number of interesting analyses have also emerged from the Berkeley longitudinal studies relating patterns of the CPI in adulthood to earlier data on adolescent personality and socialization experiences (see Block, 1971). We had some interest in attempting a cross-cultural replication of some of these longitudinal analyses. Thus the CPI appeared the self-report instrument of choice at this stage of the study. It was mailed out to the subjects along with the brief personal questionnaire, and usable returns were obtained from 41 subjects in Boston, 40 in Rome, and 51 in Palermo. While these rates of return are too low to ensure representativeness of our original samples, the results may still be of some interest and will be reported briefly here.

The composite CPI profiles for the three groups are on the whole very similar, with all of the mean scores falling within a decile of the means for the standardization groups. This similarity of profiles tends to dispel the notion of any dramatic differences in personality types between our three groups, or between our Italian and Italian–American subjects as a whole and the relevant reference groups of American young male adults. A more detailed comparison of the respondents from our three study groups did yield significant differences in mean scores on five out of the eighteen CPI scales. These scales were Social Presence, Self-Control, Achievement through Conformity, Achievement through Independence, and Flexibility. In all cases the mean score for the Boston group was significantly higher than the means for both of the Italian groups; t's for the comparisons for the first two scales were significant at the .05 level and for the latter three at the .01 level. There were no significant differences between the two Italian groups. These findings reinforce the impression we have gained from our earlier data that the Italian–American group is characterized by higher achievement motivation, and suggest that they may also be more flexible, more self-controlled, and more socially poised than their Italian counterparts. The Italian–American group, in their early twenties, may appear more socially mature, more ambitious, and a bit less tied to traditional values.

We next turned to a consideration of possible differences (as well as similarities) between our groups in the socialization antecedents of personality characteristics in early maturity as measured by the CPI. We note first that the family's socioeconomic status is unrelated to any of the CPI scales among the Boston subjects, while among both groups of Italian subjects higher SES is related to greater sense of well-being, self-control, tolerance, achievement through independence, intellectual efficiency, and psychological mindedness Thus we see a closer association among our Italian subjects between socioeconomic origins and personality characteristics, especially those that would appear to be related to intellectual functioning. The affective quality of the boy's relations with parents in adolescence, as judged by the social workers who interviewed the families, seems to predict a number of personality characteristics in common in all three groups, although it would seem that the relationship with the mother was more important for the Boston subjects, while that with the father was more influential for the Italian subjects. In Boston positive relationship with parents, especially the mother, is predictive of higher scores on sociability, self-acceptance, sense of well-being, socialization, communality, and intellectual efficiency. In Rome, a positive relationship with the father is predictive of a higher sense of well-being and socialization but lower flexibility, while overall affection received from the family predicts higher scores on both socialization and responsibility. Similarly in Palermo, affection from family predicts higher socialization, while a positive relationship with the father predicts higher socialization, self-control, and femininity. Thus positive family relationships seem to be predictive of a more conforming pattern among the Italian subjects when they reach early maturity. The pattern of indulgent early socialization, which we found to be more characteristic of the Italian than the Boston parents, predicts lower self-acceptance in both Boston and Rome, lower communality but higher responsibility, self-control, good impression, and flexibility in Boston and lower psychological mindedness in Palermo.

Freedom of expression, which we also found to be more characteristic of the Boston families, predicts achievement through independence, psychological mindedness, and flexibility among the Boston subjects. Two of these three scales were also found to differentiate the Boston group in early maturity from the Italian samples, so that we have some evidence of the connection between differences in family life and later personality dispositions. Among the Roman subjects, high self-expression in the family predicts dominance, sociability, and self-acceptance, while in Palermo this socialization variable predicts only communality, a finding easily attributable to chance. The general socialization dimension of control versus permissiveness seems also to have somewhat different implications for the Italian and the Italian–American subjects. In Boston, higher scores on parental control predict greater dominance and sociability. In Rome, the relationships are in the opposite direction, with more controlling parental attitudes also predicting lower self-acceptance and femininity but higher self-control and good impression, whereas in Palermo high parental control predicts low responsibility and low intellectual efficiency. Restrictive attitudes toward sexual behavior, which were also much more characteristic of the Italian parents, are associated with low social presence and intellectual efficiency in Palermo, and in Rome with low self-control, low intellectual efficiency and psychological mindedness, low achievement through conformity but higher self-acceptance. It would seem, then, that the more restrictive attitudes of the Italian parents when their sons are adolescents, particularly with respect to overt expressions of sexual impulses, may be associated with generally more conforming personality dispositions and with suppression of intellectual curiosity, as psychoanalytic theory would suggest.

For the Boston group, parental intervention in peer relations (which generally implies encouragement of sociability) seems to have been associated with many positive characteristics on the CPI: dominance, capacity for status, sociability, social presence, self-acceptance, sense of well-being, responsibility, good impression, communality, achievement through conformity, and intellectual efficiency. The few correlations that do appear for the Italian subjects are generally in the opposite direction, with parental intervention in peer relations being associated with lower scores on achievement through independence, intellectual efficiency, and flexibility for the Roman group. This is a further illustration of the differential importance of peer relations for the Italian–American group.

It is difficult to arrive at any definitive conclusions from these correlations, and we should remember that less than half of our original subject group contributed to these data. They do suggest, however, that differential patterns of socialization are the relevant antecedents to personality characteristics that differentiate young men of Italian origin who have grown up in Boston from young Italians. Also, as we have suggested in several other places, certain dimensions of family relations or child-rearing attitudes (e.g., indulgence or suppression of sexuality) may have different implications in different cultural contexts.

These CPI data and the information available on parental socialization practices and family relations when our subjects were early adolescents suggested the possibility of a partial replication of a study by Block, von der Lippe, and Block (1973). (We are grateful to Jack and Jeanne Block, who were visiting the project in 1973, for suggesting this possibility and facilitating the necessary data analysis.) In their paper, based on data from the Berkeley longitudinal studies, Block *et al.* (1973) have distinguished four types of sex-role orientations, characterized by different combinations of scores on the CPI Femininity and Socialization scales. (They applied this analysis to the sexual identifications of both males and females; our data involve only males, of course.) Among the Berkeley male subjects whose CPI scores would characterize them as High Masculine, those with high scores on the Socialization scale were characterized as competent, self-confident, and optimistic, and as coming from homes where parents were generally supportive but nonintrusive and the father was available to and accepting of his son. The High Masculine, Low Socialized group, on the other hand, showed a self-centered, irresponsible, and exploitive "machismo" orientation. They tended to come from homes where the father was weak and rejecting, providing an ineffectual masculine model, and where the mother was dissatisfied and probably seductive toward the son. The Low Masculine, High Socialized males presented the opposite picture from the preceding group, being productive and conscientious but overcontrolled and conventional. These subjects had experienced positive relations with both parents, who seemed to have been comfortable with themselves and each other and to have presented models of social responsibility and control of impulse in favor of long-range goals. The Low Masculine, Low Socialized group, on the other hand, presented a generally neurotic and ineffectual personality picture and came from families where both parents seemed to have been similarly ineffective and conflict-ridden.

We applied the same criteria as those used by Block *et al.* to define four groups among our CPI respondents as a whole, and then examined the parental attributes and socialization attitudes characterizing each of these four types as compared to the rest of the group. These comparisons were made for the total group of respondents and also for the sample from each of the three cities separately. These latter sets of comparisons are based, of course, on very small numbers of subjects, but may still hold some interest for their cross-cultural implications. The socialization variables found to be differentially characteristic of each of the four sex-role types are as follows:

High Socialized, High Masculine (SO 34 or more, FE 17 or less)
Total group (30 vs 102 subjects): Mother more educated, better relationship with father, more encouragement of aggression.
Boston (11 vs 30 subjects): Earlier maturity demands (less indulgent socialization), more encouragement of aggression, higher family income.
Rome (8 vs 32 subjects): Higher control, higher achievement pressure.
Palermo (11 vs 40 subjects): More intervention in peer relations, lower achievement pressure, higher SES.

Low Socialized, High Masculine (SO 33 or less, FE 17 or less)
Total group (40 vs 92 subjects): Higher intervention in peer relations, lower SES, poorer relationship with father, seen by parents as less truthful.
Boston (13 vs 28 subjects): More permissive with respect to sexuality.
Rome (12 vs 28 subjects): Less permissive with respect to sexuality, more intervention in peer relations, lower affection from family, later in birth order and lower SES.
Palermo (15 vs 36 subjects): Higher achievement pressure, poor relation with father, lower income.

High Socialized, Low Masculine (SO 34 or more, FE 18 or more)
Total group (36 vs 96 subjects): A tendency toward more indulgent socialization, higher affection from family, perceived by parents as truthful, less encouragement of aggression.
Boston (11 vs 30 subjects): More indulgent early socialization and less encouragement of aggression.
Rome (12 vs 28 subjects): No variables significant.
Palermo (13 vs 38 subjects): Less intervention in peer relations, seen by parents as truthful.

Low Socialized, Low Masculine (SO 33 or less, FE 18 or more)
Total group (26 vs 106 subjects): A tendency toward later birth order.
Boston (6 vs 35 subjects): Higher freedom of expression, poor relation with father.
Rome (8 vs 32 subjects): More encouragement of aggression, later birth order.
Palermo (12 vs 39 subjects): Lower education of both parents.

While these findings are much sparser than those available to the Berkeley group, they do tend to confirm their conclusions of rather different patterns of parental relations characterizing high masculine subjects who are also high in sense of social responsibility, as compared to the high-masculine–low-socialized ("machismo") group. The former tend to come from higher SES families and to have had more positive relations with their fathers. In Boston, but not among the Italian subjects, well-socialized masculinity is also associated with parental encouragement of appropriate aggression toward peers. This finding seems supportive of our earlier conclusion that the Boston families had been influenced by the emphasis in American culture on self-assertive aggression as a necessary component of appropriate masculine sex-typing. Except for the Palermo group, the subjects who fall into this type also conform to the Block *et al.* finding that they would be likely to have experienced greater demands for maturity and responsibility.

By contrast, the subjects who fall into the "machismo" type tend to come from lower SES families, and like those in the Block *et al.* study have generally experienced poor relations with their fathers, and less affectionate and probably more conflictful family relations in general. One interesting cross-cultural reversal emerges in our data: while "machismo" in Boston is associated with greater parental permissiveness of sexual behavior, in Rome it is associated with more restrictive parental attitudes toward sexuality and more intervention in peer relations, and thus may carry the connotation of late-adolescent rebellion against parentl restrictions.

Our findings for the two low masculine groups are sparser and less supportive of those of Block *et al.*, except for the tendency for low-socialization–low-masculinity to be associated with a poor relation with the father among the Boston group. High socialization and low masculinity, especially among the Italian–American subjects, seems to be associated with an indulgent and affectionate pattern of family relations, with less encouragement of aggression than for the high masculine group, but without the emphasis on self-control and conformity found by Block *et al.* Overall these findings do support the usefulness of the distinction between more and less highly socialized types of masculine gender role development, and the importance of a positive relation with the father for masculine sex-typing.

SUMMARY

In this and in the following two chapters we report on information gathered between 1965 and 1968, when our subjects were entering their twenties; thus we have some picture of differences among the three groups in early maturity. The Boston subjects were much more likely to report that they were married and living away from home, though this was still only a minority in this group; *none* of the Italian young men was yet married in 1968 and 85–90% still lived at home. However, the pattern of more frequent contact with relatives, in Boston as well as in Palermo as compared to Rome, continued into the early adult years; the Italian–American young men seemed almost as involved with extended family as their Sicilian counterparts. More of the young men in Boston reported extensive work histories, and for our Italian–American subjects both job status and educational achievement beyond high school seemed an expression of more individual, internalized goals and aspirations rather than being a function of family economic status and continued support, as in the Italian South. A slightly greater number of boys in Palermo had dropped out of school early to go to work but a higher proportion of Italian subjects planned to obtain a university degree. In other respects, the three groups reported remarkably similar patterns of interests and social life, and there was less of the emphasis on having many friends which had characterized the American group in early adolescence.

Data on alcohol usage collected by Jessor indicated that the Boston sample had diverged from both the Italian groups in the direction of more typically American drinking patterns; beginning to drink 3 years later, on the average, and much more frequently outside rather than at home; substituting beer for wine as the alcoholic beverage most frequently consumed; reporting much more frequent drunkenness. Only in Boston did drinking behavior seem to be an expression of personal frustration and alienation, as assessed by a personality inventory.

The Jessor scales administered in 1966 indicated that the Italian–American subjects had significantly higher expectations of goal attainment, more internal locus of control, and felt less alienated than their Italian compeers. Responses to the California Personality Inventory from smaller subsamples of the three groups in 1968 confirm these findings. While the three groups generally have remarkably similar and "normal" profiles, the Italian–American subjects tended to score higher on scales measuring achievement motivation, social poise, self-control, and flexibility. Socialization antecedents of individual differences in response to the CPI do show some interesting cross-cultural contrasts. Personality dispositions seem much more closely associated with family socioeconomic background in Italy, and greater parental restrictiveness in adolescence seems to have had a more debilitating effect among the Italian young men. A comparison of socialization variables associated with different patterns of sex-role identification yielded findings somewhat similar to those of Block *et al.* based on the Berkeley longitudinal sample, with closer correspondence among the Italian–American subjects.

CHAPTER 7

Values and Personal Philosophy

STABILITY OF MORAL VALUES

The measure of moral judgments described in Chapter 4, the "EV 3," first administered to our three groups of subjects in 1960, was readministered in 1965 when they were just entering their twenties. It is thus possible to examine the stability of moral judgments among our Italian and Italian–American subjects across a temporal span of 5 years that, for most of them, represents the period of development from early to late adolescence. The results of this second administration of the EV 3 are shown in Table 7-1. Comparing these results to those shown in Table 4-12, we note that moral judgments have, overall, become slightly more severe in Boston and Rome, but not in Palermo. Again, the Boston subjects as a group render more severe moral judgments than do the Italian subjects. While the internal consistency of the scale is again quite good for each of the three groups of subjects, temporal stability is very poor—only the correlation for Rome is significantly different from 0, and it is quite low. Thus we cannot conclude that individual differences in moral judgments, at least as measured by this instrument, represent stable or consistent attributes of the individual. This view is confirmed when we examine the correlates of overall scores on the second EV 3 in the rest of our data; the correlates for both the Palermo and the Boston groups are generally of low magnitude and no more are significant

TABLE 7-1

EV 3 — SECOND ADMINISTRATION

	Boston	Rome	Palermo
N	65	102	112
Mean	38.06	34.66	33.38
Standard Deviation	4.10	5.06	6.96
Internal Consistency r	.74	.64	.66
Temporal Stability $r_{1.2}$	-.15	.21	.16

than one would expect by chance. There are a few more significant correlates for the Roman subjects, as one might expect from the slightly higher stability of moral judgments among this group. None of these correlations exceeds .27, but they do form a consistent pattern. Severity of moral judgments among the Roman subjects seems to be associated with higher SES (especially mother's education), interviewer ratings when the boy was in early adolescence of higher affection expressed in the family, higher support to the home, a great sense of community responsibility, and capacity to work with others. Severity of moral judgments is related to lower need for affiliation and higher need for autonomy expressed in the Imagination Test, and to reports in the Personal Questionnaire (about 3 years later) that the subject was less likely to live with his parents or to visit other relatives frequently. Severity of moral judgment in early maturity is also positively correlated with time perspective, expectations of goal attainment, and the alienation score derived from the Jessor questionnaire. Thus it would seem that stricter moral judgment, for the subjects in our Rome sample, does represent a generalized sense of personal responsibility, of autonomy, and of orientation toward future goals to be achieved by one's own efforts. Just why this particular measure should seem to tap stable, internalized moral standards among the Roman group and not among our Boston or Palermo subjects we are at a loss to explain. One possibility is that there was a higher proportion of genuinely middle-class families in that group, despite the initial effort to control for SES.

The responses to individual EV 3 items were submitted to a three-factor analysis of variance with repeated measurements (Winer, 1962, p. 319)— modified for unequal N's. The results can be summarized as follows:

1. Responses to the items varied as a function of the item ($F = 691.717$, $p < .005$). (See Chapter 4, pp. 120–121, for the list of items.) The three items (11, 2, and 9) in which the protagonist was most severely condemned involved stealing in order to pamper one's self or stealing from a sister. The three items (1, 3, and 6) in which the protagonist's behavior was least condemned involved stealing to support a sick, widowed mother, and stealing in order to get food after going hungry for 3 and for 2 days, respectively.

2. Differences between youths of the three cities varied as a function of the nature of item (interaction between items and cities, $F = 16.456$, $p < .005$). Boston youth were especially more condemnatory than Rome and Palermo youth in response to items 1, 3, 5, 6, and 10. In item 1, the protagonist steals to support a sick, widowed mother; in item 3, the unemployed protagonist steals after being hungry for 3 days; in item 5, the protagonist picks up and does not return money a peer has dropped, the peer having not returned a borrowed ball; in item 6, the protagonist steals after being hungry for 2 days; and, in item 10, the protagonist, not having money, steals to buy a birthday gift for his girl friend.

   On two items, 9 and 11, Rome and Palermo youth were *more* condemnatory than Boston youth of the behavior of the protagonist. While these differences are not statistically significant, it is of interest to note that both items involve stealing solely for self-gratification under conditions of no or little distress—to buy something good to eat before dinner, and to buy candy.

3. While responses on the occasion of the 1965 administration were, in general, more condemnatory of the protagonist than on the 1960 administration (F for occasions is 14.55, $p < .005$), the difference in levels of response for the two administrations varied as a function of the item (F for the occasion by item interaction was 3.343, $p < .005$). Items 5, 7, and 9 showed the largest increase in condemnation of the protagonist over time while responses to items 1, 2, 3, 6, and 8 showed low levels of change (items 6 and 8) or a *decrease* in level of condemnation (due solely to the responses of Rome and Palermo youth). In these latter items (1–3), the Italian subjects became *less* condemnatory of the protagonist who stole from his sister (this result obtains solely for Palermo youth) or who stole for himself after being hungry for 3 days.

These differential responses to items may well reflect, in part, the greater economic hardships and near-starvation experienced by some of the Italian families during World War II, as well as the generally poorer economic conditions of the Italian South.

SOCIAL ATTITUDES

The V-Scale

These data derive from a study planned and executed by Irving Torgoff (see Torgoff & Tesi, 1965) while he was visiting the project in 1964–1965. This scale (see Table 7-2) was designed to measure "achievement potential" and to discriminate between overachieving and underachieving high school students, ages

TABLE 7-2

V-SCALE RESPONSE LEVELS

| | Percentage Who Disagree* | | | | |
| | Strodtbeck Study | | Harvard-Florence Study | | |
Items	Jews	Italians	Boston	Rome	Palermo
1. Planning only makes a person unhappy since your plans hardly ever work out anyway.	90	62*	86	58	47*
2. When a man is born, the success he's going to have is already in the cards, so he might as well accept it and not fight against it.	98	85*	95	90	87
3. When the time comes for a boy to take a job, he should stay near his parents, even if it means giving up a good job opportunity.	91	82*	91	88	89
4. Nowadays, with world conditions the way they are, the wise person lives for today and lets tomorrow take care of itself.	80	79	84	91	86
5. Nothing in life is worth the sacrifice of moving away from your parents.	82	59*	96	60	73*
Percentage who disagreed with at least 4 items*			89	63	67

	Boston (N=67)	Rome (N=99)	Palermo (N=117)
Mean Scale Values	4.34	3.80	3.79
Standard Deviations	1.01	.99	.997

*Differences are significant at the .05 level or greater, using a chi-square test.

14–17, of Jewish and Italian descent residing in New Haven, Connecticut (Strodtbeck, 1958). In the Strodtbeck study, a subject was classified as Italian if "one or more paternal and one or more maternal grandparents" had been born in Italy, a looser criterion than that used here. From an ethnographic analysis and inferences based on status mobility, Strodtbeck predicted that Jewish youths would have higher achievement-related responses than would the youths of Italian descent.

A factor analysis revealed that three items (1, 2, and 4) had a high loading on a factor Strodtbeck labeled "Mastery" (loadings of .64, .49, and .58, respectively). The content of these items related to a rejection of fate and a "belief that the world is orderly and amenable to rational mastery; that, therefore, a person can and should make plans that will control his destiny [Strodtbeck, 1958, p. 186]." Three other items (3, 4, and an item not used in the present study) had a high loading on a factor labeled "Independence of Family," indicating a willingness to leave home to make one's way in life (loadings of .60 and .68 for items 3 and 4, respectively). Strodtbeck found that the scale significantly differentiated overachieving from underachieving students, and Jewish from Italian–American students. When the scale was administered to a stratified sample of students and their parents, however, no Italian–Jewish differences appeared in the responses of fathers or sons when differences in socioeconomic status were taken into account. Jewish mothers, however, did have higher V-Scale scores than did Italian–American mothers. For purposes of this study only five of Strodtbeck's original eight V-Scale items were administered.

The percentage of Boston subjects (89%) who scored high on the V-Scale (disagreed with at least four items) was significantly higher than that of subjects from Rome (63%) or Palermo (67%), and the mean scale score for Boston is accordingly higher (see Table 7-2). Significant intercity differences emerge on only two of the five items (items 1 and 5), however.

Faith in the efficacy of planning (item 1) was more likely to be expressed by subjects from Boston (86%) than by those from Rome (58%) or Palermo (47%). Did this difference in orientation toward planning reflect a difference in metaphysical belief in preordained fate or *"destino"* as suggested by Strodtbeck (1958) and by Gans (1962)? Apparently not—the percentages of subjects who rejected the fatalistic view described in item 2 ("When a man is born, the success he is going to have is already in the cards, so he might as well accept it and not fight against it.") were high for each of the three groups (Boston, 95%; Rome, 90%; Palermo, 87%) and the intercity differences were not significant. An alternate view, based on differences in reality appraisal rather than metaphysical belief, suggests that subjects from Rome and Palermo are more pessimistic (rather than fatalistic) than are Boston subjects regarding the efficacy of planning—this difference in pessimism, in turn, reflecting differences in the estimate of the chances an individual has to manipulate the direction of his future in a given socioeconomic-political environment rather than a belief in a preordained fate. In effect, then, while all three groups rejected the fatalistic *"che, sera, sera"* view, the Boston group was more likely to view changes in their life-space as more amenable to personal control, while Rome and Palermo youth were more pessimistic and saw less chance of success in effecting control over the conditions that shape their lives. This explanation might also account for the pattern of responses to item 4 ("Nowadays, with world conditions the way they are, the wise person lives for today and lets tomorrow take care of itself."). This is the only one of the five items that was rejected by a higher percentage of subjects from Rome and Palermo than from Boston—although, it should be noted, these differences were not significant. Life for Italian youth, more so than for the Boston group, is far from the *dolce vita* sterotype and demands constant concern and hustling to survive in a life experienced as *dura*. Further, it may also be of value to consider the possibility that the continuing involvement of the United States in international conflicts during that period (1964–1965), the possibility of personal involvement (e.g., being drafted), and the consequent possibility of not being able to plan for and to control one's future would result in the Boston group's being more prone than at other periods to accept the thesis: "the wise person lives for today and lets tomorrow take care of itself." These findings parallel those yielded by the Jessor measures of expectations of goal attainment and *internal control* administered the following year. It should be noted that within each of our samples the V-Scale and the two Jessor scales correlate to different degrees. In Boston, the V-Scale correlates .31 with *internal control* and .34 with *expectations of future goal attainment* (both significant at the .05 level); in Rome the correlations are .14 and .20 (not significant) and in Palermo .04 and .00. Thus a sense of mastery over one's fate is not only more prevalent among the Boston subjects, but is a more stable trait across different sets of measures and different points in time.

Only one of the two items relating to independence from family elicited significantly different responses as a function of residential location. Subjects from Rome and Palermo were less likely to disagree with the proposition that "Nothing in life is worth the sacrifice of moving away from your parents" (item 5) than were subjects from Boston (60%, 73%, and 96%, respectively). Disagreements to item 3, "When the time comes for a boy to take a job, he should stay near his parents, even if it means giving up a good job opportunity," were uniformly high for subjects from Boston, Rome, and Palermo (91%, 88%, and 89%) and showed no significant differences among the groups.

These results suggest that while the Italian subjects may place stronger value on the concept of retaining family cohesion, subjects in all three groups when faced with a situation concretely posing a realistic choice between intergenerational family cohesion and economic opportunity will overwhelmingly avail themselves of "a good job opportunity" even if it means they will not be near their parents. The extent to which this lack of difference among the groups is a function of increasing dispersion of economic opportunities for those willing to leave home and a decrease in economic opportunities for those remaining in southern Italy is, of course, a matter of conjecture. The continuing migration of members of families and total families in search of economic opportunity was as true in the 1960s of Italian–Americans in Boston (Gans, 1962) as in Rome and Palermo. However, when surveyed 3 years later, the Boston group (as we have seen in the previous chapter) were significantly less likely to be living with their parents.

Concern for Others[1]

Banfield (1958), in an analysis of certain segments of Italian society, pointed to the presence of a particular type of moral ethos he termed "amoral familism."

[1]We are further indebted to Irving Torgoff for this discussion of "amoral familism."

According to Banfield, an "amoral familist" is one who follows the rule: "maximize the material, short-run advantage of the nuclear family, assume that all others will do likewise." For the "amoral familist," moral standards are appropriately applied only to those behaviors that affect his immediate family; his interactions with others outside the nuclear family are evaluated in regard to *interesse*—self-interest and private advantage—rather than a moral code based on a concern for others. Gans (1962), in his study of second-generation working-class Americans of Sicilian and southern Italian descent living in an inner-city Boston neighborhood called the West End, noted a similarity between Banfield's findings and his own, especially in regard to an "amoral familistic" ethos characteristic of the patterns of political participation of the two groups: "In a society of amoral familism, only officials will concern themselves with public affairs, for only they are paid to do so. For a private citizen to take a serious interest in a public problem will be regarded as abnormal or even improper [Banfield, 1958, p. 87]." However, it is important to note that the bifurcation between the immediate family and the rest of society that characterizes a society based on amoral familism is less total in the West End than in the southern Italian village described by Banfield. Gans (1962), in comparing the lives of second-generation with those of the immigrant West Enders, pointed to the presence of ongoing change.

> For the West Enders, life is much less of a struggle than it was for their parents. There are more jobs, more secure ones, and better paid as well. As economic conditions improve, the ethos which Banfield calls amoral familism has begun to recede in importance. Most West Enders, for example, no longer need to fear their neighbors and unrelated people as a threat to their own existence. These "others" are no longer competitors for a small number of scarce jobs, but people with whom one can associate. Consequently, social life and mutual aid are not entirely restricted to the family circle; West Enders can and do make friends more easily than their ancestors . . . the attitude toward caretakers, the law, city government, and other phases of the outside world is no longer based on total incomprehension and fear [p. 209].

The changes in the lives of the West Enders have not been all-pervasive, however. "American culture . . . could not pervade the family circle. Thus, whereas the children who became the adults of the second generation retained little of the Italian culture, they did retain most of its social structure [Gans, p. 208]."

In an effort to account for the persistence of similarity in social structure between southern Italian society and the West Enders, Gans suggests, after reviewing three generations of West Enders, that many basic features of the way of life and in the environment have *not* changed as drastically as it appears; that

> the environment that the immigrants and the West Enders have encountered in America has differed in degree rather than in kind; it is less hostile and depriving, of course, but it is otherwise still the same. There have been no radical changes in the position of the working class vis-a-vis other classes, or in the position of minority ethnic groups vis-a-vis the majority.

As a result, there have been as yet no strong pressures or incentives among the West Enders for any radical change in the basic social structure with which they respond to the environment [p. 213].

Gans points out, however, that an increase in the extent and rate of change would be more prevalent for the third generation (those most similar to the Boston subjects in the present study)—especially as these relate to occupational opportunities, education, and consequent impact on the nuclear family.

Gans's analysis of the similarities and differences obtaining between southern Italian society and the various generations of West Enders suggest some leads in examining areas of similarities and differences among subjects in the present study. If, as Gans suggests, "West Enders are almost, but not entirely, representative of the mainstream of second-generation Italian life in America," then the moral ethos characteristic of our Boston subjects should be comparable to that of the West Enders. In contrast to the subjects from Rome and Palermo, therefore, Boston subjects should be more likely to indicate a greater extension of moral concern to members of the peer community who are not members of the nuclear family. In order to measure the extent of concern for the rights, needs, and welfare of others, a ten-item questionnaire was developed to measure "amoral familism" among Italian adolescents (Torgoff & Tesi, 1965). Content of the items (e.g., item 3, "It is best to support only those community programs that are of benefit to yourself and your family, but other people concern themselves with programs that have no personal benefit to you," and item 8, "Everyone is a little bit responsible for an injustice committed in the town in which he lives") was based on Banfield's description. Chi-square analysis of the levels of response to each of the items revealed no significant differences among youths from the three cities on any of the items. Nor are the scale means significantly different. At the level of avowed concern for others, the three groups are indistinguishable. The high levels at which the amoral familistic position was rejected further suggest that for these groups, using this measuring instrument, there is no evidence indicating the prevalence of an amoral familistic ethos in any of our three groups. This failure to substantiate Banfield's ideas may be a reflection of the rather obvious item content. The influence of *interesse* might emerge with more subtle or more behavioral measures.

Viewed as a measure of individual differences, the C O scale yields too few significant correlations for us to interpret them with any degree of confidence. Rejection of the amoral familist position is significantly correlated, however, with the EV 3 in both Boston and Rome, with measures of creativity among all three samples, with father's occupational status and the boy's own occupational and educational attainment in Boston, and with favorable self-judgments (expressed in the earlier interview with the boy) in Palermo. Thus this scale may have some validity as a measure of moral standards and as a reflection of independent thinking.

PERSONAL PHILOSOPHY

The Inventory of Personal Philosophy, developed by Frank Barron (Barron, 1952), was administered to the Boston and the Rome groups when the subjects were, on the average, 20 years of age. Unfortunately, the Palermo group was not included in this round of data collection. Thus we are limited to a comparison of the two emigrant groups on this particular measure, and for this reason as well as the limited rate of return no analysis of the longitudinal antecedents of individual differences in personal philosophy has been attempted. The comparisons between Boston and Rome were carried out by Frank Barron and have previously been reported (Barron & Young, 1970).

This rather lengthy questionnaire was distributed to the subjects by mail and returned by only 56 (59%) in Boston and 82 (65%) in Rome. An analysis of Raven scores of those who failed to respond as compared with those who responded to the questionnaire shows no significant difference in either the Boston or Rome samples; there is also no significant difference in social status classification of the immediate families. Thus we may have some confidence in the representativeness of the reduced sample.

The Inventory of Personal Philosophy consists of three parts. The first part deals with basic beliefs in matters of religion. Each item consists of a triad of statements that the respondent is asked to rank in terms of the extent to which it expresses his belief. The first item may serve as an example. It presents the following triad of statements:

a. I believe in God.
b. There is no God.
c. We cannot know for sure whether there is a God or not.

The respondent chooses the alternatives with which he is in *most agreement* and *least agreement*.

In the second part of the inventory, 80 statements are presented in the form of declarative sentences. The respondent is asked to indicate for each statement whether he *Agrees* or *Disagrees* with it. Here are three examples:

1. Divorce is practically never justified.
2. In illegitimate pregnancies, abortion is in many cases the most reasonable alternative.
3. No war is justifiable.

In the third part of the inventory, the respondent is presented with 30 pairs of personal traits and asked to choose the one trait of each pair that he *would rather be known to possess*. Here are three examples:

I would rather be known as
a. imaginative   a. obliging   a. logical
b. clear-thinking   b. independent   b. intuitive

As we have indicated, 56 members of the Boston sample and 82 members of the Rome sample responded to the Inventory of Personal Philosophy. The results were analyzed first by comparing *for each item* the percentage of Boston *agrees* with the percentage of Rome *agrees*. When a significant percentage difference occurs, the response is said to characterize one group or the other. A comparison in terms of differences on various scales of the inventory will also be considered, but we shall begin by taking a look at the individual items that differentiate the Boston young men from the group in Rome. The exact percentages are given in Barron and Young (1970); only the significant items are presented.

Basic Religious Beliefs

Here are the items that show a percentage difference significant at the .05 level of statistical significance.

Boston agrees	*Rome agrees*
Heaven and Hell are real places.	Heaven and Hell are just ideas.
The church is the house of God.	The church is a worthwhile social institution, whether or not its teachings concerning God are true.
God is an eternal and all-powerful person.	I do not believe in God in the conventional sense, but I think that nature expressed the existence of some abstract principle of order which might be called God.
It is a good thing to pray when you need help.	Prayer is useless.
God hears our prayers.	Prayer may bring spiritual comfort, but has no other power.
All children should receive formal religious training.	Children should be taught to respect religion, but they should not be indoctrinated in the beliefs of one particular church.

We must begin by noting an important similarity in the Boston and Rome responses (i.e., on an item that does not appear in the preceding). There is *no significant difference* between the two groups on the question of belief in God. None of the Boston respondents espoused an atheistic position, and only 5% of the Rome respondents did so. Eighty-five percent of the Bostonians affirmed the statement, ''I believe in God,'' compared with 76% of the Romans; this is not a significant difference.

There the similarity ends, however. Succeeding items in the inventory provide the opportunity for qualifying the basic position, and here Boston and Rome go in different directions. The Boston group holds to a much more fundamentalist version of Christian theology than does the Roman. Thus to the Bostonians, heaven and hell are real places; to the Romans, they are "just ideas." The Bostonians characteristically state that "God hears our prayers" and "It is a good thing to pray when you need help." The Romans feel either that prayer is useless or that while it may bring spiritual comfort it has no other power. Church and religion are seen as worthwhile by the Rome group, but they characteristically deny that the church is the house of God and that all children should receive formal religious training. Essentially, their position is expressed by the statement, "I do not believe in God in the conventional sense, but I think that nature expresses the existence of some abstract principle of order which might be called God."

An analysis of the religious belief scales scored from the first part of the inventory bears out the item analysis. In Table 7-3 are shown the means and sigmas for these four scales. Boston scores significantly higher on Fundamentalist Belief, while Rome is significantly higher both on Enlightened Belief and on Enlightened Disbelief. On Fundamentalist Disbelief there is not a significant difference.

These findings are easy to understand in the light of another survey of religious belief and practice in "Catholic Italy," by Burgalassi (1968). Titled *The Religious Behavior of Italians* (*Il comportamento religioso degli italiani*) and written by a Catholic priest, Father Silvano Burgalassi, the report in book form of this survey caused a great stir in religious circles in Italy. What the survey shows, in brief, is that only a small percentage of Italians today observe the prescribed regularities of religious practice, and that the fundamentals of catechism belief of only a generation ago are no longer accepted by the majority of nominally Catholic Italians. In Boston, on the other hand, to be of Italian descent is still to be conventionally Catholic and largely fundamentalist in acceptance of standard

TABLE 7-3

COMPARISON OF BOSTON AND ROME GROUPS ON BASIC BELIEF SCALES
OF INVENTORY OF PERSONAL PHILOSOPHY

		Boston		Rome		t-Ratio	Significance Level
		Mean	SD	Mean	SD		
1.	Fundamentalist Belief	8.92	3.13	6.59	3.89	3.57	.01
2.	Enlightened Belief	1.90	2.07	3.57	2.65	-3.77	.01
3.	Enlightened Disbelief	4.52	2.95	5.99	3.68	-2.38	.05
4.	Fundamentalist Disbelief	0.42	1.18	0.66	1.05	-1.17	NS

Church dogma. The unorthodox Dutch catechism that has so profoundly influenced European Catholicism has had little circulation or acceptance in the United States, and so what at first may seem an odd result is perhaps best understood as reflecting the much greater conservatism and conformity of American Catholicism in general. The Boston parishes within which our Italian emigrant families have lived were served, at least a generation ago, predominantly by Irish clergy. The influence of the Irish–American clergy has certainly been in the direction of fundamentalism, and it may be that both the national and the urban culture in this instance worked to keep the descendants of Italian immigrants conformist in their belief patterns. Incidentally, in another study by Barron (1969), it was shown that the Irish in Ireland, unlike the Italians in Italy, remain strongly fundamentalist in their interpretation of Catholic theology.

Social Attitudes and Personal Opinions

The results of a comparison of the two groups on the second part of the inventory, again based on the chi-square method, are presented here. Only items showing a difference so great that the chi-square value is significant at the .05 level of confidence are given. First are shown the items with which the Boston group *agrees* significantly more often, and then the items with which the Rome group *agrees*. The items in each set are grouped according to the magnitude of the percentage difference (given in parentheses after each item).

Items with which *Boston agrees* (.05 level or better):

ITEM	Boston	Rome	% Difference
5. All people are somewhat evil at heart.	50.0	26.3	23.7
37. English version: The United States should look after its own national interests more, and give less of its resources to building up other countries	65.4		
Italian version: The more developed countries should look after their own national interests more, and give less of their resources to building up other countries.		2.6	62.8
47. Voters should disregard the party and vote for the men.	87.5	39.5	48.0
48. Negroes are basically less intelligent than Caucasians, on the average.	42.3	19.7	22.6
57. I think I take primarily an aesthetic view of experience.	61.5	17.1	44.4
65. I would enjoy the experience of living and working in a foreign country.	83.7	55.3	28.4
75. It is the duty of a citizen to support his country, right or wrong.	61.5	43.4	18.1

Items with which Rome agrees (.05 level or better):

ITEM	Boston	Rome	% Difference
3. It is a good rule to accept nothing as certain or proved.	38.5	65.8	−27.3
7. There will always be war as long as there are men.	51.9	75.0	−23.1
9. There is something noble about poverty and suffering.	40.4	82.9	−42.5
10. A criminal is not really responsible for his evil deeds, since he himself is the product of so many unhappy circumstances over which he had no control.	18.2	47.4	−29.2
14. Above almost everything else, I like to deal with and comprehend others.	59.6	80.3	−20.7
18. Purely social conversation generally bores me.	44.2	71.1	−26.9
33. It is hard to see how most juvenile delinquents could have been anything else, considering the environments in which they were reared.	51.9	71.1	−19.2
35. Children should be allowed more sexual freedom.	8.6	38.2	−29.6
40. Capital punishment should be done away with.	50.0	69.7	−19.7
41. It would be a good thing if a popular international language could be established.	79.9	93.4	−13.5
44. There should be a widespread effort to maintain a very low birth rate among the less competent classes of our society.	36.5	57.9	−21.4
45. Divorce should be made easier.	18.2	38.2	−20.0
49. No war is justifiable.	42.3	69.7	−27.4
50. Communism is the most hateful thing in the world today.	30.7	53.9	−23.2
61. People would be happier if sex experience before marriage were taken for granted in both men and women.	26.9	51.3	−24.4
62. I often get the feeling that I am not really part of the group I associate with and that I could separate from it with little discomfort or hardship.	34.6	53.9	−19.3
69. A person who doesn't vote is not a good citizen.	42.3	82.9	−40.6
71. I enjoy the company of strong-willed people.	67.3	89.5	−22.2

Perhaps we should note first of all that 25 items out of 80 in this part of the inventory emerge as significantly different at the .05 level of confidence when the Rome group is compared with the Boston. It is clear that large real differences between the two groups have developed.

We shall attempt to summarize these differences by generalizing about the belief systems of the young men in *Rome*.

1. They express liberal, rational, enlightened attitudes toward marriage, sexual relations, and the planning of family size. Some of these attitudes are frowned upon officially by the Church (such as more sexual freedom for children, sex experience before marriage, easier divorce, and efforts at birth control, especially for the less competent).

2. They think in terms of social and psychological causation rather than punitively regarding crime (a criminal is produced by unhappy circumstances, juvenile delinquents have hardly any choice or freedom of self-determination, capital punishment should be done away with).

3. They evince a greater sense of social and political responsibility (a person who does not vote is not a good citizen, voters should respond to a political party's platform rather than the candidate's personality, Communism is hateful, the more developed countries—which presumably would include Italy—ought to help the underdeveloped by giving of their own resources, no war is justifiable, and finally the citizen should *not* support his country if it is in the wrong).

4. They are more intellectual and skeptical in the scientific sense (it is a good rule to accept nothing as certain or proved, purely social conversation is boring, ideas above all are interesting and challenging).

5. They are less ethnocentric, more international-minded (the Boston group, by contrast, believes that Negroes are basically less intelligent; they are also less interested in establishment of a popular international language).

The second part of the Inventory of Personal Philosophy may be scored for eight factor scales developed by Barron on the basis of a series of factor analyses carried out by C. Naranjo. Results of a scale analysis are presented in Table 7-4.

As Table 7-4 shows, there is no difference between the Rome and Boston groups in religious conservatism, in spite of the higher Boston scores on Fundamentalist Belief in the first part of the inventory. That difference apparently was compensated for by the higher Rome scores on Enlightened Belief, since the Religious Conservatism scale encompasses both attitudes at the positive end.

TABLE 7-4

FACTOR SCALE DIFFERENCES PART II,
INVENTORY OF PERSONAL PHILOSOPHY

	Boston			Rome			t-Ratio	Significance Level
	Mean	SD	N	Mean	SD	N		
1. Religious conservatism	6.54	2.06	52	5.77	2.60	76	1.77	NS
2. Political-social conservatism	8.21	2.80	52	8.80	2.38	76	-1.28	NS
3. Authoritarianism	5.50	2.38	52	5.62	2.02	76	-0.30	NS
4. Artistic values	9.52	2.41	52	9.68	2.29	76	-0.39	NS
5. Skepticism	3.40	1.56	52	4.13	1.43	76	-2.73	.01
6. Personal-sexual freedom	1.96	1.44	52	2.74	1.68	76	-2.71	.01
7. Refined sense of justice	3.92	1.81	52	5.14	1.72	76	-3.86	.01
8. Intolerance of ambiguity	2.50	0.98	52	2.35	0.90	76	0.86	NS

The finding is consistent with the earlier observation that the groups were quite similar as to the basic theistic position, their differences occurring in qualification of that position.

In terms of political-social conservatism there again is no significant difference between the groups, and the same is true of authoritarianism. The significant differences that do occur are on scales thought to reflect *skepticism, high valuation of personal and sexual freedom*, and a *refined sense of justice*, on all of which the Rome group is higher. These findings are consistent with the general picture that emerges from the item analysis.

Valued Personality Characteristics

This part of the inventory revealed striking differences between Boston and Rome in the personality characteristics on which the groups typically place a high value. The significantly different percentages in preferences are shown.

Boston Values

Would rather be:

logical (84% vs 44%)
  than a first-rate student
casual and friendly with everyone (76% vs 51%)
  than a person with few but intense friendships
a person who is concerned about the opinions of society (50% vs 16%)
  than a person who does not care what others may think
king and considerate (25% vs 3%)
  than honest and forthright
popular and a leader (67% vs 51%)
  than a first-rate student
obliging (40% vs 25%)
  than independent

Would rather be:
good-looking (19% vs 5%)
  than intelligent
boastful (19% vs 8%)
  than self-effacing

Rome Values

Would rather be:

warm and sociable (83% vs 65%)
  than self-contained
the life of the party (47% vs 23%)
  than a good sport

good-humored (78% vs 58%)
  than clever

quickwitted (39% vs 23%)
  than dependable
pleasure-seeking (47% vs 29%)
  than earnest
a person easily downed in an argument (29% vs 14%)
  than a person who almost always has the last word

There are three outstanding differences here. The Boston-Italians place a very high value on logic as opposed to intuition, they would rather be casual and friendly with everyone than have a few but intense friendships, and in contrast to the Romans they are much more concerned about the opinion of society. Although a majority of them (65%) would rather be warm and sociable than independent and self-contained, this is a significantly smaller percentage than in the Roman group, and the fact that 35% of them would opt for the Yankee stereotype as opposed to the Italian stereotype (neither of which may be accurate) is itself quite significant. In this they seem to have taken on the coloration of Boston rather than of the United States in general, for national male norms on the test reveal that some 80% of American men prefer to be considered warm and sociable, a figure close to the Italian average.

In the three most significant differences, the Rome group affirms the values that in earlier studies have been found to be associated positively with creativity: intuitiveness, intensity of feeling, and nonconformity or unconventionality. These are also the characteristics of artists, and it is therefore not surprising to find through scale analysis that on the Artistic Sensibility scale of the Inventory of Personal Philosophy the Rome group is significantly higher (means of 5.91 vs 5.23, t significant at $p < .01$). This finding seems consonant with the differences reported in earlier sections of this and the previous chapter.

The Boston group values earnestness, kindness, considerateness, dependability, responsibility, and conscientiousness. These differences seem consonant with the higher scores obtained by the Boston subjects on our measures of moral values. They would also rather be "popular and a leader" than "a first-rate student" and more of them admit to being boastful and to preferring good looks to intelligence than do their Roman counterparts. As Child (1943) found through interviews with second-generation southern Italians in New Haven, young male Italian–Americans were insecure about their physical attractiveness compared with other American groups. The relatively high valuation of "good looks" may perhaps best be understood in terms of a sensed deficit of unfavorable comparison of self with others by the parents of the young men in the Boston group. In general this last set of differences confirms our conclusions about the relatively greater importance of peer relations for the Boston subjects at an earlier stage of adolescence.

SUMMARY

Self-report inventories contributed to the project by Torgoff and by Barron give further insight into the value orientations of our subjects. The measure of severity of moral judgments (EV 3) first administered in 1960 was repeated 5 years later; individual subjects' judgments did not prove stable over time, except for a low degree of consistency in Rome. Mean judgments were consistently more severe in Boston than in Italy; Italian youth were more likely to accept economic hardship as an excuse for stealing. The Italian–American group also obtained, on the average, higher scores on the V-Scale, designed as a measure of achievement potential, but a scale designed to tap Banfield's construct of "amoral familism" failed to distinguish among the three groups. Responses to Barron's Inventory of Personal Philosophy were obtained from subsamples only in Rome and Boston. While both groups professed belief in God, the religious beliefs of the Roman subjects were characterized as less fundamentalist and more enlightened than those of the American immigrant group. The Roman subjects expressed beliefs that were generally more liberal (particularly on sexual matters), more intellectually sceptical, less ethnocentric, and less punitive in ideas of justice. The Bostonians tended to place greater value on friendliness, popularity, consideration for others, self-assertion, and logical thinking, while the Romans were more likely to value being warm, intuitive, and pleasure-seeking—attributes associated with creativity in other studies.

CHAPTER 8

Political Orientations

While the Harvard–Florence Project had attracted many well-known behavioral scientists for short periods of study, there was no one particularly concerned with the development of political attitudes associated with the project until 1967. At that time a brief report on data of political interest gathered by the project was prepared for the Specialist Meeting on Youth and Politics, Seventh World Congress, International Political Science Association, Brussels, by the author of this chapter.*

The few data of political relevance that had been collected suggested a confirmation of previous research findings that political attitudes may be related to childhood experiences, particularly relations with parents. The existence of such a large amount of information on the adolescent development of these subjects presented an unusual opportunity for the testing of hypotheses about political socialization, if in addition to the developmental data we could obtain information on the subjects' political attitudes and behavior as young adults. A questionnaire designed to gather such political information was mailed to the subjects in

*LeRoy C. Ferguson, Professor of Political Science, Michigan State University, East Lansing, Michigan.

1968-1969; and the information it yielded has been briefly reported previously (Ferguson, Ferguson & Young, 1972).

In the 13 years of the project, there was, as is inevitable in longitudinal studies, a certain amount of shrinkage of the size of the sample available from the original N of 340. In the later years an important shrinkage factor was the fact that the young men were reaching the age of military service. In the Boston group a number of them were serving in Vietnam at the time our political questionnaire was distributed. Political questionnaires were mailed to all subjects with whom the project was still in touch in 1968-1969, and one follow-up was sent to those who did not respond to the initial effort. Eventually satisfactory returns were obtained from 65 subjects in Boston (70% of the original sample), 83 subjects in Rome (65%), and 77 subjects in Palermo (64%). Of the subjects who could actually be said to be "available" in 1968-1969, the replies represented approximately 77% in Boston, 78% in Rome, and 72% in Palermo.

Obviously it would have been more desirable to have been able to collect the political data in a personal interview, but neither the time nor money were available to make this possible. It is equally obvious that neither the original group of subjects nor the subgroup who replied to the political questionnaire can be assumed to be a representative sample of the total population of young men in the areas where they resided. In the case of Boston, it would have been particularly desirable to have administered the same questionnaire to a group of young men who were matched with the original group in all characteristics except Italian ethnic background.

An additional problem inherent in the cross-cultural nature of the study is that of language. Most of the items were taken directly, or with slight modifications, from questionnaires or interview schedules that had already been used in Italy. (Professor Alessandro Pizzorno of the University of Ancona was particularly helpful in providing such items.) Backtranslations were used to try to insure that the questions had the same meaning in both languages. This effort appears to have been largely successful, but there were a few differences in response that may have been due to language. Cultural differences other than language are also to be noted. The subjects were invited to comment on the questionnaires and there were numerous objections by the Rome and Palermo subjects to the "forced answer" questions. They would have preferred (as, indeed, would we) to carry on a dialogue rather than merely to check an agree or disagree response. The Boston subjects, possibly because they were more accustomed to objective tests in schools, made very few comments of this nature.

Despite the foregoing limitations, the data obtained from the political questionnaires provided some interesting glimpses into cross-cultural differences in political attitudes. While there was a similarity among the three cities in the amount of interest in and attention to politics, there were quite different levels of emotional involvement with politics and sense of political efficacy between Boston and the Italian cities.

POLITICAL INTEREST AND ATTENTION

In the first question on the political questionnaire the subjects were asked whether they had a strong interest in politics, a slight interest, or almost no interest at all. There were negligible differences in the proportions from each city who indicated a strong interest (Palermo, 32%; Rome, 30%; Boston, 31%) but, compared to the Italian cities, Boston included a somewhat higher proportion who reported that they had no political interest at all.

In order to measure political attention, the subjects were asked whether they generally kept up with what is going on in politics, and how often they followed reports of political events in the newspapers, and on television and radio. They were also asked how often they had occasion to talk about political problems. The proportions who said that they did generally keep up with political goings on were Palermo 49%, Rome 58%, and Boston 61%.

All three groups reported a considerable amount of attention to political news. The proportions who followed political reports in the newspapers "almost every day" were Palermo 39%, Rome 46%, and Boston 45%. Daily attention to political reports on television and radio was reported by 46% in Palermo, 45% in Rome, and 54% in Boston. Almond and Verba (1963) found much less attention to political news reported by their Italian national sample.[1]

There was great similarity in the amount of political talk reported from the three cities. In each case about one-fourth talked about political problems almost every day, slightly more than one-half talked from time to time, and a little less than one-fourth rarely or never talked about politics. Replies to a similar question by an Italian national sample in the Almond–Verba study suggest that our subjects talk much more about politics than do Italians generally.

Most of the talk was reported to be with friends in all three cities. Somewhat less talk with relatives was reported from Palermo, and somewhat more from Rome. The Boston subjects were somewhat more likely to report political talk with persons other than friends or relatives. Most of this was with fellow workers. Table 8-1 is based on the responses to all five of the attention items in the questionnaires. Those in the "high" category reported that they had a strong interest in politics, that they generally kept up with what is going on in politics, and that they followed media reports and talked about politics almost every day.

EMOTIONAL INVOLVEMENT WITH POLITICS

In contrast to the generally similar pattern of political interest and attention, there were marked cross-cultural differences in reports of emotional involvement

---

[1] Our comparisons of responses to similar or identical items were based on the code book of the Almond–Verba study, which they have kindly made available to other scholars.

TABLE 8-1

POLITICAL INTEREST AND ATTENTION

	Boston	Rome	Palermo
Low	31%	20%	31%
Medium	40%	50%	38%
High	29%	30%	31%
Total	100%	100%	100%
Number of cases	65	83	77
Mean of raw scores	8.23	8.46	8.16

with politics shown in Table 8-2. The Boston subjects were much less likely than those in Italy to report that they had been made to feel excited or indignant by political events. It will be noted, additionally, that there was somewhat more excitement and indignation reported from Palermo than from Rome. In some previous Italian studies the subjects had been asked in a single question whether they had ever been made excited or indignant by political events. It appeared to us that, in English anyway, one could be excited without being indignant, and so the two kinds of involvement were dealt with in separate questions. As it turned out there were more who reported frequent indignation than who reported frequent excitement in all three cities, though the difference in Boston was negligible. In all three cities there was a high correlation between excitement and indignation, and to simplify further analysis we assigned each of our subjects a score based on their combined responses to the two questions.

SENSE OF POLITICAL EFFICACY

Sense of political efficacy (Table 8-3) is a measure originally developed at the University of Michigan Survey Research Center. It was "designed to capture differences between individuals in a basic sense of control over the workings of the political system" (Campbell, Converse, Miller, & Stokes, 1960, p. 516). Since it was first used by the Survey Research Center in 1952, this measure has been used in various forms and with various levels in a wide variety of empirical and theoretical studies. Subjects who are high in sense of political efficacy are likely to feel that they, personally, can influence political events. This element of the efficacy variable has been called "political effectiveness" (Abramson, P.R., 1977; Douvan & Walker, 1956; Lane, 1959) or "political competence" (Almond & Verba, 1963). Political efficacy also includes the feeling that public officials are responsible and that the political system is just. This element has been called "political trust" or "governmental responsiveness" (Lane, 1959).

TABLE 8-2

EMOTIONAL INVOLVEMENT WITH POLITICS

Do you ever find that you get excited by political events?

Response	Boston	Rome	Palermo
Never	19%	8%	10%
Sometimes	66%	70%	57%
Frequently	15%	22%	33%
Total	100%	100%	100%
Number of cases	65	83	77
Mean of raw scores	1.97	2.13	2.22

Do you ever find that political events make you feel indignant?

Response	Boston	Rome	Palermo
Never	36%	18%	4%
Sometimes	47%	40%	48%
Frequently	17%	42%	48%
Total	100%	100%	100%
Number of cases	65	83	77
Mean of raw scores	1.81	2.24	2.44

Combined scores for excitement and indignation.

Scores	Boston	Rome	Palermo	Total Group
Low*	80%	57%	55%	63%
High	20%	43%	45%	37%
Total	100%	100%	100%	100%
Number of cases	65	83	77	225
Mean of raw scores	3.8	4.4	4.7	

*"Low" and "high" mean below or above the median for the total group. Due to clustering, it was not possible to divide the total group into exactly equal proportions.

The final element in the efficacy measure has to do with political understanding and awareness. This was called "comprehensibility" by Easton and Dennis (1967, 1969). The latter authors (1967) have also called attention to the fact that efficacy can be conceived as a norm (what people think should prevail); as a disposition (how people feel about their own effectiveness and the responsiveness of the government); or as a form of behavior. As we shall see below, the

TABLE 8-3

SENSE OF POLITICAL EFFICACY

Scores	Boston	Rome	Palermo
Low	18%	31%	35%
Medium	36%	49%	47%
High	46%	20%	18%
Total	100%	100%	100%
Number of cases	65	83	77
Mean of raw scores	8.22	6.46	6.22

perception of what should be the norm may sometimes have an effect on the measurement of the disposition or feeling.

Although the concept of political efficacy has encountered criticism for theoretical ambiguity and methodological reliability, it has continued to be widely used, mainly because since it was first introduced by the Survey Research Center it was found to be highly correlated with political participation. People who were high in sense of political efficacy were much more likely to vote and to participate in other ways (Campbell *et al.*, 1960). Almond and Verba (1963, p. 257) called subjective political competence a "key political attitude," and it was the major dependent variable in their five-nation study, where they found that it was related both to participation and to other values related to democratic politics.

To the four efficacy items originally used by the Survey Research Center we added two additional ones that had previously been used in Italy.[2] Subjects in the "high" category in Table 8-3 gave efficacious responses to at least four of the six items. Those in the "low" category gave efficacious responses to no more than two of the six items. As has already been indicated, the Boston youth were much more likely to be high in sense of political efficacy than those in the Italian cities.

The total efficacy scores upon which Table 8-3 was based conceal some important differences in responses to individual items. The subjects in Palermo were more likely than those in Rome to agree with the items expressing political

---

[2]The following four items were used by Campbell and his associates: A. I don't think public officials care much about what people like me think. B. Voting is the only way that people like me can have any say about how the government runs things. C. People like me don't have any say about what the government does. D. Sometimes government and politics seem so complicated that a person like me can't really understand what's going on. To these we added the following: E. In general do you think that: 1. American (or Italian) citizens have ample opportunity to react against unjust laws; or 2. Unjust laws are rather easily imposed. F. Faced with an unjust law, do you feel that you, personally, could somehow contribute to changing it?

cynicism (unjust laws easily imposed; public officials don't care), while the Romans were more likely than the Palermans to agree with the items expressing feelings of political impotency (changing unjust law; people like me don't have any say). The most striking variation in response to individual items was in the case of the one dealing with understanding of government and politics. Although the Italian subjects were much less likely than the Bostonians to give the efficacious response to five of the six items, there was a sharp reversal on the latter item in that the Boston subjects were much more likely than those in Italy to agree that "a person like me can't understand what's going on in government and politics." This disparity between their feeling that they understand "what's going on" and their feeling of being unable to influence it may help to explain the much higher proportion of the Italians who reported frequent political indignation.

Where we have been able to find comparable data, we have looked at how the responses of our subjects compare with those of samples of their respective national populations. In general, it would appear that the young men in Rome and Palermo indicated a much higher sense of political efficacy than the national sample of the Italian population used in the Almond–Verba study. The young men in Boston also have a consistently higher percentage of efficacious responses to comparable items than were given by Survey Research Center national samples of the population of the United States. These differences probably are due partly to the fact that all of our subjects were young white males. The young tend to have a higher sense of efficacy, probably because of higher educational advantages. Women tend to feel less efficacious than men (more so in Italy than in the United States) and blacks consistently demonstrate lower feelings of effectiveness than whites in the United States. However, when we compared responses of our Boston subjects to those of their white age cohort in the Survey Research Center national sample, our subjects were still shown to be somewhat higher in efficacy (see Table 8-4).

CROSS-CULTURAL DIFFERENCES

In summary, the responses to our political questionnaire revealed a similarity among the subjects from the three cities in the amount of interest and attention devoted to politics, accompanied by much less emotional involvement with politics, but much higher sense of political efficacy, in Boston when compared to the Italian cities.

On the cognitive level, we find it difficult to believe that there is really so much more to be indignant about in Palermo than in Boston. We think it interesting to note, however, that the more frequent feelings of excitement and indignation reported from Italy are consistent with the stereotype (at least held by

TABLE 8-4

COMPARISON OF BOSTON SUBJECTS TO THOSE OF THEIR WHITE AGE

COHORT IN THE SURVEY RESEARCH CENTER (SRC) NATIONAL SAMPLE

Item	Percentage Who Disagreed	
	1967 Boston	1968 SRC National Sample (1940-1947 White Cohort)
A. Public officials don't care	69	64
B. Voting is the only way	65	61
C. People like me don't have any say	85	69
D. Can't understand what's going on	48	35

The percentages for the SRC 1940-1947 white cohort were provided
by Professor Paul R. Abramson, who has been helpful in many other
ways in the preparation of this chapter.

foreigners) of the emotional Italian. It is perhaps more socially acceptable to be excited and indignant in Italy, and we can speculate that the Italian–Americans in Boston have become more like their phlegmatic Anglo-Saxon neighbors.

Similarly, with regard to sense of political efficacy, we doubt that there is enough difference in the two political systems to explain the differences in attitude. Rather it would seem likely that political cynicism and feelings of personal political impotency are more consistent with cultural norms in Italy than in the United States. It also seems likely that various agencies of civic education (both formal and informal) do a more thorough job of inculcating the democratic ethos in America than in Italy. Whether or not he does, in fact, have more political power, the young American knows that in his system the people are supposed to have an influence. This is in line with the observation of Easton and Dennis (1967) that efficacy can be perceived as a norm as well as a disposition. With regard to possible system differences Madsen (1978) has shown that levels of efficacy may be related to ''the time during which democratic experience can accumulate in the political culture [p. 872].''

In a further effort to explain these cross-cultural differences in political orientations expressed when the subjects were young adults, we looked to the vast store of personal and family data that had been gathered in the longitudinal study. Even if these data did not help explain cross-cultural differences, we hoped that they might indicate important relationships between adolescent development and adult political orientations that would contribute to a general theory of political socialization.

AGE OF SOCIALIZATION

We began with an attempt to determine whether the political orientations expressed when the subjects were young adults could be shown to be related to the data on child-rearing practices and attitudes that had been obtained in interviews with the parents about 10 years earlier (see Chapter 2).

A major assumption in Almond and Verba's (1963) classic study was that democratic political institutions depend on democratic substructures in the family, school, and job. They found that there was some connection between democratic political orientations and democratic family relations, but that the association was a complex one affected by intervening variables such as age and education. Elder (1968) and Pinner (1965) also found evidence that family relations were related to political orientations.

With regard to democratic family participation, Almond and Verba classified the United States with the United Kingdom as high; Germany was in the middle; and Italy was, along with Mexico, in the lowest category. This was in line with our finding that the Boston parents reported quite different patterns of child rearing from those in Italy. There was some reason to believe that different treatment in childhood and adolescence might be related to differences in political attitudes and feelings expressed by our subjects as young adults. We would have much better evidence of such a relationship, of course, if we could show that the two sets of variables were related when we considered the subjects in each of the cities separately.

The first of these child-rearing variables (labeled "Age of Socialization" in Tables 8-5 and 8-6) is described in Chapter 2. It was thought that late ages of toilet and cleanliness training could be assumed to reflect relatively indulgent child-rearing attitudes on the part of parents, while earlier age of socialization would reflect greater strictness and pressure toward socialization at this early developmental state. There may be room for differences of interpretation as to what may be the effects of relatively late achievement of toilet training and other types of self-control. However it was achieved, it was apparent that in the areas of elimination control, cleanliness, and self-care the Boston boys were socialized at an earlier age than the boys in the Italian cities.

Reasoning on the basis of covariation, we might infer that this earlier attainment of self-control might be related to the higher sense of political efficacy and less frequent excitement and indignation that is characteristic of the Boston subjects. If such is indeed the case, we would expect that within each city the boys who were relatively early in being socialized would also have a higher sense of efficacy and a lower incidence of emotional involvement than those who did not learn to take care of themselves until they were older. We can see in Table 8-5 that this expectation is borne out. In each of the three cities the boys who were socialized relatively early included a higher percentage who made relatively

TABLE 8-5

PERCENT WHO WERE HIGH IN SENSE OF POLITICAL EFFICACY

	Boston	Rome	Palermo	Total
Age of Socialization				
Early	51(N=39)	47(N=38)	50(N=30)	
Late	40(N=25)	37(N=43)	39(N=39)	
Permissiveness				
Low	40(N=25)	32(N=47)	53(N=34)	
High	51(N=39)	58(N=36)	33(N=39)	
Child Rearing Pattern		P>.05		
Early Socialization-Low Permissiveness	47(N=15)	28(N=18)	61(N=13)	
Early Socialization-High Permissiveness	54(N=24)	65(N=20)	41(N=17)	
Late Socialization-Low Permissiveness	30(N=10)	34(N=29)	50(N=20)	
Late Socialization-High Permissiveness	47(N=15)	43(N=14)	26(N=19)	
Independence				
Low	27(N=15)	29(N=35)	51(N=35)	
High	54(N=48)	54(N=48)	34(N=38)	
	P<.05	P<.02		
Relations with Father				
Good	51(N=53)	53(N=34)	44(N=64)	
Poor	11(N=09)	37(N=46)	40(N=05)	
	P=.05			
Social Class				
Higher	82(N=11)	50(N=20)	41(N=22)	
	38(N=40)	39(N=33)	57(N=30)	
Lower	46(N=13)	43(N=30)	24(N=21)	
	P=.05		P<.05	
Intelligence				
Low	36(N=33)	41(N=42)	37(N=38)	
High	58(N=31)	46(N=41)	47(N=38)	
	P>.10			
Education				
Low	28(N=32)	36(N=44)	30(N=23)	
High	65(N=31)	54(N=37)	43(N=44)	
	P>.01			
School Marks				
High	60(N=38)	53(N=30)	44(N=54)	
Low	27(N=26)	37(N=51)	39(N=18)	
	P=.01			

TABLE 8-5 (continued)

	Boston	Rome	Palermo	Total
Ordinal Position				
First Born	52(N=21)	58(N=33)	47(N=36)	60(N=90)
Other	45(N=42)	34(N=50)	38(N=37)	44(N=129)
		P=.05		P>.05
Age at Puberal Maturity				
Early	54(N=17)	45(N=29)	50(N=24)	54(N=70)
Middle	44(N=25)	42(N=33)	48(N=31)	52(N=89)
Late	43(N=21)	39(N=18)	22(N=18)	44(N=57)
Sense of Expectation				
Low	43(N=28)	40(N=35)	24(N=38)	
High	47(N=30)	51(N=35)	59(N=37)	
			P>.01	
Sense of Alienation				
Low	61(N=31)	66(N=35)	37(N=35)	
High	26(N=27)	26(N=35)	45(N=40)	
	P>.01	P=.001		
Sense of Personal Control				
Low	43(N=35)	28(N=29)	37(N=35)	
High	48(N=23)	58(N=41)	45(N=40)	
		P<.01		

Probability of statistical significance was determined by chi square tests.

high efficacy scale scores. If we think of sense of political efficacy as being associated with ego strength and general self-confidence, this supports the theory already suggested that early socialization may also be associated with these same characteristics.

The data on the relation of age of socialization and emotional involvement shown in Table 8-6 do not help us further explain the difference in frequency of excitement and indignation between Boston and the Italian cities, although the data do suggest that early socialization may be related to high emotional involvement in Rome.

PERMISSIVENESS

The second variable based on the interviews with the parents had to do with the amount of control that the parents exerted over the lives of their sons in adoles-

TABLE 8-6

PERCENT WHO WERE HIGH IN TOTAL EMOTIONAL INVOLVEMENT

	Boston	Rome	Palermo	Total
Age of Socialization				
Early	67(N=39)	50(N=38)	47(N=30)	
Late	60(N=25)	37(N=43)	51(N=39)	
Permissiveness				
Low	72(N=25)	30(N=47)	41(N=34)	
High	59(N=39)	61(N=36)	51(N=39)	
		P=.01		
Freedom of Expression				
Low	53(N=32)	33(N=39)	32(N=40)	
High	74(N=31)	58(N=38)	39(N=33)	
	P=.10	P>.05		
Family Cohesion				
High	65(N=48)	46(N=43)	38(N=45)	
Low	62(N=16)	40(N=37)	61(N=28)	
			P<.05	
Intelligence				
Low	48(N=33)	45(N=42)	42(N=38)	
High	81(N=31)	41(N=41)	50(N=38)	
	P=.01			
Education				
Low	55(N=31)	28(N=39)	56(N=23)	
High	74(N=31)	64(N=36)	36(N=44)	
		P>.01		
School Marks				
High	76(N=38)	58(N=29)	50(N=54)	
Low	46(N=26)	39(N=46)	38(N=18)	
	P=.02	P=.10		
Age at Puberal Maturity				
Early	76(N=17)	38(N=29)	50(N=24)	40(N=70)
Middle	56(N=25)	58(N=33)	55(N=31)	45(N=89)
Late	57(N=21)	28(N=18)	33(N=18)	23(N=57)
				P=.05
Sense of Expectation				
Low	71(N=28)	43(N=35)	47(N=38)	
High	50(N=30)	51(N=35)	43(N=37)	
	P=.10			

TABLE 8-6 (continued)

	Boston	Rome	Palermo	Total
Sense of Alientation				
Low	68(N=31)	57(N=35)	46(N=35)	
High	52(N=27)	37(N=35)	45(N=40)	
		P=.10		
Sense of Personal Control				
Low	54(N=35)	48(N=29)	49(N=35)	
High	70(N=23)	46(N=41)	42(N=40	

Probability of statistical significance was determined by chi square tests.

cence. As reported in chapter 2, the Boston parents responded clearly in a more permissive, less controlling fashion than the parents in the two Italian cities.

Here, again, we might logically infer that there is a relation between the stricter treatment in adolescence and the lower sense of political efficacy reported by the Italians. Similarly, it seems reasonable to assume that the higher incidence of excitement and indignation demonstrated by the Italian boys might have been related to the more rigid controls that the Italian parents exerted over their sons. Again, the more stringent test of the validity of this assumption involved determining whether amount of parental control in adolescence is related to efficacy and involvement within the individual cities.

The relation of parental permissiveness to sense of political efficacy is shown in Table 8-5. The data for Boston and Rome do suggest support for the hypothesis that strict parental controls might be associated with general lack of self-confidence and ego strength, which were in turn reflected in lower efficacy scale scores. In Palermo, however, the pattern is reversed and relatively higher efficacy scores were made by the boys whose parents allowed them relatively less freedom. Perhaps "permissiveness" among Sicilian families might be interpreted as lack of concern, whereas stricter controls represent the maintenance of traditional parental authority. This indication that family permissiveness may mean something different in Palermo than in the other two samples reminds us that the latter were made up of migrant families whereas the former had not changed their location. In the more stable social situation it may be that parental disciplinary attitudes are relatively less important in the development of the personality of the boys. It may also be that in the more traditional society of Sicily, parental attitudes of permissiveness are not so conducive to a sense of personal effectiveness and political involvement as they seem to be in the more open social systems of Rome and Boston.

In the case of the relation of family permissiveness to involvement (Table 8-6), the findings for Boston are consistent with the hypothesis that strict parental controls might make the child more likely to be excited or indignant. In Rome and Palermo, however, there is a higher incidence of involvement reported by boys from the more permissive families. To explain this we are tempted to reverse our position and suggest that in Italy the more permissive families might have produced boys who felt more freedom to express their emotions. Out data do not really help us choose between these theories, but, at least, we can say that parental strictness appears to mean something different in Boston than in the Italian setting, and this might help a little to explain the greater incidence of involvement reported in Rome and Palermo.

If we consider the data on age of socialization together with those on control over the boy's behavior in adolescence reported in the interviews with the parents, very different patterns of child rearing for the Italian–American as compared with the Italian parents, emerge. The parents in Boston combined earlier pressure (or assistance) toward cleanliness and self-control with greater permissiveness and self-determination in adolescence. The Italian parents, on the other hand, particularly in Rome, combined indulgence (or benign neglect) in early childhood with greater restrictiveness and control in adolescence.

These differences would seem to constitute a consistent contrasting pattern if we assume that the parents in Boston, influenced by prevailing American values and ideas about child development, have held higher expectations of maturity in their sons than have the Italian parents. In Palermo, and especially in Rome, on the other hand, the boy is expected to remain immature and subject to parental control for a longer period of time. Thus, he is treated both more indulgently as a small child and more restrictively as an adolescent. This is precisely the pattern of child rearing that we would expect might make for lack of self-confidence, low ego strength, and a general attitude of indignation. Looking at the data on child-rearing patterns in this combined way gives the best indication as to why the Italian boys reported a much more frequent incidence of political involvement, and a much lower sense of political efficacy than the Italian–Americans in Boston. If this explanation is correct, however, it should hold up when we relate the combined child-rearing pattern to the political variables in the individual cities. To make the four-way break of our already small samples leaves us with such a small number of cases in each cell that it requires great temerity to try to make something of the findings. The possibility was so intriguing, however, that we felt compelled to see what we could do with it.

In Table 8-5 we see the relation of the four child-rearing patterns to sense of political efficacy, and the results are encouraging, despite the small numbers. In Boston it is noted that the boys with the largest percentage in the high efficacy category were those whose child-rearing pattern was the prevailing one in that city (i.e., early socialization followed by permissiveness in adolescence), and, consistent with our expectation, the Boston boys who had been raised in the pattern prevailing in Italy (i.e., late socialization combined with strictness in adolescence) had the smallest percentage in the high efficacy category. In Rome a similar finding is indicated, in part, when we note that the Roman boys who were raised in the pattern prevailing in Boston had a considerably larger percentage in the high efficacy category than the boys in the same city who came from families with different child-rearing patterns. The lack of consistency and the apparent association of late socialization/high permissiveness with low efficacy scale scores in Palermo again remind us that family attitudes may have a different meaning and thus a different impact on personality development in that city. A similar attempt to relate patterns of child rearing to incidence of political affect produced rather inconsistent results.

INDEPENDENCE

There were several other measures of family relations based on the interviews with the families. The interviewers were asked to make a judgment as to the extent to which the family favored the boy's independence respecting his personality. Subjects in the "low" independency category in Table 8-5 were judged to give little or no encouragement to the boy's independence, while those in the "high" category had favored independence to at least a fair degree. In the judgment of the interviewers there was more encouragement to the boy's independence in Boston than in the Italian cities, which is quite consistent with other findings with regard to family relations in the three cities. (See Chapter 2.) Encouragement of independence and personal autonomy would seem likely to be related to high sense of political efficacy, and this appears to give additional evidence that family relations were a possible factor related to the difference in sense of political efficacy between Boston and the Italian cities. There is considerable support for this hypothesis in the data for the individual cities of Boston and Rome, where there is shown to be (Table 8-5) a significant relation between encouragement of the boy's independence and high sense of political efficacy. In Palermo, however, the relation is in the opposite direction, which suggests that, as for several other family measures, encouragement of independence means something different in that city.

RELATIONS WITH THE FATHER

The interviewers were also asked to make judgments as to the relationships of the boys to their parents and other members of their families. More poor relationships were reported from Rome than from the other two cities, and this was especially true for relations with the father. For the sample who replied to the political questionnaire, 58% of the Rome boys were judged to have bad or indifferent relations with their fathers as compared to only 15% in Boston and 7%

in Palermo. Some of this variation is surely due to variations in interviewer judgment, but there is other evidence that the Rome boys had experienced some lack of closeness with their fathers. They were less likely to report that they discussed politics with their fathers. (See Chapters 2 and 5; also Mussen *et al.*, 1963.) Good relations with the father were significantly related to high sense of political efficacy in Boston and the data suggest a relation in the same direction in the other two cities (Table 8-5). This is consistent with what we would expect if we consider high efficacy to be related to ego strength and positive self-image. The lack of cross-cultural differences in judgments of relations with the father means that this variable does not help in explaining the differences in political orientations between the Boston and the Italian cities.

FREEDOM OF EXPRESSION

The measure labeled "freedom of expression" in Table 8-6 represents another part of the general attempt to measure variations in control of the lives of the boys. It was based on four items in the family interview that dealt with the extent with which the boys were free to participate in family decisions and to discuss problems with their families. (See Chapter 2.) The designations "high" and "low" freedom of expression refer to the relative extent (as compared to others in the same city) to which the boys were free to express themselves in relations with other members of their families. From the higher average scores in Boston when compared to the Italian cities we may infer that there was more open communication in the Italian–American families than in those in Italy, and that the Boston parents had been influenced by some of the more typically American values in favor of democratic child rearing. It seemed reasonable to infer that these more democratic child-rearing attitudes were related to the higher sense of political efficacy reported by the Boston boys, but the data for the individual cities did not support this hypothesis.

We might also infer that lower freedom of expression in the Italian families might be related to the higher frequency of emotional involvement with politics reported from Rome and Palermo. As we have previously indicated, though, there is also some logical basis for expecting that in the less strict families the child might feel more free to express his emotions. In this case our data are supportive of the latter explanation. There was (Table 8-6) a significant relation between high freedom of expression and high emotional involvement with politics in Boston and Rome, and the data suggest a relation in the same direction in Palermo.

FAMILY COHESION

Several of the items in the family interviews were intended to measure family cohesion or togetherness. On all of these items the Boston families gave replies that indicated more family cohesion than was the case for the families in the Italian cities. (See Chapter 2.) We thought that the higher family cohesion reported from Boston might help to explain the higher sense of political efficacy and lower incidence of excitement and indignation reported from that city. However, the data for the individual cities indicated no relation between family cohesion and sense of political efficacy. Family cohesion was also not related to emotional involvement in Boston or Rome, but there was a significant relation between low family cohesion and high emotional involvement with politics in Palermo. If we think of high family cohesion as being consistent with less traditional, more "democratic" family relations, this seems to provide additional evidence that the child-rearing measures had a different meaning in Palermo than in the other two cities.

SOCIAL CLASS

Since socioeconomic status has been found to be related to political attitudes and behavior in many other studies, one of our earliest concerns was whether the cross-cultural differences in political orientations in our study were due to social class differences. In the initial selection of the subjects for the study, every effort was made to insure that there were no major differences in the socioeconomic characteristics of the three groups of boys. (For a description of the social class measure, see Chapter 2.) For the subsample who answered the political questionnaire, it appears that families of the Palermo subjects are somewhat higher in social status than those in Rome, with the Boston families somewhere in between. Thus, whatever differences in SES exist can hardly explain the cross-cultural differences in political orientations that are apparent. Our data (Table 8-5) suggest that high sense of political efficacy was positively related to higher socioeconomic status in all three cities, although the association in Rome is quite small. Actually, it is more accurate to say the Boston subjects in the high efficacy category were more likely, also, to be high in social class, while the Palermo subjects who were high in efficacy were less likely to be low in class status. Social class has been found to be positively related to sense of political efficacy in other studies (Campbell et al., 1960; Easton & Dennis, 1967, p. 36; Hess & Torney, 1967, p. 124).

INTELLIGENCE

Our measure of intelligence was based on the Raven Progressive Matrices (1956 Revision) which was administered when most of the subjects were 13 or 14 years of age. The Raven was chosen as what appeared to be the most "culture-free" of available measures of general intelligence. (See Chapter 4 for more extensive discussion of the Raven and its correlation with other variables.) In their test scores the Boston subjects were at a generally similar level to the combined Rome and Palermo groups, and to the Raven standardization group. There was, however, a difference in the mean scores of the two Italian cities, with Rome somewhat higher and Palermo somewhat lower than Boston. For those who answered the political questionnaire the mean scores (in percentiles) were Palermo .42, Rome .55, and Boston .53. It does not appear likely, then, that the cross-cultural differences in political involvement and efficacy are due to differences in intelligence of the three groups.

Within our individual groups high intelligence was related to high sense of political efficacy in Boston, and the data suggest a similar relation in Rome, and somewhat more in Palermo. This is consistent with the findings in the Easton and Hess study of Chicago school children (Easton & Dennis, 1967, p. 35; Hess & Torney, 1967, p. 171; Jackman, 1970; White, 1968) and with two other more recent studies (Carmines, 1972; Harvey & Harvey, 1970). On the basis of his careful examination of the findings in this area, Abramson, P.R. (1977) observed that "there is little theoretical and somewhat questionable empirical support [p. 69]" for the assumption that low levels of intelligence contribute to low sense of political effectiveness. Our data provide some additional empirical support for the hypothesis that levels of political efficacy may be related to intelligence.

EDUCATION

When the subjects were young adults information was obtained by a personal questionnaire as to the total number of years that they had spent in school. (For a discussion of this and differences and similarities in the Italian and American educational systems see Chapters 2 and 6.) Amount of education has been found to be related to political attitudes and behavior in many studies, with the more highly educated more likely to be politically active and have a higher sense of political efficacy (Almond & Verba, 1963; Campbell et al., 1960). The differences in political orientation between Boston and the Italian cities cannot readily be explained by differences in education, but within the individual cities those with above the median amount of education were likely to be higher in sense of political efficacy, significantly so in Boston (Table 8-5). High level of education was also significantly related to high political involvement in Rome, and the data strongly suggest a similar relation in Boston, but not in Palermo (Table 8-6).

SCHOOL MARKS

Information on school marks was obtained in the parent interviews and, while it is probably not as reliable as examination of school records might have been, it does give us a broad indication as to how well the boys were doing in school at the time of the interviews (see Chapter 2). Those subjects who had been reported to be above the median in school marks were significantly likely to be high in sense of political efficacy in Boston, and the data indicate a similar relation in the Italian cities (Table 8-5).[3] The fact that intelligence, amount of education, and school marks were all more highly related to political efficacy in Boston than in the Italian cities seems to give support to our previous speculation that the higher efficacy scores in Boston might be due, in part, to differences in civic education. School marks were also positively related to high involvement in political events, significantly so in Boston (Table 8-6). Both intelligence and educational achievement are more highly related to emotional involvement with politics in Boston than in the Italian cities, and this reminds us of our previous observations that excitement and indignation may be more the cultural norm in Italy.

ORDINAL POSITION

There is a considerable literature dealing with the relation of birth order to social and psychological behavior, and several studies have indicated a relation between first-born status and political activism (Gergen & Ullman, 1977, p. 427; Renshon, 1974, p. 142; Renshon, 1975). In our study the first-born in Rome were significantly more likely to be high in sense of political efficacy, and the data suggest a similar relation for Boston and Palermo. When the three cities were combined there was shown to be a significant relation between being "first-born" and making higher scores in the political efficacy scale (Table 8-5). The percentage of first-born who replied to the political questionnaire in Boston was less than that in the Italian cities, and so it is evident that this variable was not related to the cross-cultural differences in sense of political efficacy.

AGE AT PUBERAL MATURITY

Another "biological" variable for which data were available from the longitudinal study was age at puberal maturity. We were prompted to examine the relation of this variable to political orientations by the fact that the psychological effects of early and late maturing have been well established in numerous previous studies. In their classic study of sexual behavior in the human male, Kinsey and his associates (1948, Chapter 9) noted that early maturers were more likely to be described as socially extroverted and/or aggressive, while late maturers were

---

[3]The size of our groups and the distribution of the data has made it impossible to do a satisfactory multicorrelation analysis to determine what may be the relative contributions of social status, intelligence, and educational achievement to sense of political efficacy and involvement.

more likely to be described as introverted and/or socially inept. Kinsey's findings as well as those of numerous other studies have been reviewed in Eichorn (1963, pp. 4–61). Studies based on the longitudinal data of the Institute of Human Development at the University of California have indicated that late maturers were likely to have negative self-conceptions and attitudes, while early maturers "presented a much more favorable psychological picture during adolescence" (Mussen & Jones, 1957, 1958). (See Chapter 3 for data on differences between our three groups in rate of maturation and Chapter 5 for an examination within this sample of association between early or late maturing and personality variables.) Jones (1957, 1965) reported that, even in their late thirties, early maturing males still exceeded late maturers on measures of dominance, sociability, sense of well-being, and responsibility.

Our findings as shown in Tables 8-5 and 8-6 are generally consistent with those reported. As we have reported earlier (Ferguson, Ferguson, & Young, 1976), for the total group of subjects those who were late in maturing were significantly less likely than their earlier maturing peers to report strong interest in politics and high involvement with political events. The late maturers were also found to be significantly less likely to be high in sense of political efficacy. (In the earlier report political efficacy was measured by the four original items used by Campbell *et al.,* 1960.) For the six-item efficacy measure used in Table 8-5, the relation to age of maturation was in the same direction but not statistically significant.

Difference in ages of puberal maturity between the three cities, while paralleling the cross-cultural differences in political orientations, are not sufficient to explain them, but in the individual cities the pattern established for the three-city total still holds. The data suggest that the late maturers were less likely to be high in political efficacy and involvement in the two Italian cities, but in Rome the early maturers, also, appear to have been less involved than those in the middle category. In Boston the relation of maturation to involvement and efficacy is in the same direction, but it is more accurate to say here that the *early* maturers were *more* likely to be highly politicized than those in the middle and late categories.

Obviously we cannot assume that these data suggest any direct causal relation between age at puberal maturity and politicization. The relation must be a very indirect and complex one that depends, among other things, on the importance attached to early and late maturing in a particular society. Depending on the way rate of maturation is culturally defined, it can be assumed that early and late maturers will have differing adolescent experiences that influence their personalities. Our own data give some support for this in the suggested differences in the relative effects of early and late maturing in Boston and the Italian cities (see Chapter 5).

Political socialization has conventionally been regarded as primarily a social or psychological phenomenon. Our findings suggest that the development of political orientations may sometimes be influenced by the interaction of biological and sociopsychological factors. Our data clearly suggest a relation between age at puberal maturity and political orientations, and, in terms of predictability, it is important to remember that even the late maturers had reached puberty at least 5 years prior to the time when they responded to the political questionnaire.

EXPECTATIONS, CONTROL, AND ALIENATION

At about the same time that we were collecting information on the political orientations of our subjects, Richard Jessor was using these same subjects to extend his previous work on the personal and ethnic determinants of patterns of alcohol usage. This provided us with three measures of personality for our subjects as young adults which are described by Jessor *et al.* (1968, 1970) and in Chapter 6. The first of these was "expectations of goal attainment" (perceived opportunity) in a variety of need areas (such as family, work, and friendships). The second was measure of "alienation," patterned after the Srole scale and emphasizing feelings of social isolation and lack of meaning in daily life activities. The third personality measure was a scale assessing the degree to which the subject felt he had *internal control* over his future and over the outcomes of his behavior. Differences between our three groups on these measures are reported in Chapter 6.

In general, Jessor's data showed the young men in Boston to have been feeling less frustration and dissatisfaction, higher expectations, and more control over their future than the Italian youth. These findings are in line with the observations of many writers on southern Italian culture who have emphasized the fatalism and lack of confidence in the individual's ability to control his environment. La Palombara and Walters (1961, p. 43) report that a 1958 survey showed that two-thirds of young people throughout Italy had "uniformly dismal expectations" regarding their future economic position.

Differences on the personality measures suggest some basis for the difference in political orientations. Higher expectations, lower alienation, and higher sense of personal control would appear to be consistent with the higher sense of political efficacy and lower emotional involvement with political events that characterized the Boston when compared to the Italian subjects. We remind ourselves, though, of the possible effects of differing cultural and social contexts on self-report measures of either personality or political orientations. It is surely more socially acceptable and more realistic in southern Italy than in America to express attitudes of cynicism, fatalism, and pessimism, just as it is more in line

with Italian cultural norms (and possibly realities) to report feelings of indignation over political events, and a low sense of control over the workings of the
political system.

With this reminder that both sets of self-report measures may be affected by
cultural norms, we can, none the less, take some satisfaction in the consistency
between the cross-cultural differences in both the measures of personality and
political orientations. Higher expectations, lower sense of alienation, and higher
sense of personal control can all be viewed as possible explanations of why the
Boston youth are so much less indignant, and much higher in sense of political
efficacy than those in Italy. Here again, the stricter test of this hypothesis will
come from an examination of the relation of the personality variables to political
orientations in each of the individual cities.

With regard to efficacy, there is considerable support for the hypothesis (Table
8-5). High sense of personal expectation was found to be significantly related to
high sense of political efficacy in Palermo, and the association is in the expected
direction of both of the other cities. As we would have predicted, the youth who
were less alienated were much more likely to feel politically efficacious in
Boston and Rome. This is not the case in Palermo, however, and possibly this is
related to the fact that alienation is more accepted as a way of life in that city.
Other studies have shown variable results with regard to the relation of alienation
to political attitudes and behavior (Gergen & Ullman, 1977, pp. 420–421), and
Schwartz (1973, pp. 7–8) has suggested that alienation may be related either to
withdrawal or to activism.

There was a strong positive relation between high sense of personal control
and high sense of political efficacy in Rome, and the data suggested a similar
positive relation in the other two cities. This is supportive of our hypothesis, but
seems contrary to the finding of Renshon (1974, p. 195) that persons experiencing low sense of personal control were more likely to be politically active.
Renshon (1974, pp. 35–37) suggests that the *need* for personal control, but not
sense of political efficacy, is part of personality structure. Thus, a belief that one
has control over the political process may help satisfy the need for control in
other life areas, but only if politics is salient for the person involved.

The data for the individual cities are inconclusive with regard to our general
hypothesis as to the relation of the personality measures to emotional involvement with politics (Table 8-6). Low personal expectation was related to high
involvement in Boston, and the same relation is suggested for Palermo, but not
Rome. Contrary to the general hypothesis, the data suggest that high emotional
involvement with politics was related to low sense of alienation in Boston and
Rome, but that there was no relation between the two variables in Palermo. Sense
of personal control was not significantly related to political involvement in any of
the three individual cities, but, contrary to the expectation based on the cross-
cultural differences in the two variables, there is a clear suggestion that in Boston

high sense of personal control was related to high emotional involvement with politics. Again, our data suggest that political attitudes may have differing personal meanings in different cultural contexts.

SUMMARY

Information on the political orientations of our subjects was obtained by means of a questionnaire that was distributed when they were young adults. The responses to this questionnaire revealed that the young men in the three cities were quite similar in the amount of interest in and attention devoted to politics. When compared to the young men in the Italian cities, however, those in Boston reported much less emotional involvement with politics and a much higher sense of political efficacy. In an effort to explain these cross-cultural differences in political orientations reported when the subjects were young adults, we examined their relation to the personal and family data that had been gathered in the longitudinal study. In addition to explaining the cross-cultural differences, we hoped that this might reveal relationships between adolescent development and adult political orientations that would contribute to general knowledge about the political socialization process.

The parents in the Italian cities were more indulgent than the Boston parents in the early socialization of their sons, while the Boston parents were much more likely to be permissive toward their sons in adolescence. The Boston parents were also more likely than those in Italy to encourage adolescent independence and freedom of expression. These cross-cultural differences in child rearing and family relations appear to be consistent with the comparatively lower sense of political efficacy and the higher incidence of emotional involvement with politics reported by the Italian youth.

Thinking of the relation between these two variables as a hypothesis about family influences on political orientations, we proceeded to the much stricter tests of their association within the individual cities. This effort provided considerable support for the general hypothesis with regard to political efficacy, and some support with regard to emotional involvement with politics. There were also some inconsistencies which suggested that some of the family relations measures had different meanings in the three cities.

Three measures of personality that were obtained at about the same time as the political data also showed cross-cultural differences that were consistent with the differences in political orientations, and the data for the individual cities generally were consistent with regard to personality correlates of sense of political efficacy. While our data do not speak to this, it seems probable that cognitive factors and cultural norms were major factors in determining cross-cultural differences in political orientations. This research demonstrates that differences in family relations and personality also have more than a peripheral relation to differences in political orientations.

In the case of several other measures of the adolescent development of our subjects where there were no cross-cultural differences, the correlations with political orientations proved to be generally consistent with those found in other studies of adolescent development and political socialization. Political orientations were found to be related to social status, intelligence, and educational achievement, as well as to two "biological" variables, birth order and age of puberal maturity.

CHAPTER 9

Conclusions

As this study shows, emigration to a more auspicious environment may make for more harmonious physical growth, affect patterns of health or disease, and influence ways of thought and behavior. On the other hand, the broad course of adolescent development proved very much the same for boys living in Italy and in America. The phenomena of human physical and mental growth show only limited plasticity to environmental change—at least, the kind of change provided by the "natural experiment" of migration from southern Italy on which we capitalized. We have seen also how the social institution of the family, particularly the southern Italian family, manages to perpetuate itself in changed circumstances. Bonds of relationship, customs, traditions, values, mutual expectations between generations, ways of rearing children, and patterns of family life are preserved despite geographical moves of hundreds or thousands of miles. Palermo, Rome, and Boston are very different cities, and yet a visitor acquainted with our subjects and their families in one locale would have an immediate sense of familiarity meeting those in either of the other two.

Despite these broad similarities, certain differences attributable to the contrasting environments do emerge. In the area of physical growth, it is clear that our Boston subjects are much heavier both before and after as well as during puberty. Part of this bulk is made up by extra bone and muscle, which should make for increased performance on tests of physical efficiency. While their static strength was greater, scores on a test of cardiovascular resistance were not. While most of our Boston group were not obese, some were—more than among the Italian boys. This raises some concern for the future and the possibly increased incidence of middle-aged disease processes, such as coronary thromboses. We compared blood pressures taken at the end of adolescence for our three groups of subjects, and here found more elevated levels among the Rome group. It is difficult to draw any firm conclusions about the increased risk of cardiovascular disease among the two emigrant groups; only time will tell whether this is part of the price of mobility.

While the increased weight and slight increase in height of the Boston group can be attributed to generally better nutrition and especially to the increase in protein consumption, not all of the nutritional changes in this group are for the better. (It must be noted that the weight pattern of our Boston subjects is close to the new U.S. National Standards; see Hamill *et al.*, 1977). In some way, the muscle should be retained but the fat disposed of, so that all three samples should approximate accepted standards of height and weight, instead of Boston marching proudly up to 10 kg ahead throughout the teenage period. We suspect that this tendency toward obesity among the Italian–American subjects reflects the perpetuation of southern Italian dietary patterns (lots of "pasta," etc.) in an environment where food was generally more plentiful. There is also a strong belief among southern Italian mothers that only fat babies are really healthy. Thus a program of obesity control for some adolescents (especially those from certain ethnic groups) must start in early childhood, so that other forms of gratification can come to replace high-calorie eating.

Another change in pattern of consumption evident among our Boston subjects has even more alarming implications. They show a shift away from the traditional southern Italian use of wine as a normal part of the diet, consumed in the home and sanctioned as part of normal family life, to the consumption of other forms of alcohol outside as well as at home, to the use of alcohol for tension release and the facilitation of social interchange, and to more frequent drunkenness. Again, it is too soon to tell whether these shifts presage more serious drinking problems among the Italian–American men; Italian–Americans compared with other U.S. ethnic groups, have shown low rates of alcoholism. But the indications for preventive work beginning in adolescence or before are clear.

We noted a moderate height deficit in Italy, especially before puberty. Earlier introduction of animal protein (as was characteristic for the Boston subjects) may usefully modify this, and we predict that with the current economic progress of central and southern Italy this difference will have disappeared in the next generation. This is also likely to be true of the difference we noted in the endocrine pattern: a moderate advancement in puberal development in the Boston subjects, and a disproportionate number of late maturers in Rome. It is possible that the retardation in sexual development of some of the Rome subjects may reflect the severe privations in that city during the years immediately before and after the end of World War II, just the time when many of our subjects would have been born. We cannot be sure of this interpretation, since there is little or no evidence linking pre- and postnatal malnutrition to retarded sexual development, but this seems to us a lead worth investigating in other samples. Much greater divergences in rates of maturation are found between social classes in developing countries, and these may take much longer to eliminate (Young, 1975).

If the flattening secular trend is continued, boys in Italy and other Western countries as well as in America will soon reach puberty several months earlier even than our Boston subjects. This trend has obvious implications for the practice of adolescent medicine and the need for more effective sex education, since these youths are becoming physically mature well before they are socially or psychologically prepared. This may pose particular problems in the southern Italian culture, with its traditionally repressive (at least overtly) attitudes toward sexuality.

The incremental data have shown several things. One is the close correspondence between Boston and Rome in velocity patterns of height and the consequent need of extra protein just before these periods. Another is the further weight velocity increase in Boston, which merits extra professional attention. The third is the merit of using puberal or biological age in order to smooth out the curves and make them more intelligible. This draws attention to the need to prepare medical students and physicians in the assessment of biological age during puberty. Similar techniques are useful, although more so in the social science field, in the area of geriatrics.

The use of genetic markers has been useful, but also pointed up that a possible genetic marker, that is lateral dominance, was influenced by the environment. The intercorrelations of the physical measures were much as expected; fat patterns were markedly different from body mass and linear variables. The Harvard Step Test was a disappointment, partly because it was practically identical in all three centers.

In the field of patterns of health and disease, the need for ongoing measures to improve the dental health of American children is clear. On the other hand, there are elements of the environment in Italy that seem to contribute to eye defects and especially myopia. Long hours of reading in dim lights are suspected as implicated, perhaps provoking ciliary spasm. There is also room for improvement in physical education in Italy.

We have no doubt that in the area of physical health and growth almost everything may be done to bring all children and young adults in western societies very close to their genetic potential. It may take rather longer in time to do the same for the third world, but other researches have developed techniques for confronting these problems in the most effective and least costly manner.

In the area of psychological development in adolescence, it is curious that, with the rather extensive popular literature on the Italian national character and the mythology about Italian family life, there is little or no scientific literature. Some studies exist comparing Italian–American emigrants to other ethnic groups in America, and this literature is rapidly growing, but with the one exception we have noted (Peterson & Migliorino, 1967), there exist no comparative studies of family life, child-rearing practices, or psychological development in Italy. This project was not originally designed as such a study, but we believe that the data can also make some real contributions to knowledge in this area, and contain important leads for future research.

The Italian parents, as compared to the Boston emigrant families, were both more indulgent with their sons in early childhood and exerted more control over them as adolescents. We believe that this pattern of child rearing conveys to the adolescent the expectation that he will remain a dependent and submissive child, enclosed within a warm and supportive but also restrictive family system, for a major portion of his life. American youth, on the other hand, have traditionally been reared with the expectation that they will become self-sufficient early in life and that they will, through their own efforts, achieve personal goals that will in many cases surpass the attainments of their parents. We see these prevalent American values, which many identify with the "Protestant ethic," clearly exemplified in our Italian–American families. (This despite the fact that many of these young men, as contrasted with their age-mates in Rome, have remained much more closely identified with traditional Catholic beliefs.) The Boston parents reported making earlier demands for self-help and self-control when the boys were small, but recognized their right as adolescents to participate in family decision making and to make their own choices of companions, of leisure-time activities, of future vocational goals, and even of academic program.

It is our impression that academic achievement was of equal importance to our Italian–American and our Italian families, and indeed equal numbers of the boys in the two national groups aspired to a higher education and actually continued to college. However, the pressures that the parents and the educational system placed on the boys for academic performance were much more severe in Italy, especially in Palermo. The result was higher anxiety about academic achievement and a greater number of early school dropouts in Italy, especially in the South where the economic pressures were greater. Whether the Italian boys who remained in school actually learned and achieved more than their American counterparts is an open question. Certainly the Rome adolescents, as a group, scored higher on measures of creative thinking and espoused more sophisticated aesthetic and social attitudes.

As part of the original design of the study, we attempted to equate intelligence in the three groups. However, the average scores on the Raven, a presumably culture-free test of intelligence, proved to be higher in Rome than in either

Boston or Palermo. This was one indication, and we have a number of others, that the group in Rome was different from the other two in some important respects. These families had typically emigrated to the metropolis in central Italy, in the parent generation, for reasons connected with the father's work; many of these fathers were minor civil servants. While they stayed in touch with relatives in the South and there were frequent visits to grandparents, patterns of extended family living so characteristic of the South were more disrupted in this group, which contained a greater proportion of typically modern urban isolated nuclear families. This may account for the more frequent evidences of strained family relations in this group.

On the other hand, the Boston families had emigrated from the South of Italy, many of them as impoverished peasants, in the grandparent generation. They may well have come from families originally more like those who remained in the South and constituted our Palermo sample, and they tended to emigrate in extended family groups. By now, they have experienced two generations of drastic cultural change and, in many cases, startling upward economic and social mobility. It is no wonder that they have embraced many typical American values with some enthusiasm, while at the same time retaining many customs and patterns of family relations typical of southern Italy.

Clearly the Boston families had absorbed a more "democratic" orientation to child rearing, were more permissive of impulse expression—especially sexual and aggressive impulses—and seemed to have a more open and more mutually supportive family life, although certainly they were no more affectionate or nurturant of the boys as small children. Our adolescent subjects in Boston reflected these differences in family life. They had higher achievement motivation, their vocational aspirations were more realistic, they impressed interviewers as more open and self-confident and expressed similar feelings on self-report questionnaires, their fantasy productions suggested that they had fewer feelings of being dominated and controlled by parents, and had less need to indulge in fantasies of autonomy and interpersonal power. They expressed fewer feelings of guilt and anxiety and reacted with less anxiety to a novel intellectual task, especially as compared to the boys in Palermo who seemed the most fearful of possible academic failure and were most likely to have experienced punitive parental reactions if they did poorly at school. At the same time, the Italian-American boys subscribed to more severe moral judgments, and this difference persisted into young adulthood. These higher moral standards seem to be an expression of a more generalized difference in the attitudes of the Italian-American young men, as compared to their compeers in Italy. They seem to have a greater sense of mastery over their own destinies, a belief in the usefulness of planning and working toward future goals, and a sense of real participation and influence in the political process. These are, of course, basic articles of faith in the American ethos, and one might view these attitudinal differences between the

Italian–American and the Italian resident young men as simply a reflection of different political and moral socialization. The Italian young men, especially those still living in the impoverished South, expressed profound cynicism about their own ability to influence political processes or to control in any way their own destinies and opportunities in life. This cynicism has been commented on repeatedly by Barzini and others as a prime characteristic of the southern Italian attitude toward life and the social order. It is difficult to know whether to view it as an expression of "anomie" or of greater sophistication—probably both. Certainly the American adolescents a decade or two younger than our subjects were typically more disenchanted with the social order.

We have the impression that the family's socioeconomic status still exerts a more determining influence on family life and on the boy's personal destiny in Italy, especially in the South. The young men in Palermo manifest in many ways a sense of being "locked-in" to their family's place in society and to more traditional attitudes about family life. It is also clear that the Italians attain adult status later, especially with respect to marriage and moving away from the parental home. It is only the more rebellious and self-sufficient young men in Rome, and those with a stronger sense of internalized control over their own destinies, who have moved away from their parents and are upwardly mobile occupationally. In Palermo this is a much rarer pattern.

We have observed that the southern Italian parents are more controlling and restrictive of their sons in adolescence, particularly so with respect to sex and aggression. We suspect, although in this area our data are much less satisfactory than in retrospect we wish they were, that these parental child-rearing attitudes are a reflection of a characteristic southern Italian pattern of socialization in which sexual and aggressive impulses are forcefully directed outward from the traditionally close and authoritarian family system. The Boston parents encouraged appropriate counteraggression when the boy was attacked by a peer, and this was part of a general pattern of encouraging gregarious and independent peer relations. The boys in Boston responded to this typically American emphasis on the importance of peer relations by being sociable and self-assertive, although we have the impression that their friendships may have been neither as intimate nor as enduring as those of the Italian youth.

The Italian parents are less likely to encourage aggression toward peers, and generally exert more control over their son's contacts with peers of the same and the opposite sex. They probably exert even stronger prohibitions against any form of aggression or hostility within the family, and the southern Italian boys are frankly afraid of the consequences of displaying such behavior in the family. It is tempting to infer, although we do not have direct evidence for such a conclusion, that anger and aggressive impulses must then be displaced to objects that clearly fall outside the boundaries of the closely drawn family network. This could account for some of the cynicism of the southern Italians. It could also relate to the popular impression that Sicily is the stronghold of the Mafia, and that southern Italian immigrants have made a disproportionate contribution to organized crime and violence in the United States and other parts of the world.

Although the social implications are less broad and obvious, our data also suggest that, where the Italian parents hold particularly repressive attitudes toward aggression and sexuality, the intellectual development of their sons may be impeded. In general, the structure of cognitive abilities among the Boston subjects is more coherent than among the Italians, and their performance in more novel or divergent intellectual tasks was more consistent with their scores on a measure of convergent abilities (the Raven). Perhaps the more permissive attitudes, particularly toward freedom of expression, of the Italian–American parents were helpful to their sons in fulfilling their intellectual potential as well as in leading a more independent social life. On the other hand, the Rome subjects, who were initially somewhat brighter as a group, were also clearly more creative and had a richer fantasy life. This is the group among whom we found most evidences of conflict with parents and parental control over the son's life. The Rome boys had less positive relations with their parents than the Bostonians, especially with their fathers, and tended to be somewhat closer to their mothers. We cannot be sure, of course, but perhaps these patterns of parent–son relations, combined with the much greater indulgence these boys experienced in infancy and early childhood, have contributed to their somewhat more sophisticated, more aesthetically oriented, more skeptical if less naively optimistic, more world-weary orientation to life, which has made the Italian national character as well as the national scene so appealing, intriguing, and puzzling to many generations of visitors from America and northern Europe.

Appendixes

APPENDIX A

Comparability of Groups

The findings from comparisons of a number of additional variables, which were used as indices of the genetic homogeneity of the samples, were as follows.

DATE OF BIRTH: PARENTS AND GRANDPARENTS

Table A-1 presents the mean dates of birth of parents and grandparents of our subjects. The mean dates of birth of the parents in the three groups are remarkably close. At the grandparental level, the Boston and Palermo groups are very close; the Rome grandparents are 4–5 years older.

TABLE A-1

MEAN DATES OF BIRTH OF PARENTS AND GRANDPARENTS

City	Parents		Grandparents			
			Paternal		Maternal	
	Male	Female	Male	Female	Male	Female
Rome	1912	1916	1876	1881	1879	1884
Boston	1912	1916	1881	1886	1883	1888
Palermo	1912	1917	1881	1886	1885	1889

BLOOD GROUPS

Table A-2 presents the ABO and Rh blood groups for our three study samples and a sample of comparable age related in Florence with the calculated genotype frequencies together with some data for comparison from Mourant et al. (1958) and Wolstenholme and O'Connor (1959). This table shows an increasing frequency of B genotype as one goes south in Italy. There are some differences between our southern groups; it is worth noting that 60% of the grandparents of the Boston Rh negative subjects came from Campania (the greater part from Avellino) and this may have had an effect of increasing somewhat the frequency of Rh negative in our Boston group. Our southern data, as a whole, are very close to what has so far been published both for ABO and Rh genotype frequencies.

COLOR BLINDNESS

We were informed that there is an increasing prevalence of color blindness as one proceeds south along the Italian peninsula. Color blindness was measured by Ishihara's Tables (1954) and was done at least on two occasions with each subject.

Table A-3 presents the results which confirm a greater prevalence of color blindness in all our southern groups.

LATERAL DOMINANCE

Our interest in this subject sprang from the evident differences in the Italian and North American cultures in the guidance of left-handed children in written communication, discussed in Chapter 5.

The mode of inheritance of left lateral dominance now appeared sufficiently clear to be of potential use for comparability of groups. Left-handedness was first thought to be the expression of a gene (recessive) in homozygous form (Ramaley, 1913); later it was thought that right-handedness was determined by a gene (dominant), detectable in both homozygous and heterozygous form (Trankell, 1950). Discordant expression of lateral dominance in twins and in the children of two left-handed parents led to speculation that dominance could only be explained multigenically, but

TABLE A-2

BLOOD GROUPING: PHENOTYPES AND GENOTYPES

City	No. Sub.	Rh System			A B O System								D/C
		Rh- Prevalence	Genotypes		Phenotypes				Genotypes				
			−	+	OO	AA − AO A	BB − BO B	AB	p	q	r		
Boston	91	11 12.09%	34.77	65.23	41 45.06	35 38.46	8 8.79	7 7.69	26.31	8.51	65.18		−1.75
Rome	149	6 4.03%	20.07	79.93	72 48.32	50 33.56	22 14.77	5 3.35	20.61	9.53	69.86		+0.43
Palermo	107	11 10.28%	32.06	67.94	42 39.25	40 37.39	22 20.56	3 2.80	22.69	12.47	64.84		+1.59
Florence	373	62 16.62%	40.77	59.23	167 44.77	156 41.82	36 9.65	14 3.76	23.22	6.95	66.83		−0.15

TABLE A-3

PREVALENCE OF COLOR BLINDNESS

Location	No. of Subjects Tested	Color Blind	Percentage
Rome	194	11	5.7
Boston	94	9	9.6
Palermo	120	12	10.0
Total South	408	32	7.8
Florence	590	24	4.1

The difference between Total South and Florence is significant (p<2%).

perhaps a single gene theory with the heterozygotes labile (Rife, D.L., 1951; Merrell, 1957) may fit the facts. These workers assume that the heterozygotes divide about equally but we have felt sufficiently uncertain about this to desist from calculating gene frequency and thus results will be presented as simple percent dominance of left hand and left foot in the groups and in a control group from central Italy.

We used a series of tests (three for hand, three for foot, three for ear, and four for eye) derived from Clark (1957). The group of hand tests was supplemented by the results of hand dynamometry and the subject was asked if he was left-handed. During analysis it became evident that one of the foot tests (stepping from wall) was too culturally determined to be of use and it was, therefore, eliminated. In respect to hand, foot, eye, and ear, we were able to make a 5-point judgment as follows: marked left, moderate left, ambidextrous, moderate right, marked right.

For the time being we shall present data for hand and foot. These are highly correlated. The association coefficients (Yule & Kendall, 1940) were .74, .64, .77 for Boston, Palermo, and Rome, respectively.

Table A-4 shows a relatively high prevalence of left-footedness in all three centers when they are compared with Florence. Left-hand dominance is also higher in all three centers, there being differences among them, the highest prevalence occurring in Boston, followed by Rome and Palermo, in that order. Merrell (1957) has recorded a prevalence of 7.1-7.6% of left-handedness and left-footedness in American subjects (throwing, striking, and kicking).

The differences between hand and foot in Florence and Palermo may possibly reflect the intolerance of these cultures to left-handedness, although it is difficult to explain why Rome should not also be so affected.

It is our strong impression that environmental pressures markedly influence the expression of lateral dominance. This has already been demonstrated by work on twins (Newman *et al.*, 1937; Rife, J.M. 1922; Wilson & Jones, 1932). All of our left-handed subjects residing in Italy were writing with the right hand. Those resident in Boston were writing with the left hand and there were, in addition, the two right-dominant boys also writing with the left hand. We have analyzed our total of 59 such children (including Florence); these data are discussed in Chapter 5.

TABLE A-4

PREVALENCE OF LEFT DOMINANCE IN HAND AND FOOT

Location	Original No. of Subjects Tested	No. Left-handed	Percentage	No. Left-footed	Percentage
Rome	150	14	9.3	14	9.3
Boston	91	11	12.1	10	10.1
Palermo	120	8	6.7	12	10.0
Total South	361	33	9.1	35	9.7
Florence	324	15	4.6	23	7.1
Scotland [*]	36,427	2434	6.7	--	--

[*]Writing only but the incidence of 6% to 7% of left-hand dominance correspondence to that described by others (Clark, M.M., 1957).

TASTE SENSIBILITY TO PHENYLTHIOUREA (PTC)

It has been shown that the prevalence of nontasters to the easily standardized bitter solution of phenylthiourea is of the order of 30% in adolescent subjects in northern Europe (Harris & Kalmus, 1949; Akesson, 1959). Our experience in Florence indicated a smaller number of nontasters. The solution was prepared as described by Kalmus to whom we are grateful for advice. The Boston and Rome samples were found to be similar in the prevalence of nontasters (15.6 and 19.3%, respectively) and also much less than the northern European figures that are available; some oddities in the distribution curves from Florence and Palermo have caused us to doubt the reliability of those figures. Allison and Blumberg (1959) have published the prevalence of nontasters in a number of different peoples; African and Asiatic peoples generally have a prevalence of less than 10%.

COLOR OF EYES

Hulse (1958) was not able to demonstrate that eye color and hair color changed in the children of migrants or in the offspring of exogenous marriages, although in hair color, as a phenotype almost certainly determined by several genes, this might have been expected. We, therefore, provisionally included these observations as additional controls.

Parents' eye color was recorded by the social worker and was, therefore, a crude estimate. The subject's eye color was measured by direct comparison with the London eye scale developed by Tanner. This runs from one (bluest blue) to 15 (dark brown, almost black). The comparison was made every time the subject came up for examination.

Table A-5 presents the frequency of eye colors in our three groups together with a control sample of 356 boys from central Italy. As there is some evidence that there may be changes in pigmentation of iris, hair, and skin during puberty, we have made efforts to create in the control sample approximately the same distribution of physical maturity.

It is seen that the three groups are fairly homogenous except for a high prevalence (8.4%) of blue eyes in the Palermo subjects. This corresponds closely to the prevalence reported by Correnti (1957).

TABLE A-5

EYE COLOR
(Expressed in percent groups)

City	Blue 1-5	Blue-Green 6-9	Green-Brown 10-12	Brown-Dark Brown 13-15
Florence	9.3	17.1	46.4	27.2
Boston	3.1	7.2	35.1	54.6
Palermo	8.4	9.2	31.7	50.7
Rome	1.2	10.4	43.0	45.4

The central Italian boys from Florence show a color distribution markedly different from the Boston, Palermo, and Rome subjects. The blue eyes in Sicily have been ascribed to the Norman invasion (see Correnti, 1957), but the number of Normans who are thought to have disembarked (several hundred) cannot explain such a prevalence unless they were extraordinarily fertile. A more likely explanation is the Lombard immigration encouraged by Rugero I, first Norman king of Sicily, with the object of re-Latinizing the island. The distribution suggests that iris color is insensitive to environmental change.

HAIR COLOR

This was estimated by direct comparison with the hair color scale distributed by the INECTO company to hairdressing establishments using their hair dyes and tints. The scale contains 18 samples of artificial hair ranging in color from one (black) to nine (light blond). This is not a continuous scale as there are some red tints in the middle color range under the appropriate number in Table A-6. This shows that the Rome group had by far the darkest hair. They were followed in an intermediate position by the Boston boys while Palermo and Florence occupied third place, Palermo being somewhat darker than Florence.

TABLE A-6

HAIR COLOR (INECTO SCALE) GROUPED IN SIX CATEGORIES
(Percent distribution in each group)

City	Red 7 5½ 5	Light Blond 9 8½ 8	Dark Blond 6 6 5¾	Light Brown 4¾ 4½ 4¼ 4	Dark Brown 3½ 3 2	Black 1½ 1
Florence	1.7	1.7	6.0	9.0	76.2	5.4
Boston	1.0	1.0	9.3	1.0	76.4	11.3
Palermo	1.7	-	1.6	9.3	81.5	5.9
Rome	-	-	1.2	5.2	75.0	19.6

There is a marked divergence of the Boston boys toward blond in the lower part of the scale. In estimating hair color it is not enough to have experienced observers matching color at the same point on the head under standard light conditions; cropping styles and hair washing should also be controlled and this we have been unable to do. We, therefore, suggest further investigation to determine if this shift toward blond in hair color in our Boston subjects could have been determined by environmental change.

APPENDIX B

Code for Physical Examination

1.	City
2.	Form
3.4.5.	Subject
6.	Visit
7.8.9.10.	Chronological Age
11.12.13.	Weight
14.15.16.17.	Arm span
18.19.20.	Biacromial (1)
21.22.23.	Biacromial (2)
24.25.26.	Bicondyle (humerus)
27.28.29.	Bicondyle (femur)
30.31.32.33.	Height
34.35.36.37.	Sitting height
38.39.40.41.	Leg length
42.43.44.	Arm length
45.46.47.	Foot length
48.49.50.51.	Chest circumference (1)
52.53.54.55.	Chest circumference (2)

APPENDIX B (continued)

56.57.58.	Arm circumference
59.60.61.	Calf circumference
62.63.64.	Bicrestal
65.66.	Dynamometer
67.68.	Hair - axilla
69.70.	Hair - pubic
71.72.	Testicular volume

CARD 7

1.	City
2.	Form
3.4.5.	Subject
6.	Visit
7.8.9.	Cranium length
10.11.12.	Cranium width
13.14.15.	Subcutaneous. triceps
16.17.18.	Subcutaneous. biceps
19.20.21.	Subcutaneous. subscapular
22.23.24.	Subcutaneous. supracrestal
25.26.27.	Subcutaneous. side chest
28.29.30.	Calf (1) external
31.32.33.	Calf (2) internal

34. Orthopedic Kyphosis   1. Absent 2. Mild 3. Moderate 4. Severe
                "   Scoliosis   "   "   "   "
                "   Flat feet   "   "   "   "
                "   Lordodis   "   "   "   "
                "   Winged scapular   "   "   "   "

                "   Other defects   1. Nothing
                                        2. Knock knee
                                        3. Flared chest
                                        4. Depression chest
                                        5. Others
                                        6. Multiple

40.	Carriage	1. Good
		2. Fair
		3. Poor
		4. Bad

41.	Muscle mass	1. Good
		2. Good - Fair
		3. Fair
		4. Fair - Poor
		5. Poor
		6. Poor - Bad
		7. Bad

42.	Muscle tone	1. Good
		2. Good - Fair
		3. Fair
		4. Fair - Poor
		5. Poor
		6. Poor - Bad
		7. Bad

43.	General condition	1. Good
		2. Good - Fair
		3. Fair
		4. Fair - Poor
		5. Poor
		6. Poor - Bad
		7. Bad

44.	Skin	1. Fair
		2. Fair - Intermediate
		3. Intermediate
		4. Intermediate - Dark
		5. Dark

45.	Skin infection	1. Nothing
		2. Localized
		3. Not localized

APPENDIX B (continued)

46.47.	Pulse frequency	
48.	Pulse type	1. Regular 2. Sinus rhythm 3. Extra systole 4. Other pulse irregularities
49.	Heart	1. Normal limits 2. Pathology
50.51.52.	Blood pressure. Maximum, systolic 30 - 200	
53.54.55.	Blood Pressure. Minimum, diastolic 40 - 120	
56.	Chest	1. Nothing 2. Evident infection - light 3. Evident infection - moderate 4. Evident infection - severe
57.	Abdomen	1. Nothing 2. Moderate inflation 3. Severe inflation 4. Hernia umbilical 5. Hernia inguinal 6. Palpable mass 7. Others 8. Multiple
58.	Liver - upper - lower	1. Within limits 2. Enlarged little (1½ - 2 cm) 3. Enlarged moderate (2½ - 3½ cm) 4. Enlarged greatly (3½ ...)
59.	Spleen	1. Not palpable 2. Palpable 3. Much enlarged

CENTRAL NERVOUS SYSTEM

60.	Deep reflexes	1. Normal 2. Fast 3. Slow 4. One or more elicited with reinforcement 5. One or more absent
61.	Superficial reflexes	1. Normal 2. Plantar equivocal 3. Plantar extensors 4. Abdominal reflexes absent N.B. If plantar = sluggish or hyperactive, code as 1. If both 3 and 4, put 3 only.
63.	Comportment	1. Positive 2. Neutral 3. Negative
64.	Nose	1. Clear 2. Blocked one side 3. Blocked both sides
65.	Infection	1. None 2. Cold simple 3. Cold with pus 4. Evident sinusites 5. Deviated septum 6. Multiple
66.	Tonsils - size	1. 0 2. ½ 3. 1 4. 1½ 5. 2 6. 2½ 7. 3 8. 3½ 9. 4
67.	Condition	1. 1 2. 1½ 3. 2 4. 2½ 5. 3 6. 3½ 7. 4

APPENDIX B (continued)

68.	Cervical glands Anterior	1. Not palpable 2. 1 palpable 3. 1½ palpable 4. 2 palpable 5. 2½ palpable 6. 3 palpable 7. 3½ palpable 8. 4 palpable
69.	Cervical glands Posterior	1 to 8 as above
70.	Cervical glands Lateral	1 to 8 as above
71.	Inguinal glands	1 to 8 as above
72.	Auxiliary glands	1 to 8 as above
73.	Hearing	1. Good 2. Mild unilateral impairment 3. Mild bilateral impairment 4. Moderate unilateral impairment 5. Moderate bilateral impairment 6. Severe unilateral impairment 7. Severe bilateral impairment
74.	Drums	1. Normal 2. Unilateral inflammation 3. Bilateral inflammation 4. Unilateral opacity 5. Bilateral opacity 6. Unilateral perforation 7. Bilateral perforation 8. Multiple
75.	Sundry	1. Earways both clear 2. 1 earway blocked wax 3. 2 earways blocked wax 4. 1 earway blocked foreign 5. 2 earways blocked foreign 6. Multiple
76.	Dental health	1. Good 2. Good - Fair 3. Fair 4. Fair - Poor 5. Poor 6. Poor - Bad 7. Bad
77.	Emergence teeth	1. Normal 2. Moderately late (6-12 months) 3. Very late (more than 12 mo. late) 4. Early (6-12 months early) 5. Very early

CARD 9

1.	City	
2.	Form	
3.4.5.	Subject	
6.	Visit	
7.	Temp teeth caries Filled	1. 0 2. 1 3. 2
8.9.	Permanent teeth caries Filled - number Teeth missing Permanent - number	
10.11.	Caries not filled Temporary - number	
12.13.	Caries not filled Permanent - number	
14.	Gingival health	1. Good 2. Mild gingivitis + 3. Moderate gingivitis ++ 4. Severe gingivitis +++ 5. Pyorrhea

APPENDIX B (continued)

15.	Malocclusion	1. Normal 2. Light 3. Moderate 4. Severe
16.17.	Number of milk teeth	0 - 16
18.19.	Number of permanent teeth	0 - 32
20.	Iris	1. Blue 2. Grey 3. Green - Brown 4. Light brown 5. Medium brown 6. Dark brown
21.	Sclera	1. Clear 2. Not clear
22.	Pupils	1. Regular 2. Not regular
23.	Pupils light reflex	1. Present 2. Scarce 3. Absent
24.	Accommodation	1. Regular 2. Scarce 3. Absent
25.26.	Acuity right	0 - 11
27.28	Acuity left	0 - 11
29.	Myopia right	1. Absent 2. Slight 3. Severe
30.	Myopia left	1. Absent 2. Slight 3. Severe
31.	Glasses	1. None 2. Yes, correct 3. Yes, don't correct
32.	Acuity right with glasses	Same as 29 - 30
33.	Acuity left with glasses	Same as 29 - 30
34.	Infection	1. None 2. Light conjunctivitis 3. Moderate conjunctivitis 4. Severe conjunctivitis 5. Corneal opacities 6. Multiple

IN THE PAST 12 MONTHS:

35.36.	Number of days in bed	1. None then number + 1
37.	Diagnosis	1. None 2. Upper resp. infection mild (up to 3) 3. Upper resp. infection moderate (4-6) 4. Upper resp. infection severe (7+ over) 5. Lower resp. infection 6. Gastroenteritis 7. Infectious disease 8. Others 9. Multiple
38.39.	Number of days lost at school	1. None then number + 1
40.	School report: performance	1. Good 2. Fair 3. Mediocre 4. Poor
41.	Comportment	1. Good 2. Fair 3. Mediocre 4. Poor
42.	Security	1. Secure 2. Mixed 3. Insecure

APPENDiX B (continued)

43.	Interest	1. Interested 2. Neutral 3. Indifferent
44.	Sociability	1. Sociable 2. Neutral 3. Unsociable
45.	Lateral dominance	1. D2 2. D1 3. M 4. S1 5. S2
46.47.	P.T.C.	1 to 5 as above
48.49.	Harvard step	
50.	Daltonism	1. Normal 2. Total color blind complete 3. Incomplete 4. Complete red 5. Complete green 6. Incomplete red-green
51.	Blood group	1. 0 2. A 3. B 4. AB
52.	Blood group	1. RH+ 2. RH-
53.54.	Hair scale	1. 1 deep black 2. 1½ black 3. 2 darkest brown 4. 3 dark brown 5. 3½ dark warm brown 6. 4 brown 7. 4¼ light brown 8. 4½ light warm brown 9. 4¾ light ash brown 10. 5 dark auburn 11. 5½ auburn 12. 5¾ light golden brown 13. Dark ash brown 14. 6½ ash blonde 15. 7 reddish blonde 16. 8 blonde 17. ½ golden blonde 18. light blonde

55.56.57.	C. Bone muscle upper arm: CMS		
58.59.60.	P. Bone muscle upper calf: CMS		
61.62.	Hair line	01234 if = 2.0	01234 if = 1.5
63.64.	Jaw line	"	"
65.66.	Eyebrows	"	"
67.68.	Body hair	"	"
69.70.	Facial hair	"	"

71.	Gynecomastia	1. No 2. Slight 3. Moderate 4. Severe
72.	Wet hands	1. No 2. Yes
73.	Urine albumin	1. None 2. Trace 3. Moderate 4. Much
74.	Urine sugar	1. None 2. Present little 3. Present much
75.	Urine ketones	1. None 2. Present little 3. Present much
76.	Astigmatism	1. No 2. Yes
77.	Ocular imbalance	1. No 2. Yes

APPENDIX C

Code for Medical History

Column

1.	City	
2.	Form number	
3.4.5.	Subject number	
6.	Visit number	
7.	Sickness father	0. None 1. Tuberculosis in any form 2. Other infectious diseases leading to chronic diseases, e.g. rheumatic fever 3. Allergies, e.g. asthma, eczema, hay fever 4. Heart diseases and circulatory disorders, e.g. vas. ulcers 5. Respiratory infections, both upper and lower 6. Gastro intestinal disorders e.g. ulcer, colitis 7. Endocrine disorders including obesity 8. Psychosomatic or psychiatric disorders, neurological 9. Death under 60 years
8.	Sickness mother	
9.	Sickness brother	
10.	Sickness sister	
11.	Sickness other members	
12.	Birth	1. Normal 2. Forceps 3. Complication, e.g. breech, with or without forceps 4. Grave complication, including caesarian 5. Infant distress
13.14.	Birth weight: kg	
15.-17.	Weight at 12 months	
18.19.	Breast feeding: months	
20.21.	Artificial milk started: months	
22.23.	Animal protein started: months	
24.	Quantity animal protein now consumed:	1. Bad - 20 g daily 2. Poor - 20-30 daily 3. Fair - 30-45 daily 4. Good - 45-60 daily 5. Good - 60-75 daily 6. Very good - 75-90 daily 7. Excellent - 90 daily
25.26.	Carbohydrates started: months	
27.	Vitamins	1. None 2. Infrequent 3. Frequent 4. Regular
28.	Medical care	1. No 2. Yes, clinic 3. Yes, private

247

APPENDIX C (continued)

29.30.	First teeth: months	
31.32.	First steps: months	
33.34.	First words: months	
35.	Measles	1. No 2. Yes
36.	Whooping cough	1. No 2. Yes
37.	Diphtheria	1. No 2. Yes
38.	Mumps	1. No 2. Yes
39.	Chicken pox	1. No 2. Yes
40.	German measles	1. No 2. Yes
41.	Respiratory infections	1. None 2. Mild moderate 3. Severe, e.g. pneumonia 4. Severe chronic, fatal
42.	Gastrointestinal infections	1. None 2. Mild moderate, e.g. chronic constipation, hemorrhage 3. Severe
43.	Trauma	1. None 2. Mild moderate 3. Severe
44.	Other diseases	1. None 2. Mild moderate (including bed wetting) 3. Potential severe, e.g. infection hepatic 4. Psychiatric severe
45.	Operations	1. None 2. Minor 3. Tonsillectomy and adenoids 4. Appendectomy 5. Hernia 6. Fractures 7. Multiple 8. Gastro intestinal 9. Others
46.	Hospital admissions: Number	
47.	Hormone treatment	1. No 2. Yes
48.	Vaccination smallpox	1. No 2. Incomplete or not up-to-date 3. Complete
49.	Vaccination D.F.T.	as above
50.	Vaccination Polio	as above
51.	Sleep quantity	1. Adequate 2. Inadequate
52.	Sleep quality	1. Adequate 2. Inadequate
53.	Teeth cleaning	1. Not at all or less than twice monthly 2. Less than twice weekly 3. Twice weekly 4. More than twice weekly 5. Once daily 6. More than once daily
54.	Sugar consumption	1. Unknown 2. Little 3. Medium 4. Much
55.-62.	Skin reflectometry blue	
63.-70.	Skin reflectometry green	
71.-78.	Skin reflectometry red	
79.	Parasites	1. No 2. Yes

APPENDIX D

Analysis Schedule for Interviews with Subjects

CARD D

CARD D

Column

1.	City	1. Boston
		2. Rome
		3. Palermo
		4. Florence
2.3.4.	Number of subject	
5.6.7.8.	Date of administration	
9.	Type of books preferred:	1. Novels - adventure
		2. Novels - sport
		3. Novels - secret service agent, mystery
		4. Historical, geographical, travel
		5. Science, mathematics
		6. Religious
		7. Others
		8. Novels
10.	Type of films preferred:	0. Nothing special
		1. Adventure
		2. Sport
		3. Mystery
		4. Romance
		5. Westerns
		6. War films
		7. Others
		8. Thrillers

11.   Most important interests:
     1. Collections
     2. Music
     3. Sports
     4. School
     5. Reading
     6. Modeling or other construc-
        tions (mechanics, elec-
        tricity)
     7. Art
     8. Games
     9. Meetings
     0. No response

12.   Secondary interests:
     Same as above
     0. No secondary interests

13.   Most admired famous person:
     0. None
     1. Sportsman
     2. Historical figure -
        political, military
     3. Politician - con-
        temporary military
     4. Scientist
     5. Writer, painter, sculp-
        ture, musician
     6. Religious figure
     7. Actor or singer
     8. Personal friend, member
        of family
     9. Others

14.   Do you like to tell jokes:
     1. Yes
     2. Indifferent
     3. No

15.   Preference to listen to jokes:
     1. Yes
     2. Indifferent
     3. No

16.   Career
     1. Seasonal or daily,
        irregular
     2. Manual, steady work, not
        specialized
     3. Specialized workman
        (mechanic, etc.)
     4. Minor clerical job, police
        force, sales
     5. Technical, teacher,
        clerical
     6. Managerial or professional
     7. Like all work
     0. No response

17.   Why
     1. (Do you) like the condi-
        tions and type of work
     2. (Do you) feel capable to
        do this work, or did you
        do well in this subject
        at school
     3. Interesting
     4. To become famous
     5. To earn a lot of money
     6. To help people
     7. To please someone, e.g.
        your father
     8. Trade familiar to you
     9. Other
     0. No response

18.   Who will decide your career:
     1. Boy
     2. Father
     3. Mother
     4. Father and mother
     5. Boy and father
     6. Boy and mother
     7. Boy, father and mother
     8. I don't know

19.   Parents in agreement:
     1. Yes
     2. Maybe
     3. No
     0. Don't know

20.   Three professions that would seem the nicest:
     Same as 16

21.   Same as 16
     0. No second answer -2'

22.   Same as 16
     0. No third answer -3'

23.   Three professions that you would never like to do:
     Same as 16

24.   Same as 16
     0. No second answer -2'

APPENDIX D (continued)

25.	Same as 16	0. No third answer -3'
26.	First choice of country for travels:	1. Italy 2. U.S.A. 3. Europe - apart from Italy 4. North America - apart from U.S.A. 5. Central America and South America 6. Asia 7. Africa 8. South Pacific 9. Others
27.	Subjects preferred at school - first choice:	1. Languages - except English and Italian, Latin and Greek 2. English (language and literature) 3. Italian (language and literature) 4. History, geography, economics 5. Mathematics and scienc 6. Art 7. Gymnastics 8. Religion 9. Other 0. No response
28.	Subjects liked less	Same as 27
29.	How do you get on at school:	1. Well 2. Average 3. Badly
30.	Why	0. Don't know 1. Like to study, do his best 2. Dislike of study - don't study sufficiently 3. School is easy 4. Illness, or absence for other reasons 5. Dislike of teachers 6. Not liked by teachers, not understood by teachers 7. Watched over by parents 8. Difficulties in some subject or other 9. Others
31.	How do parents react when you do badly:	1. Ignore it, don't do anything 2. Scold, threaten punishment 3. Physical punishment 4. Punishment by forfeiting pleasures, keeping in house, etc. 5. Help with scholastic work 6. Discuss the problem with you, tell you to do better 7. Others 8. Don't tell your parents 0. Never done badly
32.	Most important qualities in a teacher:	1. Nice appearance 2. Fairness 3. Strictness 4. Knowledge 5. Kindness 6. Others
33.	Do you like having friends:	1. Many 2. Few 3. None
34.	How many real friends have you:	0. None 1. One 2. Two 3. Three to five 4. Six to ten 5. More than ten
35.	Do you prefer to play alone:	1. Yes 2. With friends 3. Don't mind 4. Depends on the game

APPENDIX D (continued)

36.	Are parents pleased that you have friends:	1. Yes 2. No 0. Don't know and no response
37.	Are parents happy to leave you free to choose your own friends:	1. Yes 2. Yes with reservations 3. No 0. No response
38.	How many school companions would you like to eliminate from your class:	Scale 0 - 8 9 = 9 or more
39.	What would you do if a school friend hit you:	1. Hit him back, unconditionally 2. Hit him back, conditionally; if a friend; if provoked 3. Ignore it, laugh it off 4. Speak to him, ask the reason, etc. 5. Break the friendship; don't see him anymore 6. Threaten him protesting 7. Tell your parents, or teachers 8. Others 0. Don't know
40.	How would your parents expect you to act under these circumstances:	Same as above
41.	When are you praised:	1. Good school marks or work 2. Good at sport 3. Doing good deeds 4. Being courteous to others 5. For artistic or manual work 6. Others 0. No response
42.	Do you like being praised:	1. Yes 2. Yes, with reservations 3. No 0. Don't know
43.	Do you think adults understand you:	1. Yes, usually 2. Sometimes 3. Rarely 4. Never 0. Don't know
44.	With whom do you like to pass your free time:	1. Alone or no preference 2. Mother 3. Father 4. Grandmother and grandfather 5. Elder brother 6. Elder sister 7. Younger brother 8. Younger sister 9. Friends 0. Other relations or everyone
45.	Which parent is the more severe:	1. Father 2. Equal 3. Mother 0. Don't know
46.	What are you most afraid to do in your mother's presence:	1. Use vulgar words, to swear 2. Disobey, or answer back 3. To quarrel with brothers or sisters, or other relations 4. To smoke 5. Not to study 6. Begin trouble (troublemaker) 7. To tell lies 8. Others 9. Nothing 0. Don't know
47.	What are you most afraid to do in your father's presence:	Same as above

APPENDIX D (continued)

48.   To whom could you entrust a secret:
1. Mother
2. Father
3. Brother
4. Sister
5. Relative - other than above
6. Friend of the same age
7. Older friend
8. Grandfather/mother
9. No one
0. Other or no definite response

49.   Most important member of the family:
1. Mother
2. Father
3. Grandmother
4. Grandfather
5. Brother
6. Sister
7. Both parents
8. Others
0. Don't know

50.   Most important quality to be respected in the daily life of a family:
1. Sense of justice and the rights of others
2. Respect, faith
3. Affection and kindness
4. Manners, cordiality
5. Unity, accordance, friendship; no quarrels
6. Equality
7. Obedience
8. Authority of parents
9. Others
0. Don't know

51.   Why do family differences (quarrels) begin:
1. Difference of opinion, character
2. Criticism of other people
3. Children
4. Money
5. Bad example from parents
6. Lack of affection, or incomprehension
7. Others
0. Don't know

52.   Free to dress as you please:
1. Yes
2. Yes, within reason
3. No

53.   What makes you afraid:
1. Actual or potential fear to do oneself harm, to cause harm, or that someone harms you
2. To be alone (in the dark)
3. Offenses or refusals from others, or reproaches
4. Failures, making a mess of something
5. Natural occurrences; thunder and lightning, unexpected or sudden events
6. Harm to or loss of parents
7. Death
8. Animals, insects
9. Imaginary events, books or films
0. No response

54.   When a teacher questions you does your heart beat faster:
1. Yes
2. Sometimes
3. No

55.   Sense of "butterflies" (nervous stomach):
1. Yes
2. Sometimes
3. No

56.   Sense of guilt:
1. Yes
2. Sometimes
3. No
0. Don't know

57.   First childhood memory:
1. Positive affection
2. Neutral
3. Negative affection
4. Other
0. Don't remember

58.	What do you like most in life:	1. Amusement, adventure 2. Love, sex, dates 3. Sport 4. Change of character - strength of will 5. Among people: friends; make one's parents happy; help others 6. Personal happiness; happy family 7. School, studies, literature, work 8. Life itself 9. Others 0. Nothing or don't know
59.	In what state of mind do you usually find yourself:	1. Calm 2. Changeable 3. Depressed 4. Nervous 5. Others
60.	How do you feel when you wake up in the morning:	1. Serene 2. Indifferent 3. Worried 4. Other
61.	Intelligent - in comparison to others	1. Less 2. Equally 3. More
62.	Strength - in comparison to others	1. Less 2. Equally 3. More
63.	Unjust treatment - in comparison to others	1. More 2. Equally 3. Less
64.	Loved - in comparison to others	1. Less 2. Equally 3. More
65.	Comportment of subject	1. Laconic 2. Normal 3. Talkative
66.		1. Motionless 2. Normal 3. Restless
67.		1. Timid 2. Normal 3. Aggressive
68.		1. Embarrassed 2. Polite 3. Impolite
69.	Independence:	1. = 0 2. = 0.5 3. = 1 4. = 1.5 5. = 2 6. = 2.5 7. = 3 0. = No response
70.	Capacity to solve practical problems:	Same as above
71.	Capacity to solve emotional problems:	Same as above
72.	Open and affectionate with family:	Same as above
73.	Open and affectionate outside family:	Same as above
74.	How much support from his home:	Same as above
75.	How much support does he give to his home:	Same as above
76.	Feeling of responsibility towards the community:	Same as above
77.	Aggressive towards others:	Same as above
78.	Logical capacity to reason:	Same as above
79.	Capacity to work with others:	Same as above

APPENDIX E

Code of the Social Questionnaire

CARD A

Column

1.	City	1. Boston
		2. Rome
		3. Palermo
		4. Florence

2.3.4.   Number of boy

5.6.7.8.   Date of visit

9.   Place of birth: 1. Same as the town in which
                                            the visit was made
                                         2. Different to the town
                                            in which the visit was made

10.11.12.13.   Age of the boy at time of visit (in years and fractions
                of a year)

14.   Class (write first year in secondary modern school - 6)

15.	Informant:	1. Mother
		2. Other
		3. Mother and others
		4. Both parents

16.	Paternal grandfather - place of birth:	1. Abruzzi
		2. Calabria
		3. Campania
		4. Lucania
		5. Puglia
		6. Sicilia
		7. Lazio

255

APPENDIX E (continued)

17.	Paternal grandfather:	1. Living within the family 2. Living, not with the family 3. Not living
18.19.	Age at time of the visit or at death (in years)	
20.21.22.23.	Paternal grandmother (same data as for paternal grandfather)	
24.25.26.27.	Maternal grandfather (same data as for paternal grandfather)	
28.29.30.31.	Maternal grandmother (same data as for paternal grandfather)	
32.33.	Age of father, or age he would have been if dead (in years)	
34.	Father's birthplace (as for grandparents) plus:	7. Elsewhere in Italy 8. Boston or elsewhere in America
35.	Father's profession (scale from 1 to 8 according to Dr. Tesi's scale):	1. Unemployed 2. Seasonal or daily, irregular 3. Steady normal job, not specialized 4. Specialized workman, salesman 5. Foreman 6. Minor clerical job, police force 7. Clerical (employee), teacher, technical 8. Managerial or professional
36.	Father's education - see attached table	
37.38.	Mother's age (in years)	
39.40.41.	Same data as for the father, plus:	0. Housewife
42.	Father's health:	1. Good 2. Mediocre 3. Bad 4. Dead
43.44.45.46.	Father's height	
47.48.49.	Father's present weight	
50.51.52.	Father's weight at 20 years of age	
53.	Color of father's eyes:	1. Black 2. Brown 3. Blue 4. Green 5. Hazel 6. Grey
54.	Does he wear glasses:	1. Yes 2. No 3. Formerly, not now
55.56.	His age at time of marriage	
57.58.59.60.61.	Mother same data as for the father	
62.63.64.65.66.	Mother same data as for the father	
67.68.69.70.71.	Mother same data as for the father	
72.73.	Age at menarche	
74.75.	Age at menopause; 99. Has not come yet	
76.	Number of children	
77.	Boy's chronological position in family:	1. Only child 2. Oldest (of two or more children) 3. Youngest (of two or more children) 4. Middle on (of three or more children
78.	Sex distribution in the family:	1. Only child 2. All males 3. All females - in addition to subject

APPENDIX E (continued)

79.	Other people live in the same house:	1. No one 2. Grandparents 3. Relations 4. Non-relations 5. A combination of the preceding possibilities
80.	Card	

CARD B

Column

5.	Social class (scale from 1 to 5); see Dr. Tesi	
6.	Family income:	1. $600+ or 200,000+ Lire 2. $450 - 600 or 150,000 - 200,000 Lire 3. $300 - 450 or 100,000 - 150,000 Lire 4. $150 - 300 or 50,000 - 100,000 Lire 5. $ - 150 - 50,000 Lire
7.	Earnings of 10 years ago:	1. Much more 2. The same 3. Less 4. Much less
8.	Boy's average marks:	1. 85% = A (i.e. mostly A, 1 or 2 B) 2. 70-85% = B (possibly 1 C) 3. 60-70% = C, C+ 4. Below C, any D
9.	Has the boy repeated a class:	1. Yes 2. No
10.	Hours of study at home:	1. None 2. Less than an hour 3. 1 - 2 hours 4. 2 - 3 hours 5. 3 - 4 hours
11.	Special interests and preferences (scholastic):	1. Latin 2. Mathematics 3. Italian 4. History and geography 5. English 6. Shop, electronics, etc. 7. Art, music, etc. 8. Sports 9. Others 0. None
12.	Second preference	
13.	Is he helped and encouraged in his work:	1. Yes 2. No
14.	By whom:	1. By his father 2. By his mother 3. By other people 4. By no one 5. Both parents 6. Parents and others 0. Not helped
15.	Choice of future occupation by boy (as for the father's profession, item 35, card A)	
16.	Choice of future occupation by the family (as above)	
17.	Comparisons between occupations chosen by the boy and those chosen by the family:	1. Lower occupation chosen by the boy 2. The same occupation 3. Lower occupation chosen by the family 0. Hasn't chosen
18.	Opinion on health:	1. Well now and previously 2. Well now and some illness previously 3. Poor now and well previously 4. Poor now and previously

APPENDIX E (continued)

19.	Mother's work when child was small:	1. She has never worked 2. Has worked but only in the home - in addition to normal housework and child care 3. The mother has worked outside the home for a short time 4. The mother has worked outside the home for extended periods but not full time 5. The mother has worked outside the home for extended periods full time 0. Unknown
20.	If the mother worked who looked after the child:	1. Grandmother 2. Relations 3. Other people 4. Servant 0. Mother did not work
21.	Cuddled:	1. Much 2. Average, little 3. Little, very little 4. Yes, but not known how much
22.23.	Bladder control - age commenced in months (if age is uncertain, state the lesser):	
24.25.	When toilet trained - age in months	
26.27.	Difference between initial bladder control and being toilet trained (in months)	
28.29.30. 31.32.33.	Anal control (same as for bladder control)	
34.	Eating habits:	1. Excessive and regular 2. Excessive and irregular 3. Normal and regular 4. Normal and irregular 5. Little and regular 6. Little and irregular
35.	Quality: 1,2,3,4,5 (see scale)	
36.	Quantity: 1,2,3,4,5 (see scale)	
37.	Did he suck his thumb:	1. Yes 2. No 0. Not known
38.	Does he bite his nails:	1. Now yes 2. Yes previously 3. Never 4. Not known
39.	Sleep:	1. Deep 2. Normal 3. Light
40.	Disturbed sleep:	1. Yes 2. No
41.42.	Hours of sleep	
43.	Teeth cleaning:	1. Regular 2. Irregular
44.45.	When teeth cleaning started (in months)	
46.	Does he tell the truth:	1. Yes 2. Yes, but not always; not certain 3. No, but uncertain 4. No
47.	Is he obedient: as for 46	
48.	Type of paternal upbringing:	1. Rigid 2. Moderately severe 3. Indulgent
49.	Type of maternal upbringing: as for 48	
50.	Type of upbringing by others: as for 48, plus:	0. Inapplicable
51.	Relationship with father:	1. Good 2. Indifferent 3. Bad 0. Inapplicable

APPENDIX E (continued)

52.	Relationship with mother (as for 51)	
53.	Relationship with brothers (as for 51), plus:	0. No brothers
54.	Relationship with sisters (as for 51), plus:	0. No sisters
55.	Relationship with other people in household (as for 51), plus:	0. No others in household, uncertain
56.	Type of friendships:	1. Scholastic 2. Non-scholastic 3. Both
57.	Friendships:	1. Free 2. Arranged 3. Both 4. Uncertain
58.	Pastimes:	1. Passive - cinema, television, sport (as spectator) 2. Participation in sport 3. Collections 4. Constructing 5. Reading 6. Imaginary games 7. Other things 8. Automobiles 0. Nothing special
59.	The same for the second answer among which:	0. No second pastime
60.	Group activities:	1. None 2. Only one group 3. Two groups 4. Three or more groups 5. Not known
61.	Work apart from study (schoolwork):	1. None 2. Some previously but not known 3. Some now not more than one job 4. A great deal (several jobs, has worked for some time)
62.	In the case of conflict between siblings, do the parents intervene:	1. Yes 2. No 3. Only child or doesn't argue
63.	Are they pleased that the boy has friends:	1. Yes 2. No
64.	Are they opposed to games and friendships between friends of the opposite sexes:	1. Yes 2. No 3. No definite response
65.	What is your opinion of the intervention by the family in the solution of problems that he might have with others:	1. Not at all 2. A little 3. A fair amount 4. A great deal 0. Not indicated
66.	In his scholastic failures, do the parents sustain and understand the boy:	1. Yes 2. No 3. Neither 4. No failures
67.	With regard to his school work, do they push him or slow him up:	1. Push him 2. Slow him up 3. Neither
68.	In the case of difficulties with teachers, the parents have supported:	1. The boy 2. The teacher 3. Have not taken sides 0. Has not occurred
69.	How much do they follow the boy in his homework:	1. They aren't interested 2. They let him do it being sure of him 3. They remind him he has work to do 4. They supervise him and make him repeat things 5. They help him actively

APPENDIX E (continued)

70.	To summarize how much does the family intervene in the solution of the boy's scholastic problems:	0. Has no scholastic problems 1. Not at all 2. Little 3. A fair amount 4. A great deal
*71.	Does the boy discuss his personal problems with his parents:	1. Yes 2. No 0. No problems
*72	May he question an order:	1. Yes 2. No 3. Mother yes, father no 4. Father yes, mother no
*73.	Do the parents explain the why and wherefore of orders or prohibitions:	1. Yes 2. No
*74.	When there is an important decision which affects the whole family, do they take his opinion into consideration:	1. Yes 2. No
*75.	May he go out along outside of going to school:	1. Yes 2. No
∵76.	Must he seek permission every time:	1. Yes 2. No
∵77.	Must he be home by a fixed hour:	1. Yes 2. No
*78	May he choose any friends he wishes:	1. Yes 2. No
*79	May he develop interests and hobbies on his own:	1. Yes 2. No
80.	Card	

CARD C

Column

*5.	On holidays may the boy have fun on his own or must he go along with the family:	1. On his own 2. Sometimes one and sometimes the other 3. With the family
*6.	May the boy belong to youth clubs, or similar organizations of his own:	1. Yes 2. No
*7.	May the boy dress as he likes:	1. Yes 2. No
*8.	Has the boy chosen his own school curriculum:	1. Yes 2. No
*9.	Will the boy have full freedom to choose his own profession:	1. Yes 2. No
*10.	Would the boy's parents like him to achieve what they themselves have been unable to achieve:	1. Yes 2. No
*11.	Does the boy have pocket money (weekly or otherwise):	1. Yes 2. No
∵12.	Do his parents control the way in which the money is spent:	1. Yes 2. No
13.	Do his parents make sure the boy is neat and clean:	1. Yes 2. No
14.	Freedom of expression: number of all the answers from 71 - 74 Form B	
15.16.	Permissiveness-strictness: "yes" or 1 of all the numbers Form B—75.78.79; Form C—76.77; Form C—12. ('Yes' numbers marked *; 'No' numbers marked ∵)	

APPENDIX E (continued)

17.
Responsibility in the home:
1. A great deal
2. Yes, a little
3. Yes, but not known how much
4. No

18.19.20.21.
Age at which he began to dress and wash himself

22.23.
Age up to which he slept in the same room as mother

24.
Do his parents prefer that he plays:
1. At home
2. At the house of others
3. No preference
4. Outside
0. No information

25.
Do they prefer:
1. That he takes the lead
2. That he is led
3. Depends upon the situation
4. No preferences
0. No information

26.
Do they think he is capable of facing up to his own difficulties:
1. Yes
2. Uncertain
3. No
0. No information

27.
The three most important things that the boy should learn to do (1):

28.
The three most important things that the boy should learn to do (2):

29.
The three most important things that the boy should learn to do (3):
1. Ability in relationships with others
2. Moral and religious
3. Get a diploma, hard work, a profession, intelligence
4. A happy family, a good marriage
5. Others

30.
On the whole to what extent do you feel that the family favors the boy's independence, respecting his personality:
1. Not at all
2. Little
3. A fair amount
4. A great deal

31.
Sexual education - Do the parents prefer to inform the boy themselves or do they prefer him to be informed by others, i.e. friends, teachers, priests, books, etc.:
1. Themselves
2. Others
3. No preferences
4. Both 1 and 2

32.
Do they speak of sexual problems in the boy's presence:
1. Yes
2. No

33.
Do they prefer to inform him in a realistic manner or have they taken refuge in tales of storks, gooseberry brakes, etc.:
1. In a realistic manner
2. With various stories
0. No positive answer

34.35.
When did the boy ask the first questions about sexual matters (age in years):
0. Has not asked

36.
If the child is reticent about this subject do his parents feel the need to encourage his confidence and to explain:
1. Yes
2. No
3. Not clear - not reticent

37.
To what extent has the family faced up to the problem of the sexual education of the boy:
1. Not at all
2. Little
3. A fair amount
4. A great deal

38.
Do they encourage him to act immediately to a hostile act from peers or to retire and avoid all fights:
1. To act immediately
2. To act immediately on certain conditions
3. To withdraw on certain conditions
4. To withdraw
0. Has not been in fights

APPENDIX E (continued)

39.	Do they suggest other ways of reacting:	1. Yes 2. No
40.	If so, how:	1. Tell parent or adult 2. Other 0. Not applicable
41.	Do they influence him indirectly to take a decision or certain attitude by means of adages, proverbs, etc.:	1. Yes 2. No
42.	In the face of aggressive acts from peers what is the family influence on the boy? Do they encourage him to defend himself? Do they let him make his own decisions or do they advise him to hold back:	1. Withdraw 2. Make his own decision 3. Defend himself
43.	How much affection has the boy received in the family from the father:	1. None at all 2. Little 3. A fair amount 4. A great deal
44.	How much affection has the boy received in the family from the mother:	Same as above
45.	From other members of the family:	Same as above 0. Not applicable
46.	To summarize how much affection does the boy get from his family:	Same as above
*47.	Do they take all their meals together:	1. Yes 2. No
˅48.	Does the mother work outside the house:	1. Yes 2. No
*49.	Do they have fun together:	1. Yes 2. No
50.	Have they common interests:	1. Yes 2. No
51.	Do they talk a lot together:	1. Yes 2. No
*52.	Do husband and wife go out alone together:	1. Yes 2. No
53.	Cohesion: Sum of "yes" answers on items 47.49.52. and "no" on number 48 Card C ("yes" marked *; "no" marked ˅ as before)	
54.	Does the mother take care of the house and the children:	1. Alone now and previously 2. Alone now but her husband helped her previously 3. Her husband helps her now but not previously 4. Her husband helps her now and previously 5. Help other than husband
55.	Are they both pleased with their work:	1. Mother and father are satisfied 2. Father yes, mother no 3. Mother yes, father no 4. Both unsatisfied
56.	Would they advise their children to marry:	1. Yes 2. Yes conditionally 3. No
57.	Does each member of the family participate in the life of the other members of the family:	1. Yes 2. Some yes, others no 3. No
58.	How united do you feel the family is on the whole:	1. Not at all 2. Little 3. A fair amount 4. A great deal

APPENDIX E (continued)

59.	Involvement in sports:	1. None
		2. Watches as spectator
		3. Active participation
		4. Both
60.	Interests of parents:	1. Professional
		2. Cultural
		3. Sporting
		4. Other
		0. No information
61.	Do they get together with friends:	1. A great deal
		2. A fair amount
		3. A little
		4. No
		0. Not known how much
62.	What do they do:	1. Cinema
		2. Touring
		3. Visiting friends
		4. Television
		5. Reading
		6. Sports
		7. Other
		0. Do not get together
63.	Do they read books:	1. Yes
		2. No
64.	Do they read newspapers and periodicals:	1. Yes
		2. No
65.	Attitude to school:	1. Positive
		2. Positive with reservations (not much interest)
		3. They disapprove
		0. No response
66.	Do they approve or disapprove of the amount of schoolwork (homework):	1. They approve
		2. They approve with reservations
		3. They disapprove
		0. No response
67.	On the whole to what extent does the family's cultural level influence or stimulate the boy's interests:	1. Not at all
		2. Little
		3. A fair amount
		4. A great deal
68.	The mother is anxious or worried:	1. Not at all
		2. Little
		3. A fair amount
		4. A great deal
69.	Is she tolerant:	Same as above
70.	Does she understand the emotional needs of the boy:	Same as above
71.	Is she an authoritative person:	Same as above
72.	On the whole to what extent do you feel that the mother is able to deal with the boy's practical problems:	Same as above
73.	On the whole to what extent do you feel that the mother is able to deal with the boy's emotional problems:	Same as above
74.	Attitude towards this research:	1. Positive
		2. Positive with reservations
		3. Negative
75.	Are the parents more favorable towards a particular section of the research:	1. Medical
		2. Psychological
		3. Social
		4. No preference
76.	Education category now (last exam or later information)	
77.	Education finished:	1. Yes
		2. No
78.79.	Age now	
80.	Card	

APPENDIX F

Imagination Test

Name   School   Grade

Age   Sex   Location and date of testing

Instructions

(Read carefully before turning page)

This is a test of your creative imagination. On the following pages you are to write out some brief stories that you make up on your own. In order to help you get started, there are brief plot suggestions at the top of each page. For example, suppose one of them reads: "A boy and his dog." Then your task would be to write up a story about a boy and his dog. To help you even further, you will find four questions spaced out over the page that cover the main parts of a story. They are

(1)   What is happening?
(2)   What has led up to this situation? That is, what happened in the past?
(3)   What is being thought? What is wanted? By whom?
(4)   What will happen?

So you might imagine that the boy is trying to teach his dog some tricks, that he was led to do it because he saw a dog performing tricks in a circus, that he is angry because the dog does not learn faster, and so forth. You would then write all this out on the page under the various questions. This is *not* one of the themes that will be suggested but the others will be very much like it.

264

The object of the test is to show how imaginative you can be. Make your stories vivid and dramatic. Do not worry whether there are right and wrong kinds of stories to write because any story is all right. You also do not have to answer each of the questions. They are just meant to be *guides* to help you think of the plot of a story.

You will be allowed only 40 min for the whole test, after you get started, although you may finish in less time if you like. Since there are eight stories to write, this means you will have *about 5 min for each story*. So make your stories brief and dramatic. Show how much imagination you have. If you have no questions as to what you are to do, you may now turn the page, read the first plot suggestion, think of a story, and write it out in the space provided. When you have finished go on to the next page and so on through the test.

PLOT 1   A mother and her son. They look worried.   (5 minutes)

(1)   What is happening?

(2)   What has led up to this situation? That is, what happened in the past?

(3)   What is being thought? What is wanted? By whom?

(4)   What will happen?

The next 7 pages are the same except the story plots printed at the top.

PLOT 2   A boy sitting in a schoolroom with an open book in front of him.   (5 minutes)

(1)   What is happening?

(2)   What has led up to this situation? That is, what happened in the past?

(3)   What is being thought? What is wanted? By whom?

(4)   What will happen?

PLOT 3   A boy and a girl walking together.   (5 minutes)

(1)   What is happening?

(2)   What has led up to this situation? That is, what happened in the past?

(3)   What is being thought? What is wanted? By whom?

(4)   What will happen?

PLOT 4   Two men in a workshop, standing by a machine. One is older.   (5 minutes)

(1)   What is happening?

(2)   What has led up to this situation? That is, what happened in the past?

(3) What is being thought? What is wanted? By whom?

(4) What will happen?

PLOT 5 A young man alone at night.   (5 minutes)

(1) What is happening?

(2) What has led up to this situation? That is, what happened in the past?

(3) What is being thought? What is wanted? By whom?

(4) What will happen?

PLOT 6 A father and son talking.   (5 minutes)

(1) What is happening?

(2) What has led up to this situation? That is, what happened in the past?

(3) What is being thought? What is wanted? By whom?

(4) What will happen?

PLOT 7 Two small children, a boy and a girl, walking together.   (5 minutes)

(1) What is happening?

(2) What has led up to this situation? That is, what happened in the past?

(3) What is being thought? What is wanted? By whom?

(4) What will happen?

References

Abramson, E., & Ernest, E. Height and weight of school boys at a Stockholm secondary school, 1950, and a comparison with some earlier investigations. *Acta Aldiatrica*, 1954, *43*, 235–246.

Abramson, P. R. *The political socialization of Black Americans: A critical evaluation of research on efficacy and trust.* New York: Free Press, 1977.

Acheson, R. M. Effects of nutrition and disease on human growth. In J. M. Tanner (Ed.), *Human growth* (Vol. 3). Oxford: Pergamon Press, 1960.

Akesson, H. O. Taste deficiency for phenylthiourea in southern Sweden. *Acta Genetica, Medica,* 1959, *8,* 431–433.

Allison, A. C., & Blumberg, B. S. Ability to taste phenylthiocarbamide among Alaskan Eskimos and other populations. *Human Biology,* 1959, *31,* 352–357.

Almond, G., & Verba, S. *The Civic Culture.* Princeton, N.J.: Princeton University Press, 1963.

Anderson, F., & Cowan, N. R. Survival of healthy older people. *British Journal of Preventive Social Medicine,* 1976, *30,* 231–232.

Atkinson, J. W. *Motives in fantasy, action, and society.* Princeton, N.J.: Van Nostrand-Reinhold, 1958.

Bacchetta, V. Alimentazione e stato di nutrizione dei bambini italiani dopo la guerra. *La Ricerca Scientifica,* Supplemento A, 1951.

Banfield, E. C. *The moral basis of a backward society.* Glencoe, Il.: Free Press, 1958.

Barron, F. *Inventory of personal philosophy.* Berkeley: Univ. of California Press, 1952.

Barron, F. The disposition toward originality. *Journal of Abnormal and Social Psychology,* 1955, *51,* 478–485.

Barron, F. The measurement of creativity. In D. Whitla (Ed.), *Handbook of measurement in behavioral sciences.* Palo Alto, Calif.: Atherton Press, 1968.

Barron, F. *Creative person and creative process.* New York: Holt, 1969.

Barron, F., & Young, H. B. A tale of two cities and their differing impact on the creativity and personal philosophy of southern Italian immigrants. *Journal of Cross-Cultural Psychology,* 1970, *1,* 91–144.

Barron, F., Guilford, J. P., Christenson, P. R., Berger, R. M., & Kettner, N. W. *Interrelations of various measures of creative traits.* Tech. Memo. A.F. 18(600)-8. Berkeley, Calif.: Institute of Personality Assessment and Research, 1957.

Barron, F., & Welsh, G. S. Artistic perception as a factor in personality style: Its measurement as a figure-preference test. *Journal of Psychology,* 1952, *33,* 199–203.

Barsley, M. *The left-hand book.* London: Souvenir Press, 1966.

Barzini, L. *The Italians.* New York: Atheneum, 1964.

Barzini, L. *From Caesar to the mafia.* New York: Library Press, 1971.

Baumrind, D. Child care practices anteceding three patterns of pre-school behavior. *Genetic Psychology Monographs,* 1967, *75,* 43–88.

Belmont, L., & Birch, H. G. Lateral dominance, lateral awareness, and reading disability. *Child Development,* 1965, *36,* 57–70.

Belousov, V. A., & Gilman, M. A. Nitrogen retention in school children fed on a diet containing different ratios of animal and vegetable protein. *Problems of Nutrition,* 1934, *3,* 54. (Abstracted in *Nutritional Abstracts Review,* 1935, *5,* 189.)

Belousov, V. A., & Gilman, M. A. Das Eiwessoptimums in der Nahrungsration von Schulkindern, 2. Stickstoff Retention bei wechselndem Verhaltnis von tierischem zu pflanzlichem Eiweiss in der Ration von gesunden Schulkindern. *Problems of Nutrition,* 1936, *5,* 69. (Abstracted in *Nutritional Abstracts Review,* 1936, *6,* 450.)

Bene, E. Suppression of heterosexual interest and of aggression by middle class and working class grammar school boys. *British Journal of Educational Psychology,* 1958, *28,* 231–266.

Block, J. *Lives through time.* Berkeley, Calif.: Bancroft Books, 1971.

Block, J., von der Lippe, A., & Block, J. H. Sex role and socialization patterns: Some personality concomitants and environmental antecedents. *Journal of Consulting and Clinical Psychology,* 1973, *41,* 321–341.

Bower, E. M. *A process for early identification of emotionally disturbed children.* Bulletin 27, No. 6. Sacramento: California State Department of Education, 1958.

Bowles, G. T. *New types of old Americans at Harvard and at eastern women's colleges.* Cambridge, Mass.: Harvard University Press, 1932.

Boyne, A. W., & Leitch, I. Secular change in the height of British adults. *Nutrition Abstracts Review,* 1954, *24,* 255–269.

Editorial (1). *British Medical Journal,* 1976, p 415.

Bronfenbrenner, U. Developmental research, public policy, and the ecology of childhood. *Child Development,* 1974, *45,* 1–5.

Burgalassi, S. *Il comportomento religioso degli Italiani.* Florence, Italy: Vallenchi, 1968.

Burks, B. S., & Roe, A. Studies of identical twins reared apart. *Psychological Monographs,* 1949, *63*(5).

Campbell, A., Converse, P., Miller, W., & Stokes, D. *The American voter.* New York: Wiley, 1960.

Campisi, P. J. Ethnic family patterns: The Italian family in the United States. *American Journal of Sociology,* 1948, *53,* 444–446.

Campisi, P. J. The Italian family in the United States. In R. F. Winch & R. McGinnis (Eds.), *Selected studies in marriage and the family.* New York: Holt, 1953.

Carmines, E. G. Race, intelligence and sense of political efficacy: A multivariate political socialization study. M.A. thesis, College of William and Mary, 1972.

Castenada, A., McCandless, B. R., & Palermo, D. S. The children's form of the manifest anxiety scale. *Child Development.* 1956, *27,* 317-326.

Cattell, R. B. *The high school personality questionnaire, forms A and B.* Urbana, Il.: Institute for Personality and Ability Testing, 1958.

Cattell, R. B. Personal communication, 1965

Cattell, R. B., & Beloff, J. *The high school personality questionnaire.* Champaign, Il.: Institute for Personality and Ability Testing, 1957.

Cattell, R. B., Beloff, J., & Coan, R. W. *The high school personality questionnaire.* (Translation and adaptation into the Italian language and culture by the Harvard Florence Research Project in collaboration with the Psychological Division of the Italian National Research Center.) Florence, Italy: Organizzazione Speciali, 1961.

Child, I. *Italian or American: The second generation in conflict.* New Haven, Conn.: Yale University Press, 1943.

Clark, M. M. *Left-handedness, laterality characteristics and their educational implications.* London: University of London Press, 1957.

Compendio statistico Italiano. Rome: Instituto Poligrafico dello Stato, 1960.

Conant, J. B. *The American high school today.* New York: McGraw-Hill, 1959.

Correnti, V. Frequenza del colore dell'iride in soggetti di 8-9-10 anni delle province di Palermo e di Agrigento. *Rivista di Antropologia,* 1957, *44,* 3-26.

Costanzo, A. La statura degli italiani ventenni nati dal 1854 al 1920. *Annali di statistica Serie,* 1948, *8,* 59-123.

Covello, L. *The social background of the Italo-American school child: A study of the southern Italian family mores and their effect on the school situation in Italy and in America.* Leyden, Netherlands: E. J. Brill, 1967.

Crandall, V. Achievement. In H. W. Stevenson (Ed.), *Child psychology: The 62nd yearbook of the National Society for the Study of Education.* Chicago: Univ. of Chicago Press, 1963.

Douglas, J. W. B., & Blomfield, J. M. *Children under five.* London: Alen & Unwin, 1958.

Douvan, E., & Walker, A. M. The sense of effectiveness in public affairs. *Psychological Monographs,* 1956, *70*(32).

Dunn, L. C. Personal communication, 1957.

Durnin, J. V. G. A., & Weir, J. B. de V. Statures of a group of university students and of their parents. *British Medical Journal,* 1952, *1,* 1006-1008.

Easton, D., & Dennis, J. *Children in the political system.* New York: McGraw-Hill, 1969.

Easton, D., & Dennis, J. The child's acquisition of regime norms: Political efficacy. *American Political Science Review,* 1967, *41,* 25-38.

Economist diary. London: The Economist Newspaper, Ltd., 1961.

Eichorn, D. W. Biological correlates of behavior. In H. W. Stevenson (Ed.), *Child psychology: The 62nd yearbook of the National Society for the Study of Education.* Chicago: Univ. of Chicago Press, 1963.

Elder, G. H. Democratic parent-youth relations in cross-national perspective. *Social Science Quarterly,* 1968, *54*(2), 216-228.

Ellis, R. W. B. Growth and health of Belgian children during and after the German occupation. *Archives of the Diseases of Childhood,* 1945, *20,* 97-109.

Endler, N. S., Hunt, J. M., & Rosenstein, A. J. An S-R inventory of anxiousness. *Psychological Monographs,* 1962, *76*(536).

Feminella, F. X. The Italian-American family. In M. Barash & A. Scourby (Eds.), *Marriage and the family.* New York: Random House, 1970.

Ferguson, L. C., Ferguson, L. R., & Young, H. B. Comparative political attitudes of Italians and Italo-Americans. *Comparative Political Studies,* 1972, *5,* 85-92.

Ferguson, L. C., Ferguson, L. R., & Young, H. B. An attempt to relate age at puberal maturity to political orientations. *Social Science Information*, 1976, *15*, 943-952.

Fishberg, M. Materials for the physical anthroplogy of the eastern European Jew. *Annals of the New York Academy of Science*, 1905, *16*, 155-257.

Franzblau, R. N. Race differences in mental and physical traits: studied in different environments. *Archives of Psychology*, 1935, (177), 44.

Freud, S. *Civilization and its discontents.* Reprint. London: Hogarth Press, 1955. (Originally published 1930.)

Gallagher, J. R., & Brouha, L. Physical fitness: Its evaluation and significance. *Journal of the American Medical Association*, 1944, *125*, 834.

Gans, H. J. *The urban villagers: Group and class in the life of Italian Americans.* Glencoe, Il.: Free Press, 1962.

Gardiner, P. A. Physical growth and the progress of myopia: Progress of myopia closely related to rate of growth. *Lancet*, 1955, 952-953.

Gardiner, P. A. Observations on the food habits of myopic children. *British Medical Journal*, 1956, *5*, 699.

Gardiner, P. A. In myopic children, a group who received extra animal protein determined more sturdy. *Lancet*, 1958, 1152-1155.

Garn, S. M., & Rohmann, C. G. Interaction of nutrition and genetics in the timing of growth and development. *Pediatric Clinics of North America*, 1966, *13*, 353-379.

Gergen, K. J., & Ullman, M. Socialization and the characterological basis of political activism. In S. Renshon (Ed.), *Handbook of political socialization.* New York: Free Press, 1977.

Gilbert, M. *Comparative national products and price levels.* Paris: Organization for Economic Cooperation and Development, 1958.

Goldstein, M. S. *Demographic and bodily changes in descendents of Mexican immigrants with comparable data on parents and children in Mexico.* Austin, Tex.: Institute of Latin American Studies, 1943.

Gottschaldt, K. Über den Einfluss der Erfahrung auf die Wahrnehmung von Figuren und ihre Sichtbarkeit in umfassenden Konfigurationen. *Psychologische Forschung*, 1926, *8*, 261-317.

Gough, H. G. *The California personality inventory.* Palo Alto, Calif.: Consulting Psychologists' Press, 1956. (Italian edition: Florence: Organizzazioni Speciali.)

Gough, H. G. A cross-cultural study of achievement motivation. *Journal of Applied Psychology*, 1964, *48*, 191-196.

Gough, H. G. Appraisal of social maturity by means of the CPI. *Journal of Abnormal Psychology*, 1966, *71*, 189-195. (a)

Gough, H. G. A cross-cultural analysis of the CPI femininity scale. *Journal of Consulting Psychology*, 1966, *30*, 136-141. (b)

Graffar, M. Une méthode de classification sociale d'échantillons de population. *Courrier*, 1956, *6*, 455-459.

Grasso, P. G. Valori morali-sociali in transizione. *Orientamenti Pedagogici*, 1961, *8*, 233-368.

Gray, H. Increase in the stature of American boys in the last fifty years. *Journal of the American Medical Association*, 1927, *88*, 908.

Greely, A. M., & McCready, W. C. Does ethnicity matter? *Ethnicity*, 1974, *1*, 91-108.

Greulich, W. W. A comparison of the physical growth and development of American-born and native Japanese children. *American Journal of Physical Anthropology*, 1957, *15*, 489-516.

Greulich, W. W. Growth of children of the same race under different environmental conditions. *Science*, 1958, *127*, 515-516.

Greulich, W. W., Dorfman, R. L., Catchpole, H. R., Solomon, C. L., & Culotta, C. S. Somatic and endocrine studies of puberal and adolescent boys. *Monographs of the Society for Research in Child Development*, 1942, *24*(3).

Greulich, W. W., & Pyle, S. I. *Radiographic atlas of skeletal development of the hand and wrist* (2nd ed.). Stanford, Calif.: Stanford University Press, 1959.

Grotevant, H. D., Scarr, S., & Weinberg, R. A. Patterns of interest similarity in adoptive and biological families. *Journal of Personality and Social Psychology,* 1977, *35,* 667–676.

Guilford, J. P. Intelligence has three facets. *Science,* 1968, *160,* 615–620.

Guthe, C. E. Notes on the cephalic index of Russian Jews in Boston. *American Journal of Physical Anthropology,* 1918, *1,* 213–223.

Hamill, P. V. V., Drizd, T. A., Johnson, C. L., Reed, R. R., & Roche, A. F. *N.C.H.S. growth curves for children: Birth to 18 years.* Washington, D.C.: U.S. Dept. of Health, Educ. and Welfare P.H.S. Publication No. 78-1650, 1977.

Hardyck, C., Goldman, R., & Petrinovich, L. Handedness and sex, race, and age. *Human Biology,* 1975, *47,* 369–375.

Harris, H., & Kalmus, H. The measurement of taste sensitivity to phenylthiourea (P.T.C.). *Annals of Eugenics,* 1949, *15,* 24–31.

Harvey, S. K., & Harvey, T. G. Adolescent political outlooks: The effects of intelligence as an independent variable. *Midwest Journal of Political Science,* 1970, *14,* 565–594.

Havighurst, R. J.. & Breese, F. H. Relation between ability and social status in a midwestern community. III. Primary mental abilities. *Journal of Educational Psychology,* 1947, *38,* 241–247.

Havighurst, R. J., & Janke, L. J. Relation between ability and social status in a midwestern community. I. Ten year old children. *Journal of Educational Psychology,* 1944, *35,* 357–368.

Hess, R. D., & Torney, J. V. *The development of political attitudes in children.* Chicago: Aldine, 1967.

Hirsch, N. D. M. Cephalic index of American-born children of three foreign groups. *American Journal of Physical Anthropology,* 1927, 10, 79–90.

Hoffman, M. L. Child-rearing practices and moral development: Generalizations from empirical research. *Child Development,* 1963, *34,* 295–318.

Hoffman, M. L. Moral development. In P. H. Mussen (Ed.), *Manual of child psychology.* New York: Wiley, 1970.

Holmogren, I. The increase of the height of Swedish men and women from the middle of the 19th century up to 1930, and the changes in height of the individual from the ages of 26 to 70, based on measurements of 46,000 persons. *Acta Medica Scandinavia,* 1952, *142,* 367–390.

Holt, L. E., & Fales, H. L. The food requirement of children. II. The protein requirement. *American Journal of Diseases of Childhood,* 1921, *22,* 371–380.

Honzik, M. P. Developmental studies of parent–child resemblance in intelligence. *Child Development,* 1957, *28,* 215–228.

Horwitz, A. Recent developments in maternal and child health in the Americas. *American Journal of Public Health,* 1960, *50,* 20–27.

Hulse, F. S. Exogamie et hétérosis. *Archives Suisses d'Anthropologie Générale,* 1958, *22,* 103–125.

Hulse, F. S. Adaptation, selection, and plasticity in ongoing human evolution. *Human Biology,* 1960, *32,* 63–79.

Ianni, F. J. The Italo-American teenager. *Annals of the American Academy of Political and Social Science,* 1961, *338,* 70–78.

Ianni, F. J., & Ianni, E. R. *A family business: Kinship and social control in organized crime.* New York: Russell Sage Foundation, 1972.

Ihinger, R. G. Some relationships among laterality in groups at three grade levels in performances on the California Achievement Tests. In *Toward a professional identity in school psychology,* Los Angeles: California Association of School Psychologists and Psychometrists, 1963.

Ishihara, S. *Test for color-blindness.* Tokoyo: Kanehara Shuppan Co., Ltd., 1954.

Ito, P. K. Comparative biometrical study of physique of Japanese women born and reared under different environments. *Human Biology, 1942, 14,* 279–351.

Ivanovsky, A. Physical modifications of the population of Russia under famine. *American Journal of Physical Anthropology,* 1923, *6,* 331–353.

Iyenga, T., & Sato, K. *The Japan and California Problem.* New York: Putnam, 1911.

Jackman, R. A note on intelligence, social class, and political efficacy in children. *Journal of Politics,* 1970, *32,* 984–988.

Jenss, R. M. Gain in weight and its association with ancestry and economic status. *Human Biology,* 1940, *12,* 532–544.

Jessor, R., Graves, T. D., Hanson, R. C., & Jessor, S. L. *Society, personality, and deviant behavior: A study of a tri-ethnic community.* New York: Holt, 1968.

Jessor, R., Young, E. B., Young, H. B., & Tesi, G. Perceived opportunity, alienation, and drinking behavior among Italian and American youth. *Journal of Personality and Social Psychology,* 1970, *15,* 215–222.

Jones, M. C. The later careers of boys who were early or late maturing. *Child Development,* 1957, *23,* 113–128.

Jones, M. C. Psychological correlates of somatic development. *Child Development,* 1965, *36,* 899–911.

Juel-Nielsen, N., & Morgenson, A. Uniovular twins brought up apart: Preliminary report of a psychiatric–psychological study. *Acta Genetica,* 1957, *7,* 430–433.

Kagan, J., & Kogan, N. Individual variation in cognitive processes. In P. H. Mussen (Ed.), *Manual of child psychology* (3rd ed.). New York: Wiley, 1970.

Kagan, J., & Moss, H. A. *Birth to maturity.* New York: Wiley, 1962.

Kaplan, B. Environment and human plasticity. *American Anthropologist,* 1954, *56,* 780–800.

Kinsey, A. C., Pomeroy, W. R., & associates. *Sexual behavior in the human male.* Philadelphia, Pa.: Saunders, 1948.

Klineberg, O. A. A study of psychological differences between "racial" and national groups in Europe. *Archives of Psychology,* 1931, (132), 58.

Kodlin, D., & Thompson, J. D. An appraisal of the longitudinal approach to studies of growth and development. *Monographs of the Society for Research in Child Development,* 1958, *23*(1).

Kohlberg, L. Moral development and identification. In H. Stevenson (Ed.), *Child psychology: The 62nd yearbook of the National Society for the Study of Education.* Chicago: Univ. of Chicago Press, 1963.

Kohlberg, L. Development of moral character and moral ideology. In M. L. Hoffman & L. W. Hoffman (Eds.), *Review of child development research* (Vol. 1). New York: Russell Sage Foundation, 1964.

Kraus, H. Comparative survey of muscular fitness in school children. *Proceedings of the 1954 convention of the American Association for Health, Physical Education, and Recreation.* Washington, D.C., 1954.

Kraus, H., & Hirschland, R. P. Muscular fitness and health. *Journal of the American Association for Health, Physical Education, and Recreation,* 1953, *24,* 17.

Kraus, H., & Hirschland, R. P. Minimum muscular fitness tests in school children. *Research Quarterly of the American Association for Health, Physical Education, and Recreation,* 1954, *125,* 178–187.

Lane, R. E. *Political life: Why and how people get involved in politics.* Glencoe, Il.: Free Press, 1959.

LaPalombara, J., & Walters, J. Values, expectations, and political predispositions of Italian youth. *Midwest Journal of Political Science,* 1961, *5,* 39–58.

Lasker, G. W. Migration and physical differentiation: A comparison of immigrant with American-born Chinese. *American Journal of Anthropology,* 1946, *4,* 273–300.

Lasker, G. W. Environmental growth factors and selective migration. *Human Biology*, 1952, *24*, 262–289.

Lee, M. M. C., & Lasker, G. W. The sun-tanning potential of human skin. *Human Biology*, 1959, *31*, 252–260.

LeVine, R. A. Cross-cultural study in child psychology. In P. H. Mussen (Ed.), *Manual of child psychology* (3rd ed., Vol. 2). New York: Wiley, 1970.

Levy, N. A short form of the children's manifest anxiety scale. *Child Development*, 1958, *29*, 153–154.

Lolli, G. *Alcohol in Italian culture*. Glencoe, Il.: Free Press, 1958.

Lundman, B. J. Ueber die Körperhohensteigerung in den nordischen Ländern nach dem Weltkriege. *Zeitschrift fur Rassenkunde*, 1940, *11*, 1–5.

Madsen, D. A structural approach to the explanation of political efficacy levels under democratic regimes. *American Journal of Political Science*, 1978, *22*, 867–883.

Martin, W. J. *The physique of young adult males*. Medical Research Council Memorandum No. 20. London: Her Majesty's Stationery Office, 1949.

Matheny, W. D., & Meredith, H. V. Mean body size of Minnesota school boys of Finnish and Italian ancestry. *American Journal of Physical Anthropology*, 1947, *5*, 347–355.

Maxwell, J. *Social implications of the 1947 Scottish Medical Survey*. London: Univ. of London Press, 1953.

McLaughlin, V. Y. Patterns of work and family organizations: Buffalo's Italians. *Journal of Interdisciplinary History*, 1971, *2*, 299–314.

Meredith, H. V. Stature of Massachusetts children of north European and Italian ancestry. *American Journal of Physical Anthropology*, 1939, *24*, 301–346.

Meredith, H. V. Stature and weight of children of United States with reference to influence of racial regional, socioeconomic and secular factors. *American Journal of Diseases of Childhood*, 1941, *62*, 909–932. (a)

Meredith, H. V. Stature and weight of private school children in two successive decades. *American Journal of Physical Anthropology*, 1941, *28*, 1–40. (b)

Meredith, H. V., & Meredith, E. M. The stature of Toronto children half a century ago and today. *Human Biology*, 1944 *16*, 126–131.

Merrell, D. J. Dominance of eye and hand. *Human Biology*, 1957, *29*, 314–327.

Miller, F. J. W., Court, S. D. M., Walton, W. S., & Knox, E. G. *Growing up in Newcastle-upon-Tyne*. London: Oxford University Press, 1960.

Mills, C. A. Climatic effects on growth and development with particular reference to the effects of tropical residence. *American Anthropology*, 1942, *44*, 1–13.

Mills, C. A. Temperature dominance over human life. *Science*, 1949, *110*, 267–271.

Mills, C. A. Temperature influence over human growth and development. *Human Biology*, 1950, *22*, 71–74.

Morant, G. M. Secular changes in the heights of British people. *Proceedings of the Royal Society of Britain*, 1950, *137*, 443–452.

Morant, G. M., & Samson, Ò. An examination of investigations by Dr. Maurice Fishberg and Professor Franz Boas dealing with measurements of Jews in New York. *Biometrika*, 1936, *28*, 1–31.

Mourant, A. E., Kopec, A. C., & Domaniewska-Sobczak, K. *The ABO blood groups*. Oxford: Blackwell, 1958.

Mussen, P. H., & Jones, M. C. Self-conceptions and interpersonal attitudes of late and early-maturing boys. *Child Development*, 1957, *23*, 129–148.

Mussen, P. H., & Jones, M. C. The behavior inferred motivations of late and early maturing boys. *Child Development*, 1958, *29*, 61–67.

Mussen, P. H., & Young, H. B. Relationships between rate of physical maturing and personality among boys of Italian descent. *Vita Humana*, 1964, *7*, 186–200.

Mussen, P. H., & Young, H. B. Gaddini, R., & Morante, L. Influence of relationship with father upon personality development in boys of Italian descent within diverse cultures. *Journal of Child Psychology and Psychiatry*, 1963, *4*, 3–16.

Nelson, W. E. (Ed.). *Textbook of pediatrics* (6th ed.). Philadelphia, Pa.: Saunders, 1954.

Newman, H. H., Freeman, F. N., & Holzinger, K. J. *Twins: A study of heredity and environment.* Chicago: Univ. of Chicago Press, 1937.

Palmer, R. D. Hand differentiation and psychological functioning. *Journal of Personality*, 1963, *31*, 445–461.

Paton, D. N., & Findlay, L. *Poverty, nutrition and growth: Studies of child life in cities and rural districts of Scotland.* Medical Research Council Special Reports Series, No. 101, London, 1926.

Peckham, C. S., Gardiner, P. A., & Goldstein, H. Acquired myopia in 11 year old children. *British Medical Journal*, 1977, *26*, 542–545.

Penrose, L. S. Evidence of heterosis in man. *Proceedings of the Royal Society of Britain*, 1955, *144*, 203–213.

Peterson, D. R., & Migliorino, G. Pancultural factors of parental behavior in Sicily and the United States. *Child Development*, 1967, *38*, 967–991.

Piaget, J. *The Moral judgment of the child.* New York: Harcourt, 1932.

Pinner, F. A. Parental overprotection and political distrust. *Annals of the American Academy of Political and Social Science*, 1965, *361*, 38–70.

Puzo, M. *The godfather.* New York: Putnam, 1969.

Ramaley, F. Inheritance of left-handedness. *American Naturalist*, 1913, *47*, 564.

Raven, J. C. *Guide to using progressive matrices* (Rev. ed.). London: H. K. Lewis, 1956.

Renshon, S. A. *Psychological needs and political behavior: A theory of personality and political efficacy.* New York: Free Press, 1974.

Renshon, S. A. Birth order and political socialization. In D. Schwartz & S. Schwartz (Eds.), *New directions in political socialization.* New York: Free Press, 1975.

Rettig, S., & Pasamanick, B. Changes in moral values among college students: A factorial study. *American Sociological Review*, 1959, *24*, 856–863.

Rey, A. Centration soutenue sur une tache intellectuelle simple. *Archives de Psychologie*, 1957, *36*, 29–61.

Rife, D. L. Heredity and handedness. *Scientific Monthly*, 1951, *73*, 188–191.

Rife, J. M. Types of dextrality. *Psychological Review*, 1922, *24*, 474–480.

Roche, A. F., Wainer, H., & Thissen, D. Predicting adult stature for individuals. *Monographs in pediatrics*, 1975, *3*, 67–69.

Scarr, S., & Weinberg, R. A. I.Q. test performance of black children adopted by white parents. *American Psychologist*, 1976, *31*, 726–739.

Scheinfeld, A. *Twins and supertwins.* London: Chatto and Windus, 1968.

Schwartz, D. C. *Political alienation and political behavior.* Chicago: Aldine, 1973.

Sears, R. R., Maccoby, E. E., & Levin, H. *Patterns of child rearing.* New York: Harper, 1957.

Shapiro, H. L. *Migration and environment.* London and New York: Oxford University Press, 1939.

Shields, J. *Monozygotic twins brought up apart and brought up together.* London and New York: Oxford University Press, 1962.

Sheldon, W. H. *Atlas of men.* New York: Harper, 1954.

Sielicka, M., Bodganowicz, I., Dilling-Ostowska, E., Szelozynska, K., & Kaczenska, M. Forced use of the right hand in left-handed children as a cause of neurosis. *Pediatrische Polska*, 1963, *38*, 405–408.

Skodak, M., & Skeels, H. M. A final follow-up study of one hundred adopted children. *Journal of Genetic Psychology*, 1949, *75*, 85–125.

Snyder, C. R. *Alcohol and the Jews: A cultural study of drinking and sobriety*. New Brunswick, N.J.: Rutgers University Center of Alcohol Studies, 1958.

Sorsby, A. *Modern opthalmology* (Vol. 3). London: Butterworth, 1972.

Sorsby, A., & Leavy, G. A. *A longitudinal study of refraction and its components during growth*. Medical Research Council Special Reports Series, No. 309, London, 1970.

Sorsby, A., Sheridan, M., & Leavy, G. A. *Refraction and its components in twins*. Medical Research Council Special Reports Series, No. 303, London, 1962.

Sorsby, A., Sheridan, M., Leavy, G. A., & Benjamin, B. Vision, visual acuity and reader refraction of young men. *British Medical Journal*, 1960, *9*, 139.

Spence, J., Walton, W. S., Miller, F. J. W., & Court, S. D. M. *A thousand families in New Castle upon Tyne*. London: Oxford University Press, 1954.

Spiegel, J. *Transactions: The interplay between the individual, family, and society*. New York: Science House, 1972.

Spier, L. Growth of Japanese children born in America and in Japan. *Univ. of Washington Publications in Anthropology*, 1929, *3*(1), 1–30.

Strodtbeck, F. L. Family interaction, values and achievement. In D. C. McClelland, A. L. Baldwin, U. Bronfenbrenner, & F. L. Strodtbeck (Eds.), *Talent and society*. Princeton, N.J.: Van Nostrand-Reinhold, 1958.

Stuart, H. C., & Stevenson, S. S. Physical growth and development. In W. E. Nelson (Ed.), *Textbook of pediatrics* (6th ed.). Philadelphia, Pa.: Saunders, 1954.

Susanne, C. Genetic and environmental influences on morphological characteristics. *Annals of Human Biology*, 1975, *2*, 279–287.

Suski, P. M. The body build of American-born Japanese children. *Biometrika*, 1933, *25*, 323–352.

Sutow, W. W. Skeletal maturation in healthy Japanese children 6 to 19 years of age: Comparison with skeletal maturation in American children. *Hiroshima Journal of Medical Science*, 1953, *2*, 181–191.

Tanner, J. M. *Growth at adolescence* (2nd ed.). Oxford: Blackwell, 1962.

Tarrow, S. G. *Peasant communism in southern Italy*. New Haven, Conn.: Yale University Press, 1967.

Teng, E. L., Lee, P. H., Yang, K. S., & Chang, P. C. Handedness in a Chinese population: Biological, social, and pathological factors. *Science*, 1976, *193*, 1148–1150.

Thomas, A., Birch, H. C., Chess, S., Hertzig, M. E., & Korn, S. *Behavioral individuality in early childhood*. New York: New York University Press, 1963.

Tomasi, L. F. *The Italian American family: The southern Italian family's process of adjustment to an urban America*. New York: Center for Migration Studies, 1972.

Torgoff, I., & Tesi, G. Achievement, motivation, morality and conflict: A study of Italian working class apprentices. Paper presented at the Biennial Meeting of the Society for Research in Child Development, Minneapolis, Minnesota, 1965.

Torrance, E. P. *Education and the creative potential*. Minneapolis: Univ. of Minnesota Press, 1963.

Torrielli, J. *Italian opinion on America*. Cambridge, Mass.: Harvard University Press, 1941.

Trankell, A. *Wänsterhänthet has Barn i skolaldern*. Helsingfors: Mercators Trycheri, 1950.

Trevor, J.C. *Race crossing in man: The analysis of metrical characteristics*. London and New York: Cambridge University Press, 1953.

U.S. Department of Health, Education and Welfare. Monthly Vital Statistics Report. H.C.H.S. Growth Charts (HRA) 76-1120, vol. 25, no. 3, supplement. Washington, D.C.: June 22, 1966.

U.S. Congress. Senate. *Changes in bodily form of descendants of immigrants,* by F. Boas. S. Doc. 208, 61st Cong., 2nd Sess., 1911.

Vandenberg, S. G., Stafford, R. E., & Brown, A. M. The Louisville twin study. In S. G. Vandenberg (Ed.), *Progress in human behavior genetics.* Baltimore, Md.: Johns Hopkins Press, 1968.

Vernon, P. E. The distinctiveness of field dependence. *Journal of Personality,* 1970, *40,* 366–391.

Wartegg, E. *Reattivo di disegno per la diagnostica degli strati della personalita.* Florence, Italy: Organizzazioni Speciali, 1957.

Weir, J. B. de V. The assessment of the growth of school children with special reference to secular changes. *British Journal of Nutrition,* 1952, *6,* 19–33.

White, E. S. Intelligence and sense of political efficacy in children. *Journal of Politics,* 1968, *30,* 710–721.

White, R. W. Motivation reconsidered: The concept of competence. *Psychological Review,* 1959, *66,* 297–333.

Widdowson, E. M. *A study of individual children's diets.* London: Medical Research Council Special Report Series, No. 257, 1947.

Wilson, P. T., & Jones, H. E. Left-handedness in twins. *Genetics,* 1932, *17,* 560–571.

Winer, B. J. *Statistical principles in experimental design.* New York: McGraw-Hill, 1962.

Witkin, H. A., Dyk, R. B., Faterson, H. F., Goodenough, D. R., & Karp, S. A. *Psychological differentiation.* New York: Wiley, 1962.

Wolstenholme, G. E. W., & O'Connor, C. M. *Medical biology and Etruscan origins.* London: Churchill, 1959.

Young, H. B. Detection and encouragement of the talented in Italian schools. In G. Z. F. Bereday & J. A. Lauwerys (Eds.), *The yearbook of education.* New York: Harcourt, 1962. (a)

Young, H. B. Epidemiology of dental caries: Results from a cross-cultural study in adolescents of Italian descent. *New England Journal of Medicine,* 1962, *267,* 843–849. (b)

Young, H. B. Handbook of methods of assessing pubertal age. Mimeographed, Florence, Italy, 1969.

Young, H. B. Growth and development during puberty and adolescence in both an industrialized and a developing country. Speech given at The First International Symposium on Adolescence, 4–8 August 1974, at Helsinki. (Summary in *Acta Paediatrica Scandinavica Supplement 256,* 17, 1975.)

Young, H. B., & Knapp, R. Personality characteristics of converted left-handers. *Perceptual Motor Skills,* 1966, *23,* 35–40.

Young, H. B., Young, E. B., & Flori, A. G. Dieta e accrescimento. *Pediatria in Calabria,* 1957, *2,* 15–30.

Young, H. B., & Tesi, G. Estimation of social class. *Modern Problems in Pediatrics,* 1962, *7,* 171–177. (a)

Young, H. B., & Tesi, G. A standardization of Raven's Progressive Matrices, 1938 (revised order 1956). *Archivi Psicologi Neurologie Psichiatrici,* 1962, *23,* 445–464. (b)

Yule, G. U., & Kendall, M. G. *An introduction to the theory of statistics.* London: Charles Griffin, 1940.

Index